The Continent Without Qualities

Phorkyas:
Have you the patience to hear the long-drawn-out tale
In silence? It is made up of many stories.

Chorus:
Patience enough! We will live and listen.[1]

Peter Sloterdijk

The Continent Without Qualities

Bookmarks in the Book of Europe

Translated by Robert Hughes

polity

Originally published in German as *Der Kontinent ohne Eigenschaften. Lesezeichen im Buch Europa*

The text on pages 1–14 is taken from Peter Sloterdijk's inaugural lecture at the Collège de France on Thursday April 4, 2024, published by Éditions du Collège de France in 2024 under the title *Le Continent sans qualities: des marque-pages dans le livre de l'Europe*. A freemium open-access digital edition is available through OpenEdition Books: https://books.openedition.org/cdf/156.

The translation of this work was supported by a grant from the Goethe-Institut.

Polity Press
65 Bridge Street
Cambridge CB2 1UR, UK

Polity Press
111 River Street
Hoboken, NJ 07030, USA

ISBN-13: 978-1-5095-7015-7 – hardback
ISBN-13: 978-1-5095-7016-4 – paperback

A catalogue record for this book is available from the British Library.

Library of Congress Control Number: 2026932746

Typeset in 11.5 on 14 Adobe Garamond
by Fakenham Prepress Solutions, Fakenham, Norfolk NR21 8NL
Printed and bound in Great Britain by Ashford Colour Ltd

For further information on Polity, visit our website:
politybooks.com

Contents

First inaugural address
Excuses, obituaries, *aprèsludes*

Of all the accusations made in recent times against the strange political entity called Europe and its inhabitants – and they would make for a long litany if one were to hear them in full – probably the mildest is that it is conspicuous for its unreachability by telephone. The veteran political scientist Henry Kissinger, a former US Secretary of State, who died in November 2023, is said to have joked that he didn't know which number to dial if he wanted to get Europe on the line. The story is too well formulated not to be retold, despite the fact that Kissinger himself could not remember ever saying such a thing. He said that an Irish colleague had come up with the *bon mot* – which, considering the somewhat marginal location of Dublin, does not sound altogether implausible. But he never objected to the anecdote's attribution because it was "a good story."

In the autumn of 2012, this quiet reproach of Europe's abstraction into a noble weakness of address, which could almost be interpreted as sclerosis, returned when the European Union was awarded the Nobel Peace Prize by the Norwegian Nobel Committee in Oslo. The EU was commended for having ensured peace and prosperity for more than six decades, even among nations that had previously considered each other sworn enemies – the accolade concealed a quiet amazement that modern states can exist side by side without, as was common in historical times, attacking each other at least once per generation. Apparently, the

Norwegian capital could not decide to whom, exactly, the good news should be conveyed – perhaps to the European Parliament? Then the German Martin Schulz would have been the appropriate recipient of the call. Or they might have tried the European Commission, represented by the Portuguese José Manuel Barroso, or perhaps the European Council – in which case the phone of the Belgian Herman Van Rompuy should have rung. In Oslo, they chose not to inform anyone, allegedly because they did not want the news to leak prematurely. They relied on the fact that the European Union, if it could not afford a telephone for surprise calls from the outside world, would be informed of their honor in good time by the newspaper or the evening news.

If Europe's accessibility is already somewhat uncertain at the level of its highest political representatives, to put it mildly, it is not surprising that attempts to reach Europe at the popular level, at its social base, so to speak, seem similarly unpropitious. Naturally, a people as a whole or as a population, whether European or not, will not be reachable at a particular postal address or telephone number. To remedy this, one might settle upon a statistical or, better, an aleatoric procedure that would allow one to phone up the inhabitants of this part of the world, in the person of their typical representative: let us imagine it would be possible to select a single person capable of speaking as *vox populi* for the multitude of their peers! Such a person could take up this role by embodying all the traits that compose the "average European" of 2024, the regionally typical version of *l'homme moyen*, as might have been conceived by Adolphe Quetelet (1796–1874), if the Belgian master thinker of average values were still to be entrusted with such a task. Individuals cannot be average if, like the hero of Robert Musil's novel, they sink into an abyssal lack of qualities; they transfigure their averageness by conjoining in themselves locally and globally relevant qualities in the mode of a well-tempered inconspicuousness. The average European has no distinguishing features – from the ears to views and passions, everything is rounded off to median values. The person in question would embody the average European, who, according to statistical yearbooks, annually consumes 11 kilograms of pure alcohol, 6.2 kilograms of boiled sausage and 900 grams of honey, has a working life of 35.9 years, has 0.75 to 0.85 offspring, of whom one in ten is conceived in an Ikea bed, travels 12,000 kilometers per year, produces 7.8 tons of CO_2 and spends 13 percent of the household budget on transportation.

All that is needed now is a random generator fed with all the necessary contact details and tasked with tracking down the average European, without passion, preference, or zeal. It would be best to call at a reasonable hour of day, so as not to discriminate against those who arrive at a later hour into the waking world; citizens under the sway of southern European siesta culture should likewise not be disadvantaged from the outset. The time has come, the attempt is underway, the electronic ball rolls and, within minutes, it selects one, disinterestedly and impersonally, from the 450-million candidates in the pool of virtual accessibility. Somewhere in the Eurosphere a receiver rings. The user picks up, and, to no one's surprise, asks the obvious questions, beyond all irritation and curiosity: Who is calling? What is this all about? The response is that the call is coming from an office outside of Europe, and that they would like to get to know a *European*, a real European, an ordinary citizen from this part of the world, in a sense representative of countless peers, but without any official or even political charge. They would like to hear a voice of the people from the continent that has been called the "Old World" since the days of Columbus's voyages, an individual with whom they could communicate as with an advocate of the local center in the most favorable sense, as unbiased as possible, free from ulterior motives of any kind. Of course, the first thing they would like to know is *who* they have been lucky enough to meet.

Let's give the person called a few seconds to decide whether to stay on the line or else to hang up. In these seconds, we suggest, a crevice in the inner space of Old European memory opens up – from which there emerge long-hidden, long-discarded memories. The average European suspects that nothing good is in store when singled out so suddenly and unexpectedly from the mass of one's peers. There is a sudden feeling as if muffled noises were coming from a dark distant cave. There is an instinctive flash of realization: whoever calls unexpectedly to ask about your identity is most certainly trying to set a trap for you. If they have been looking for you, it is probably because they want someone to charge. They are contacting you to get an address where they can send the allegations in the case. But why? What could we have done wrong?

Of what could they possibly accuse us? Well, okay, long ago, out there on an island full of dangers, we once got a one-eyed giant drunk; we had every right to blind him because we didn't want to perish in his cave like some of our companions. We certainly have more than a few questionable deeds to confess from our travels around the world – if this were the moment for confessions, which it is not.

How should the average European escape the situation? Will Homeric memory come to the rescue with the saving excuse? Like Odysseus, one could answer: Nobody is my name! I am called *Outis*. Indeed, I am none other than Nobody – "My father and mother call me Nobody, as do all the others who are my companions."[1]

The oldest bookmark in the Book of Europe, of which a few chapters will be opened here (and on the pages to come), indicates the first excuse used by a European, later named as such, to save his own skin after a clash with the civilization of the Cyclopes. By outwitting Polyphemus and his allies through a trick with names, Odysseus provided an unforgettable example of how in early Europe, as in Chinese thought patterns, cunning (*metis*, *mechané*) entered upon the stage as a prologue to discursive reason – and as its constant companion.[2]

From today's standpoint, looking at the situation in Europe as a whole, one can hardly resist the impression that the inhabitants of the continent have once again, and for some time now, adopted the ruse of Odysseus in order to withdraw into a "no man's land" after having triggered the sequence of events called "world history." But at this point, the Polyphemic Alliance refuses to be deceived again. The ships of the Europeans have taken flight back to their own waters, but their pursuers are chasing them all the way home. What is more, the attackers, the humiliated and insulted from the bygone days of Western supremacy, have much on their minds to the discredit of the Old World, and are now recruiting their young people from the inhabitants of the nobody's land itself and from their American partners. Even as average Europeans between Lisbon and Szczecin are increasingly consigning themselves to becoming nobodies, their antagonists from Beijing to Ankara are forming a Polyphemic International.

Moreover, it would be trivializing the European situation to emphasize only the escape into excuses, or, to speak psychologically, the escape from discomfort into disidentification. The fall of Europe after its displacement from the political center of the world is more serious than just the embarrassment of one who has been exposed. To put it bluntly: many Europeans have ceased to be interested in themselves; they wave their hands in refusal when it comes to forming a new project out of the remnants of the old continent. They would, if they could, exchange themselves for some other – perhaps in the way Giorgio Agamben had in mind when he suggested taking the *citoyen*, who became the bearer of inalienable claims through the right of birth on European soil, and swapping in the figure of the refugee.[3] It would be frivolous to pretend to explain such utterances solely by way of the coquettish extremism that made itself heard in the last third of the twentieth century through a renewed interest in questions of political theology. One grasps that the subtle contempt for Europe that can be detected in Agamben's propositions draws from a contempt of older origin;[4] it percolated into the sphere of Christian orthodoxy from the eastern fringes of the Mediterranean world in late antiquity. In their view, the world as a whole was a place that should not recognize any inhabitants as enjoying stronger rights of residence; if need be, it should provide necessities to accommodate people in transit; newborns should therefore be treated here no differently from illegal immigrants, even if some arrive via various Mediterranean routes, and others through the notorious maternal portal. For depth of contempt with respect to European and general worldly conditions, Alain Badiou matches Agamben's predilection for the extreme – he believes that contemporary Europe is altogether sunk in boredom, and indeed he sees in it nothing other than "a fleeting structure of various conservatisms."

Expressions of this tendency, and, in similar-sounding tones, were circulating even before the 1990s. From the chorus renouncing Western civilization on both sides of the Atlantic, the dictum of young Susan Sontag (1933–2004), published in the winter 1967 issue of *Partisan Review*, has lost little of its piercing sting: "The white race *is* the cancer of human history."[5] There it was, written and signed and soon to become a leitmotif of Western self-negation – there it was, printed and put into circulation, a sentence inspired by the spirit of New York Gnosticism, which could not have been better formulated in the Latin Quarter. Susan Sontag's frivolous remark – borne out of the certainty that exaggeration is the mother tongue of ingenious girls – has circled the globe and solidified into a stable axiom of leukophobia – the aversion to the color white – above all in the so-called Global South. It also serves indirectly as a code word for anti-Semitic sentiment, since the descendants of Abraham, Isaac, and Jacob – including Rachel, Ruth, and Miriam – tend to be offhandedly assigned to the genetic pool of white-skinned people, without regard for the philologically and phenomenologically remarkable fact that the biblical Genesis does not know any color words.

The Europhobia native to Europe, sometimes reduced to skepticism with respect to one's own, did not need to wait for the support of intellectuals from America's East Coast. It was, after all, not only the "specter of communism" that had been stalking the Old World since the middle of the nineteenth century; at the same time, in this same part of the world, an even more frightful specter was abroad under the name of "decadence." It was not unwilling to present itself in national costume – as with Maurice Barrès (1862–1923), who was as concerned about sub-replacement fertility in France as he was about the continuing weakening of the "social bond," which he could conceive only in resolutely national terms. Even so, the specter appeared as a supranational apparition. All across ethnic borders, a vague fear of decadence found expression as a concern about what was supposedly an all too visible "decline" of peoples often equated with "races" – a fatal process mostly attributed to harmful mixings with foreigners and foreign elements. Concern for some "imperiled substance," inspired by bizarre theories, plunged into sinister speculations about the rampant spread of venereal diseases, lung ailments, neurasthenia, and the recalcitrance of women, of which the much-commented-upon hysteria was a mere harbinger. A vague suspicion of decrepitude spread across the continent, not sparing the British Isles. The *fin-de-siècle* chord of creeping weariness and technical bravura was heard everywhere; in it there was something stirring of what Nietzsche would have called "new music for new ears." Looming up over the astonished capital city of the French was the Eiffel Tower, commissioned just in time for the centenary of the French Revolution, as the last word in European constructional will and prowess. In the novels of the time, for example those of Joris-Karl Huysmans (1848–1907), whose *À rebours* was published in 1884, one encountered men who were too refined to survive a journey from home to the train station. They indulged in colonies and migraines, but suspected that both would sooner or later lead to what could only be described as intolerable conditions.

Michel Winock (b. 1937), the historian of ideas, has described in detail the hothouses of national exhaustion in France in the years before the turn of the twentieth century, including the erotic temptations of "dark romanticism."[6] These were the seemingly happy decades in which understanding Europe meant understanding France. And yet: had not the great Ernest Renan already advised a young agitator named Paul Déroulède around 1880: "France is dying. Young man, do not disturb her death throes!"[7]

Europeans bore their untenable position up until 1914. By the time Paris was liberated in August 1944, if not before, they had exhausted the reserves of their presumptuous weaknesses. And yet, to this day, there is no lack of latecomers who fall into repeating the dark diagnoses of 1918 as if they were still the news of the day – the first volume of Oswald Spengler's *The Decline of the West* was published that year; we note, incidentally, Spengler's own view that his book could have been titled, just as aptly, *The Consummation of the West* or *The Fulfillment of the West.* More recently, a succession of authors, not necessarily of the first rank – from Jean-Marie Benoist to Henryk M. Broder to Douglas Murray – have acted as speakers at Europe's open grave, with some describing the deceased as a suicide[8] – whether in reproach or regret one can hardly say. In October 2018, the novelist Michel Houellebecq accepted the award of the Oswald Spengler Society, based in Belgian Limburg – perhaps in appreciation for his 1998 statement that the West was disappearing, but that its passing should be regarded as "a good thing." Which incidentally shows how declinism still feeds its man in France, Belgium, and some old-fashioned German circles. That Michel Onfray, an epigone of Spengler, also recently declared that "our Judeo-Christian civilization" is "dead" is hardly surprising. All the same, there remains a difference worth attending to between specious reports of a death in the presence of press and television cameras and the issuance of a death certificate by staff with mortuary experience.

Let us be brief: What we call "Europe" here for reasons of practical simplification represents an extremely complicated, multi-faceted structure with a certain temporal depth. Depending on temperament and school, one might begin with the victory of the Greeks in the Greco-Persian Wars or with the coronation of Charlemagne or with the expansion of Iberian seafarers into the Atlantic and the fateful discovery of its far coasts. For a while now, the spokespersons for this politico-civilizational entity have, as noted, been conspicuous for their evasiveness regarding their "identity"; frequently, they have also distinguished themselves by offering obituaries and reflections in an *après-ludial* mood. Indeed, for some time now, it has been possible to include this characteristic in the definition of the "thing itself."

One might say, almost definitionally, that the Europe that we speak of and straightaway recognize came into being at the moment when it began to displease itself. How inevitably our eyes are drawn back to the lines, vibrating with indignation, with which the Irishman Edmund Burke (1729–1797), founder of modern conservatism, commented on the execution of the Queen of France in the fall of 1793. How could he have presented his findings in anything other than an epilogical tone and with contempt for what had been announced in the morally motivated Terror, only to end a short time later in bourgeois banality?

> But the age of chivalry is gone. That of sophisters, economists, and calculators, has succeeded; and the glory of Europe is extinguished for ever.[9]

The writers of obituaries have never been at a loss for dramatic words or for learned diagnoses of the long illnesses of the Old World. Some of Nietzsche's findings, in particular, have remained relevant, although the forced neo-aristocratic tone of his judgments on the emerging mass culture may have become too alien for most readers today. His statements concerning the Zeitgeist that began to take shape after 1850 still seem clear-sighted. In the "positivist systems" of those years, whether propounded by Frenchmen like Auguste Comte or Englishmen like John Stuart Mill and Herbert Spencer, one senses, according to the cultural psychologist high up at Sils Maria, six thousand feet beyond pension reform and social issues, precarious subjects seeking for a last foothold in the sphere of the actual – driven by "weariness, fatalism, disappointment, fear of new disappointment," attended by self-dramatizing traits such as "rage, a bad mood, the anarchism of exasperation," "and whatever other symptoms or masquerades there are of the feeling of weakness."[10] Hence the *bon mot*: "Man does *not* strive for pleasure; only the Englishman does."[11] The general findings on contemporary Dasein in *Beyond Good and Evil* extend into psychodynamically darker zones:

> In an age of disintegration that mixes races indiscriminately [later, Nietzsche writes of "the hybrid European"], human beings have in their bodies the heritage of multiple origins [...]. Such human beings of late cultures and refracted lights will on the average be weaker human beings: their most profound desire is that the war they *are* [because of their conflicting inheritances] should come to an end. Happiness appears to them [...] pre-eminently as the happiness of resting, of not being disturbed, of satiety, of finally attained unity, as a "sabbath of sabbaths," to speak with the holy rhetorician Augustine who was himself such a human being.[12]

In these sentences, the outline of the postwar European comes into focus, both in Nietzsche's day and in what was to come – although the word "postwar," *Nachkrieg*, *après-guerre*, etc. here refers to more than just the long peace of the European way of life as it was realized after 1945 and honored with the Nobel Prize in 2012; it denotes the internal disarmament that began long before – certainly soon after the Battle of Waterloo – for people who no longer wanted to exist as, in their person, the scene of principles in conflict and clashing ways of world-creation. Instead, they contented themselves with being harmless and good in the future and at all times. With a demonstrative finger, Nietzsche was pointing to his contemporaries, who were suffering from uncompensated war-weariness. *Ecce Homo europaeus*![13] Their profile was clearly delineated before it appeared en masse in the second half of the twentieth century. Expressed in Quetelet's units of calculation, what Europeans demand most of all for themselves is a vacation from everything that was once their own great history. Nothing seems more necessary to them than to put as much distance as possible between themselves and the turmoil of their past. The era known as "post-history" was introduced by authors with a highly European sensibility, such as Arnold Gehlen (1904–1976), Vilém Flusser (1920–1991), and Jean-François Lyotard (1924–1998), in order to accommodate the cognitive needs of a population weary of the world and of themselves. It was as if one statement henceforth pertained: *On a raison d'être fatigués*: We are rightly weary. Gehlen, in particular, had discerned in "post-history" no less than an era of "crystallization." Its content would consist of the colorful variation of invariable results and the ongoing restaging of storms, the abatement of which requires nothing more than parliaments and glasses of water. Great history had existed for people who stepped forth to play heroic roles. Post-history celebrates the long farewell to heroes. This era has been defined, in a Wikipedia-worthy turn of phrase, as "making an exit from history for the holidays." Apart from that, it has become Europe's most successful export product in the broad category of "private life" – and it is eagerly consumed in all parts of the world. What contributes to its diffusion is that everywhere, as Nietzsche stated, "there is always a generation which feels itself to be *in opposition* [...]" – not only to conditions that are receding at this moment into the bygone past, but to every past.[14] Accordingly, Europe would not be the mere product of a successful *Verharmlosung* – a German word whose meaning and sound is only imperfectly rendered by French and English expressions such as "banalization," "minimalization," "trivialization." If it were up to the preferences of Europeans – and to their sensitive young people in particular – a general ban on emergencies would be imposed from the highest level. For them, any real crisis is tantamount to a constitutional breach, every heavy rain an attack on human dignity. After their seemingly definitive entry into a state of non-war, the room temperature of Europeans has been set to "reduced existential probation."

It would be unfair to say of Europeans today that they no longer have any guiding purpose. Their unquenched ambition consists in ensuring that the difference continues to narrow, from decade to decade, between politics and administration, democracy and the provision of public services, as was experienced and welcomed (with a grain of salt) from the 1950s until the implosion of the Eastern Bloc around 1990.

Since September 11, 2001, the growing securitarian ambitions of the Europeans have encountered unexpected obstacles – there is no need to discuss them here. We still find it difficult to explain where we stand with ourselves and the rest of the world. The very formula "the rest of the world" – superb as it is – sounds anachronistic in the mouths of Europeans today, and there is a hint of bitterness to it: the impression cannot be dismissed that "the world" has for a long time been happening somewhere else and that we ourselves have become part of "the rest."

In his essay, "The Other Heading: Memories, Responses, and Responsibilities," written shortly after the fall of the Berlin Wall for a conference in Turin, Jacques Derrida addressed the concern that a new monstrosity might arise from the "residuality" of Europe – from its "decentering" or "provincialization," or however one wants to call it. Indeed, at that moment, it seemed reasonable to ask whether new dragon heads would not sprout in the "West" with the collapse of the Soviet Union.[15] It was as if we were hearing a stern warning to beware of the thoughts that must inevitably stir in our heads after the colossus in the East had fallen from its feet of clay! There could be dragon thoughts lurking in the background, ready to seize upon the first opportunity to return. Derrida's warning came as if on tiptoe and yet it wanted to have an urgent effect. In order to correctly understand the Europe of the future, one must think of it as a severed head. The dragon body of yore, composed of a dozen so-called mother countries together with their colonial extensions, this monstrous multi-imperial composite, which we believed to have died in the "African Year" of 1960 at the latest,[16] or at the very latest with the signing of the Évian Accords in March 1962 marking the end of the Algerian War, should have been thought finally dead and buried and sealed under a massive slab. The fact that the half-carcass of imperial Russia could be shaken by a convulsive reawakening after playing dead under the Soviet shroud for 69 years should not disconcert us in the midst of our satisfaction at the course of events, nor should we be put off by the triumphalism of American liberals, who suddenly saw the way cleared for unrivalled world domination by the United States.[17]

Ideas that would sprout from the severed head of a no longer monstrous Europe would have to draw their strength from sources other than those of the early seafaring era and its programs of expansion. Looking back with a critical eye, it cannot be denied that in the era of nautical globalization, people had all too unscrupulously drawn on Christian motifs and civilizational phantasms to claim for the ambitions of European states the best places under the sun in America, Asia, and Africa. The papacy itself, embodied in exemplary corruption by Alexander VI (1431–1503) of the House of the Spanish Borja (Borgia), had blessed the partition of the world between the plundering explorers of Portugal and Castile with the Treaty of Tordesillas in the summer of 1494. We know that the consequences of this partition were consolidated after a series of disturbances;[18] since the days of Simón Bolívar, South America, often called Latin America, has been seeking a *modus vivendi* beyond colonialism, although, under the influence of the ideas of 1789 and in the wake of Napoleon's actions, its "liberator," *El Libertador*, acted almost exclusively within European categories. It would be premature to claim that South America has outgrown the phase of its anti-European *ressentiment* – anyone seeking evidence of its continued existence need only open the daily newspapers.

As concerns Europe, politically reduced to itself as a continent without colonies, no one will claim that alternative sources of power are flowing particularly strongly at the moment. It can nevertheless be explained why this flow will not necessarily run dry. Within a few decades, the severed head has attached itself – from above and without any specific energy from below – with a complex, but no longer monstrous body made up of 27 organs – people are still looking for names and terms to describe this absurdity, for which there is no precedent in the history of large political bodies. Various attempts to give the novelty some shape or contour – for example defining it as a "quiet power"[19] – have yet to yield a satisfying result. Derrida's reflections from 1990, written under the impression of something new in the East, read today as a masterpiece of obscurity – an attempt to present hypothetical imperatives and precious subjunctives as formal guarantors of historically required prudence and caution. Derrida was one of those thinkers who seemed to seriously believe that a precipitous word from the mouth of a philosopher could – as examples from the nineteenth century had shown – lead to new major wars, even world wars, via ideological multiplications and opportune power-political constellations. He chose the tone of a security consultant for a phantom that was only tentatively seeking its own embodiment. For better or for worse, Derrida's tortuous deliberations and somewhat vapid games with the words *cape*, *capital*, and *capitals*, remain of testimonial value with regard to the embarrassments of this region, which emerged as a broken entity from the double war between 1914 and 1945. Derrida posed the rhetorical question:

> [Europe:] Has it ever existed? And yet we are like these young people who get up, at dawn, already old and tired. We are already exhausted.[20]

Accordingly, we live in the most compromised part of the world, where every attempt at a new beginning has been forestalled by the burdens of an extremely difficult history. Anyone who faces the task of rethinking Europe in such a situation must know that it will involve forming concepts for a political and cultural novelty whose existence is largely taking place under yet unknown auspices: concepts for a continent without qualities.

Inhabited by half a billion people and sought after as a refuge by countless potential immigrants, it has been searching since the end of the Second World War for a new purpose for itself and its peoples, whom it prudently calls "populations" so that their *populus* or *demos* qualities do not go to their heads. In the form of the European Union, it has succeeded in launching a political improvisation not provided in the existing scripts of world history. The quasi-continent has created a large political body that, despite its scale, does not exhibit the attitudes or behavior of an empire. Its capital cities may offer all the amenities of urban life, but they have lost the phallic radiance that was once accorded to the metropolises of colonial powers. They attract tourists without being stations of dispatch for major missions. The inhabitants of Europe honor the state of their ascriptively assigned new Europeanness with the stubborn habit of abstaining from half the elections to the European Parliament – only Belgians and Luxembourgers vote in European elections as diligently as if they were national ballots. And, although the citizens of the new construct are overwhelmingly on the winning side through their membership in the difficult-to-understand superstructure, many still find it difficult to vest the abstraction with emotions that would be felt toward a homeland. This reflects the fact that post-imperial Europe, which emerged in the 1950s from the meager outlines of an association for the interests of the mining industries, known as the European Coal and Steel Community, was from the outset a project of concerned, hopeful, and far-sighted elites. Their successors still refuse to be deterred from their belief that majorities would follow as soon as the advantages of the new *modus vivendi* became generally apparent, even as mining has since become a rather un-European activity.

One cannot help fearing that Dostoevsky may have succeeded, in a sudden intuition, in defining under the optics of Orthodox Christianity the contemporary man of this part of the world when, in his *Notes from the Underground* – that cruel novella of 1864 that catapulted *ressentiment* onto the stage of world literature – he had his protagonist say that man is a being that goes on two legs and is ungrateful.[21]

The average Europeans of today, living with a sometimes warranted rancor against often opaque, virtually extraterrestrial processes in Brussels and Strasbourg, and disinclined to reflect on the premises of their existence, are the incarnation of ingratitude – insofar as this means floating along in the drift of quasi-post-historical sensitivities and not knowing, let alone wanting to know, the sources from which the present *modus vivendi* has emerged. All too often, Europeans of today are the end-consumers of comfort and convenience, without the least notion of the conditions of its formation. In their existences, perforated by gaps in memory, Stephen Dedalus's declaration has become reality: "History … is a nightmare from which I am trying to awake."[22]

In what follows, we will try to counter this spirit of ingratitude just a little. In doing so, we proceed from the assumption that ingratitude is only a synonym for a certain lack of reading and a curable symptom of it. We define Europe here as a book too little read by those whom it concerns, and which its haters leaf through only to document their accusations. The ensuing chapters are to be understood as bookmarks in a volume almost daunting in its scope. They highlight certain passages, asking a distracted readership to give a minute of attention to the marked pages.

Second inaugural address
Latin Europe:
The continent, the imperium, and its transfers

To designate as a "continent" a region of the earth such as Europe seems at present like a linguistic convention without risk. Such a view profits from the fallacy of cartographers and geographers, ingrained since the eighteenth century, of denoting cohesive landmasses as continents, as if sprawling mainland territories were containers that made "contents" of whatever lay within them or whatever was established upon them. The planetary modernity inaugurated with the voyages of Columbus and Magellan ought to have taught us that the relationship between container and content had been reversed. The effective containers that deserve the name *continens*, "that which holds together," are the global seas, named after the Greeks' world-encircling river *Okeanos*, while the large land masses, rightly understood, are not continents, *containers*, but rather *contents*, contiguities of soil and population girded on all sides by the seas.

When we seek suitable terms for the content of "Europe," we bump up against an elusive phenomenon to which we try in vain to attach an "identity." What then is Europe? Does this entity have an essence, a core, a substance? The negative answers to the frequently asked questions are too numerous to recapitulate in detail. Is it a misunderstanding to regard Europe as a continent of its own, separate from its aspect as a Western adjunct to the Asian landmass – from Valéry's point of view its agile "promontory," in Derrida's eyes the "other cape," in the conception of the

Slavophile Danilevsky no more than a confused aggregate of peninsulas – or is Europe nonetheless something real, to which one might attach one's destiny? We would like to adopt a strictly pragmatic approach here, after more than a hundred years of contentious discussions about the "nature," the "essence," the "substance," the "limits," the "mission," the "burden," the "passion," and the "heritage" of Europe. Instead of chasing after essentialist phantoms, we settle for the question: What does Europe do when it is most itself? This amounts to asking whether there is something by which Europeans might be recognized when they behave as typical agents of their cultural pole?

In short, we acknowledge the need to make a transition from an essentialist or substantialist thinking to a dramaturgical or scenographic thinking if we want to talk about Europe. What is called intelligence or "the ability to understand things" has, from ancient times, referred not only to signs, words, and sentences, as has become "common sense" among modern philosophers of language, but always also to overall situations laden with meaning, which theater people call "scenes." Intelligence is shown not least in the ability to read scenes or grasp situations. Thinking about Europe dramaturgically and scenically implies the task of designating a privileged place within this part of the world where the script and stage direction for what follows were set down.

If, in what follows, we speak of the "Book of Europe" and announce that some bookmarks should be inserted into it – and these, as will be seen, preferably at less-read points – we should agree upon the metaphor of the book. Books and cultures have the common feature that in them "turning the page" and the continuation of ways of life in succeeding generations constitute formal equivalents. Between cultures and books, the modes of reading and the forms of re-enactment constitute a third variable. They ensure that earlier elements of a culture that have congealed into "pieces" can be re-staged. Re-enactments constitute the active middle between turning the page and propagation. The next page corresponds to the next generation.

Let us consider for a moment the gesture of turning the page and the significance of this gesture for historical consciousness, very broadly, indeed for a sense of coherence and sequentiality in general. In his 1975 short story "The Book of Sand" ("El libro de arena"), the Argentine writer Jorge Luis Borges described the nightmare of every historian and every person seeking assurance of the order of things under the law of succession.

One evening, there is a knock at the narrator's door and a stranger of Scandinavian appearance introduces himself as a Bible salesman – though, he says, he also has another holy book in his possession that would likely be of interest to a connoisseur. The Bible salesman adds that he acquired the book in India from a Dalit, an untouchable, who could not read, in exchange for a handful of rupees and a Bible. In fact, the spine of the book bears the inscription "Holy Writ" and the place of publication: Bombay. The previous owner claimed that the book was called "the Book of Sand" because neither the book nor sand itself has any beginning or any end.

The narrator now reports that he has repeatedly failed in his attempts to turn to the first or last page of the book: there were always a few pages, as if sprouting forth between his thumb and the cover. When the narrator opens the book at random to a page somewhere in the middle, the page number 40,514 appears on the left-hand page, with the number 999 on the facing right-hand page. When he turns the leaf, an eight-digit number appears in the upper corner of the following page. It proves impossible to re-find a page that has once been opened.

When the narrator stammers "This can't be," the salesman replies in a low voice:

> "It can't be, but it *is*. The number of pages in this book is no more or less than infinite. None is the first page, none the last. I don't know why they're numbered in this arbitrary way. Perhaps to suggest that the terms of an infinite series admit any number."
>
> Then, as if he were thinking aloud, he said, "If space is infinite, we may be at any point in space. If time is infinite, we may be at any point in time."[1]

Like no other story, the sinister tale of the Book of Sand points to the human interest in finitude. Only in finite relationships can one speak meaningfully of sequences, consequences, and proportions; they compose the basic figures of what must be given so that there can remain in force the benevolent fiction of the narratability of individual life stories and comprehensive collective histories. The Book of Sand signifies the impossibility of telling a story; it implies the futility of any attempt to re-find a particular page with the help of a bookmark.

One might recall here that the ancient genre of the *bioi* gave rise to the European utopia of "being toward book." It was reflected in the motto of a life led in the light of remarkable things, coined by Pliny the Younger and much quoted by humanists of the sixteenth century: *aut scribenda agere aut legenda scribere*. "Act in such a way that it is worth writing down, and write in such a way that it is worth reading!"

When Europe is represented as a "book," a scripted product is intended *eo ipso*. As a valid script, it portrays the events in question in more or less fixed places in a non-reversible time series. Some scripts, however – including the one discussed here – have the peculiar effect that whoever reads them is at risk of unexpected inclusion in a new edition, and not just coincidentally. These scripts are written to strip readers of the illusion that they might read without involvement; to the reader they present a resolute *tua res agitur!* – it concerns you too![2]

Binding the hardness of power structures in political space together with the sphere of the book is what one calls the symbolic function. As soft-power structures, books belong to the dimension of signs. Among signs, the first among equals is the command, conveyed in the imperative mode. While books, as agents of soft power, make suggestions that can be accepted or disregarded, the forces of hard power issue orders backed by the power to impose penalties. In the language of the Romans, *imperare* means to rule, to dominate. Commanding and motivating forces, voices setting goals and giving direction, are a certain kind of experience in the world; the imperative is their grammatical sediment. These things form the bridge from words to deeds and facts. Since the days of the Republic, the term *imperium* was used to describe the temporally and spatially limited command authority of the supreme commander of Roman troops. The term *imperium* was ultimately used to describe the entire area in which orders issued from Rome had to be obeyed. Over time, the command of troops had become the central power in the *res publica*, culminating in the figure of the *imperator*. After Octavian's victory in the Roman civil wars, the highest commanders were called Caesars, because the young man had been adopted as the named heir of Gaius Julius Caesar in the latter's will. The proper name became a general term.

The original play, the re-enactment of which will be the focus of "Europe," is called *imperium romanum*. In Virgil's heroic epic, Aeneas's father admonishes his "pious" son, who seeks him out in the underworld to obtain his mandate, to always remember, "as a Roman" *ante litteram*, to lead the peoples through his power of command.[3] Hence to understand Europe means, initially, to understand the metamorphoses of a structure at the center of which the imperative function of Rome remained at work.

To lay it down without any more comprehensive derivation: from a dramaturgical point of view, Europe is the scene for re-enactments of Roman command systems. These gave rise – with a delay of a thousand years or more – to modern European "states," which were mostly set up as "nation states," with the Swiss Confederation being a notable exception. They represent political systems that are doomed, sooner or later, to discover in their own ways what had already been the Roman predicament in ancient times: imperial overextension – it turns out that nation states are likewise susceptible to overextension. From the time of Augustus, the Italic heartland was authorized, competent, willing, and compelled to decide on problems it had incurred as a result of its hybrid expansion into Syria, Palestine, Egypt, North Africa, Spain, Gaul, Germania, and southern Britain. At the height of its success, the concept of "empire" implied the program of a "command without borders," from which one understands, with no further explanation necessary, why it had to fail in itself.

There is no need to recapitulate here the story told a hundred times of the fall of Rome and its division into the Western Roman zone of decline and the Eastern Roman zone of extended thousand-year decline. For the history of the part of the world that would later be called Europe, only the displacement of the motif of commanding power to the north and west is of significance here.

If we were to say when and where there came into being the Europe in which we still live, we would have to go back to a scene whose oblivion is in stark contrast with its wealth of consequences, both symbolic and factual: in the year 390 CE, Ambrose, the Bishop of Milan, refused Emperor Theodosius I communion within the church because the

Emperor had yet to do penance for the Massacre of Thessalonica (in the Roman province of Macedonia, in present-day Greece) – a city in which, it was said, thousands of visitors to the hippodrome had been massacred by Gothic troops on imperial orders, after an enraged crowd had tried forcibly to free a popular charioteer from detention. Theodosius had taken the unrest of the masses personally and interpreted it as a revolt against his imperial dignity. The primal scene of Europe testifies to Europe's peculiarity: from the very beginning, the fissure among the highest authorities was evident. Political and spiritual power, although mostly dependent on each other, never quite speak the same language in this part of the world. Augustine's teaching of the "*civitas Dei*," which would oppose the earthly state until the end of time, would consolidate the duality of political and spiritual power soon thereafter and for the next millennium and a half.[4] What Europeans consider their "freedom" results from their embarrassing privilege of being able to serve two masters at any time – the emperor and God, the fatherland and the truth. The potentiality that later became known as Europe was something that Ambrose brought into the world when he insisted on his duty to call the emperor a sinner. The Emperor, for his part, allowed this potentiality to be realized when he submitted himself to the ritual of penance, something modern misunderstanding might describe as nothing more than empty theater. The remnants of the European prerogative of dual submission that survived in the monistic climate of the late nineteenth century were what Lenin – as a pioneer of modern semi-education in matters of religion – wanted to dispose of, once and for all, with his dictum: "Freedom is a bourgeois prejudice."

In order to enter into the pragmatic horizon of the historical phenomenon of Europe, one must, as mentioned, become familiar with the dramaturgical concept of re-enactment. The current "new Europe" – a vast construct of our times that tends to be divided between professional Europeans and those who are indifferent to Europe – has emerged from the oblivion of an Old Europe, inspired by Rome and its afterlife; it can be understood, from a dramaturgical point of view, as but one stage in a wide-ranging event of re-enactment. Over its long theatrical seasons – historians call them "epochs" – it has managed to maintain its power and prestige through ever new stagings and performances. It remained in the repertoire not least because its main actors, the German kaisers and Russian tsars, the kings of Portugal, Spain, France, and England, and numerous other players on the boards of the great world, hardly ever really grasped in what show they were playing – yet they strove for the honor and privilege of being allowed to play their part with God's approval. For more than a thousand years, Europe's princes were, almost invariably, somnambulists who wandered through palaces and across battlefields, led by Charlemagne, to recite on the world stage ceremonious phrases from an anonymous author of Italian roots – always in the conviction that they were accomplishing things that were pleasing to the purposes of heaven and conducive to the welfare of their peoples.

From a scenographic point of view, Old Europe could be described as a pure effect of the script. "Enacted" Europe furnishes evidence that there are self-realizing scripts – dramas without individual authors that can be reanimated by congenial dramaturges from century to century and re-embodied by princes, politicians, and demagogues, however subject to fickle fortune.

Despite countless attempts, there is still no representation of the history of old Europe that would correspond to its dramaturgical truth over the entire course of its performances. As regards the period from the fifth to the fifteenth century, the European powers' debt to Roman models was too conspicuous not to catch the eye – even if their significance bore more upon symbolism than power-politics. For a long time, the word *imperium* denoted a canopy of sacredly charged concepts of unity and universality rather than an institutionalized entity.

Since the fifteenth century, however, Europe has in political terms transformed itself into an amphibious entity: ever since, its dramaturges, kings, ministers, and field marshals have taken up the idea that "to be" meant to be able to command in two ways. Internally they understood it as the charge of forming a *res publica* on the Roman model, something in recent times called the "state," with a capital (*urbs*) that energetically orders everything around it (*orbis*); externally they understood it as the remit of being a "motherland," a *madre patria*, that complements domestic power with nautically and militarily developed colonies, irrespective of even great distance. Imperiality now meant, once again and more than ever, the authority to command – whether about immediate or more distant matters. Internally, it created civil subordination through judicature, bureaucracy, military affairs, and regulations for weights, measures, bridges, and roads; externally, it created subalternity by compelling cooperation with foreign rule and forcing local acquiescence to extractions, with which the idea of taxation and the principle of a "legitimate plunder" of a population (Thomas Aquinas) was extended to external subjects. The ancient pattern of wanton overextension returned to the moderns: certainly, that the senate and people of Rome before the imperial age were capable of regulating their internal affairs with the means at hand is indeed to be recognized as an achievement in its own right, though it constitutes no occasion for amazement; but that, at the great *munera*, the fighting games financed by the state and patrons, Egyptian grain could be donated to the Roman masses, and that African wild animals could be slaughtered in the Colosseum before jeering crowds at so-called *venationes* (hunts), cannot be explained without the phenomenon of *imperium*. In effects of this kind – as in the permanent stationing of Roman legions on the frontiers of the empire – its meaning as the "ability to command from afar" was massively concretized.

In order to understand the phenomenon of Europe, one must therefore observe how, at the end of the Middle Ages, the crystallization of states on their "own" territories developed in tandem with vectors of command into distant regions – beginning with Portugal's incursions onto the soil of West Africa[5] – and into India soon thereafter. What's more, the territories of later European nations were arranged as spaces of internal imperiality.[6] The nation state of Spain came into being only after long campaigns against the Moorish principalities, which held their ground on Iberian soil until the fifteenth century. The country called France, which since 1792 has insisted on being *une et indivisible* as a nation, could one day exist only on the condition that orders from the Île de France were obeyed in Rouen, Dijon, Bordeaux, Montpellier, and Ajaccio – which occasionally necessitated an Albigensian Crusade, an annihilation of the Knights Templar, a siege of St. Michel, an expulsion of the Protestants, an annexation of Corsica, and a pedagogical campaign to obliterate the dialects. The urge to expand and the tendency to overextend are inherent in modern nations at an early stage.

If one searches for signs that might be considered authentic markers of Old Europe, one must first contemplate two indicators that have remained prevalent since the fifth century: *imperiality* and *Latinity*. For a full millennium, the two markers remained inextricably bound together – and they left their stamp on what historians have *formally* called the "Middle Ages."[7] After the weight of the Roman legacy shifted to the Grecophone East with the Diocletian division of power around the year 300 and the Theodosian reorganization of the empire after 395, and where it persisted in solemn stagnation until the middle of the fifteenth century, a new dynamic of re-enactments by non-Roman peoples was set in motion in the northwestern fragments of the empire. A Latinophone tone came to prevail among them. The "old Europe" – is thus nothing other than the zone whose rulers and political heads either orchestrated arbitrary transfers of empire or created the scene for such transfers – mostly by following Latin-ecclesiastical path dependencies. The Iron Age bog bodies from the Danish sites of Tollund and Grauballe or the glacier corpse "Ötzi" from the Ötztal Alps were never "Europeans" during their lifetimes – they had no concept of the later political and cultural conditions in the south of their habitat.

If one uses the traits of imperiality and Latinity as search criteria, the dramaturgical effects that were brought to bear in the re-enactments of the empire over a timespan of almost one and a half millennia become immediately apparent. First and foremost, the transfer of the Western Roman Empire to the early Latin Christian Church is worth mentioning here. The term *translatio* is too weak to describe this process: the *ecclesia triumphans* of the post-Constantinian era was not just an emulator or a spiritual concubine of the imperium. By the later fourth century, it had long since grown into its clone, its *Doppelgänger*, its better self. This was evident not only in the contours of the dioceses, which generally followed the boundaries of the Roman administrative dioceses; even Christian priestly vestments, which have left their stamp on Catholic haute couture to this day, derive from the adoption of robes worn by Roman officials at state liturgies. The church provided the political apparatus with its *raison d'être*, its legitimacy, and a pretext for its clear conscience. It was not without reason that Jacob Burckhardt remarked of Bishop Eusebius of Caesarea (c. 260–339), the author of one of the first church histories as well as the magnificently tendentious *Vita Constantini*, that the man was the first fundamentally disingenuous historian of the European tradition – today one might describe his function as being a chief ideologist; Franz Overbeck added that Constantine's eulogist had distinguished himself above all as the "coiffeur of the emperor's theological wig."[8]

Against this background, the fiction of a "fall of the Roman Empire" around the year 500, which was maintained by earlier generations of historians, becomes irrelevant in two ways: while it endured for another millennium in its eastern sphere – the key year of its end there is 1453 – it underwent a transformation in the Latinophone-dominated West, which suggests that we should speak less of a fall than of several transitions. From a dramaturgical point of view, the Roman Empire has not "fallen" to this day. It has repeated itself, marked by several intervals, in other territories in the form of more or less pathetic self-quotations. Under the name of the Roman Catholic Church, it leads, to this day, an afterlife transposed to a spiritual register. During the pontificate of Pope Gregory VII (1073–1085), Rome even claimed world-dominating supremacy for itself, as if only the Church could provide the common matrix of all power, both secular and spiritual. Still, in the face of such pretensions, one should not forget: in the mild shadow of the papacy, which up until the Reformation (and beyond) knew how to tend to its own interests in the temporal sense, the freedoms of the arts, professions, and *bene vivere* matured in the cities north of the Papal States, such that Italy could become Europe's first love. The title *pontifex maximus*, which Julius Caesar and the Caesars after him bore *ex officio*, has been claimed down to this very day by the heads of the Holy See since Pope Leo I, whose pontificate lasted from 440 to 461.[9]

Provided the ecclesiastical hyper-transmission of a virtual empire in the mode of *civitas Dei* as the matrix for subsequent filiations of Roman heritage, there emerged sprawling attempts at imperial parody in the European northwest under Merovingian and Carolingian auspices, which would one day aspire to be more than mere imitation. Charlemagne's empire of the early ninth century entered upon the stage as a dynamized copy of a power that seemed to rest strangely out of time in the East, Islamic harassment notwithstanding. Under the emperors of the Ottonian dynasty, the idea of the *translatio imperii* was invoked with "state" propaganda emphasis. The *Holy Roman Empire* proved, with God's help, to be a flexible affair – it now incarnated itself, without loss of salvation and no loss of grandeur, *in finibus Germanorum.* The empire returned as a sacred mutant amid tribes that had become capable of becoming empires through martial bravura, baptism, and the rudiments of Latin. The Battle of Lechfeld in August 955, with which the European culture of sedentism broke the back of plunder-based Hungarian equestrian nomadism, must be seen as a key moment in this event.[10] With this victory, Otto the Great (912–973) cemented his claim to have renewed the Roman Empire as an entity that could promise political salvation. The fact that an Ottonian prince was able to marry a Byzantine princess named Theophanu, who reigned as Empress Regent of the Holy Roman Empire for six years (985–991) following the early death of her spouse,[11] made it evident how the imperial transmigration of souls had seized the dynastic stratum of the western sphere. As Empress Regent, and glorified by her origins in the East, the lady signed her documents with a robust generic masculine *Theophanus gratia divina imperator augustus.* Her signature made it clear: Roman imperial salvation had definitively re-territorialized itself in the northwest of Europe. Her son, Otto III (980–1002), a servant of the end times, was completely imbued with his apostolic "mission" as, like a Paul come again, he would hurry back and forth between Poznań, Aachen, and Rome as the legate of the Holy Spirit.[12]

It would take another two centuries before the compulsion to cite the Romans was relaxed in Western architecture, with the rise of a new style of construction: French Gothic architecture, beginning with the royal necropolis at the Basilica of Saint-Denis, provided evidence that a greatness called Europe henceforth also existed in the language of cathedral builders. European declinations of imperiality under Catholic auspices attained bold new architectural forms. Gothic church towers arose as pointers to demonstrate how European builders envisaged expansions beyond just the horizontal. Hugh of Saint Victor (1097–1141) already presupposed the analogy of vertical uplift between doctrinal and architectural constructions when he declared:

> This is the whole Divinity, this is the whole spiritual building, and as many sacraments as it contains, by so many stories does it rise into the sky.[13]

It is not our task to narrate the slow drama of translations through the Carolingian, Ottonian, Salian, and Hohenstaufen periods up to the era of the Habsburgs and their Spanish branch. Academic medieval studies in Central and Western Europe have presented the essentials here. These mostly and rightly placed emphasis on the fact that, around the year 1000, the crowns of emperors and kings mostly possessed only titular significance, while the effective authority of the princes ended at the limits of their own estates. But the emperors and kings of the West were also elevated by the continual presence of clerics into a quasi-Byzantine atmosphere of sacred remoteness, which did not correspond to any reality of power politics. It took centuries for a legal entity of the state type to emerge from the patchwork of domanial economies and from local aristocratic households beyond number. This required, among other things, the conversion of royal coffers (*fiscus*) into state treasuries, a process that could hardly be left without theological and legal commentary. Even the finance ministers of republican times had little to add to this lucidity: *Ubi est fiscus, ibi est Imperium*: Where there is a treasury, there is the empire.[14] As patrons of the church, the apostolic emperors functioned for centuries like prophetic placeholders for a statehood yet to come.

In his work on the Danube, Claudio Magris depicted some of the continental effects of the expansion of empire, dipping into the wealth of cultural biotopes on the banks of the river,[15] which became, as it were, another Tiber. In a distantly analogous way, Fernand Braudel's books illuminate the rich Mediterranean dimensions of the Roman afterlife in Spain's heyday.[16] We have the Austrian historian Alexander Randa (1906–1975) to thank for his erudite book: *Das Weltreich: Wagnis und Auftrag Europas im 16 und 17 Jahrhundert*, which treats the theme in some detail – but there is still no trace of the spirit of post-colonialism to be found in it. It was devoted to the beginnings of the second translation phase, which was instigated by the tensions of the post-Columbian situation and the awakening of nation-state impulses. Here, one discovers how the Portuguese and Spanish contributed to the colossal political construct that the author, in a suggestive coinage, calls the "Catholic Commonwealth" of the modern era[17] – although the matter as such, and not only from today's perspective, encompassed a myriad of dark facts. It was the seafaring southwest of Old Europe that articulated the future powers that would shape the transfer of empire. The Iberian princes were the first to have to reckon with the fact that the earth had become round and the universe unbounded. The "Catholic Kings" in particular made efforts, after the suppression of Moorish culture, to set up a homogenous territorial state – internally on the basis of a unified political economy and a unified, tendentially post-Latin national language,[18] and externally by establishing colonial administrations, supported by viceroyalties and consolidated nautical and administrative routines. The Archive of the Indies in Seville still constitutes the secret memory of the first European modernity. Anyone wishing to gauge the powerful aura of Spanish models might pause to reflect on the fact that Oliver Cromwell (1599–1658), the puritan leader of the English Civil War and name-giver of the "Commonwealth," was interred in 1658 within Westminster Abbey and given a Spanish-type ceremony and an extravagance of solemnity that read from the 1598 obsequies of Philip II of Spain.

The historical–theological speculations of the Portuguese Jesuit, missionary to Brazil, and diplomat António Vieira (1608–1697) may be regarded as the occult culmination of Iberian conceptions of the world. Based on the four-kingdom doctrine of the Book of Daniel (according to which the dominion of Rome was interpreted as the last empire before the coming of judgment), he conceived a *Quinto Império*, a Fifth Empire, that was to embody – how else than under Portuguese leadership? – a world empire and an eschatological spiritual church in one.[19]

There is no need here to trace the further course of the imperial transfer up into modern and more recent times. Almost everywhere the motifs of imperiality, whether Imperial or Royal, preceded those of nationality; the "nationalization of the masses" was the work of only the nineteenth century.[20] By the end of the nineteenth century, Europe's map had transformed into an explosive conglomerate of ten irritable national imperialisms stretching from Lisbon to Moscow – charged with tensions enough for more than one major war. With the Congress of Vienna, the model of the five great powers devised by Metternich and Castlereagh had become established and, thanks to a series of summit conferences, remained effective as the "Concert of Europe" for much of the nineteenth century. Its task was to balance the inter-imperial relations among the great powers of Austria, Russia, and the United Kingdom, as well as among the nervous semi-great powers of France and Prussia. Meanwhile, quite a few other states certainly had imperial interests of their own, starting with the nautical pioneering states of Portugal, Spain, and the Netherlands, which had established early overseas colonial empires, through to Denmark, Belgium, and Italy, whose late but all the more emphatic demands had to be reckoned with. After the founding of the German Empire in 1871, with a Prussian emperor at the helm, discordant notes at the Concert of Europe proliferated. In the wake of Bismarck's dismissal by Wilhelm II in 1890, the dissonance became overwhelming; the Turkish problem, obsessively negotiated for nearly a century under the rubric of the "Eastern Question," brought the detuning process to its completion.

The extent to which the imperial motif shaped and overshadowed the national one[21] is revealed, among other things, in the demand made by the Austrian socialist Otto Bauer (1881–1938) at the beginning of the twentieth century to reorganize the fourteen Habsburg countries as the "United States of Greater Austria" – as if one could re-enact, on old European soil, the founding of the USA by the thirteen breakaway colonies.

If the era of nationalisms in the nineteenth century has acquired a foul reputation with historians and the educated public, this is primarily because the national motif, at the height of its potency, understandably unleashed more than just emancipatory forces. In the leading states of Europe, national ambitions had, as indicated, largely absorbed the imperial imperative. With regard to the British Isles, this observation is based on the plainest of evidence. As for France, the nation so proud of its revolution had done what was necessary during the Third Republic (1870–1940) to become the world's greatest imperial power after England. And, no sooner had Germany become nationally united than it felt its own need to claim some remnant of the African spoils for itself, notwithstanding Bismarck's vain assurance that Germany was already "saturated."

From a cultural–historical perspective, the older history of Latin Europe encompasses the fortunes of what can only be called political classicism. Wherever it got a chance, it presented itself in the sublime dialect of Romanism. It left its mark just as clearly in Aachen, Goslar, Vienna, and Paris as it did later in Lisbon, Madrid, and other imperial centers. It reached its highest – and initially least expected – culmination in the British capital: with the victory of the British fleet over the Spanish Armada in 1588, London rose to become the Rome of a great Atlantic and Pacific empire under anti-Catholic auspices. In his magnum opus *Das Inselreich: Gesetz und Größe der britischen Macht* (1936), Reinhold Schneider so sensitively portrayed the power structure that ruled from London that it was as if he had personally heard the confession of its errant prince, Henry VIII.

England clarified its imperial pretensions when it took the idea of rule, which from time immemorial had been bound to territories, and extended it to the seas: seldom, if ever before, had a monarchy believed it could rule the waves. Even the Persian Xerxes I, who condemned the sea at the Dardanelles to 300 lashes of the whip because it hindered his plans to build a bridge, considered the open water only punishable and not governable. As maritime imperialism, however, British expansion from the seventeenth century onward sailed its *translatio imperii* into oceanic dimensions. Founded on a cannon-equipped navy, coal-fired industry, and a code of gentlemanly colonialism, the Empire encompassed a quarter of the inhabited earth at its furthest extent around the start of the twentieth century. Anti-Roman in its self-conception, it nonetheless became the strongest expression of old European imperiality. The fact that, after the Great Fire of London in 1666, the city had St. Paul's Cathedral reconstructed as Christendom's most magnificent church – after St. Peter's Basilica in Rome – accords with the image of the British appearance on the global stage. The two triumphal arches, Wellington Arch and Marble Arch, erected after the victory of British arms and British money over Napoleon, lent the island's pretensions their ultimate clarity. Among its provocative effects, which can also be called its tragedies, was that it aroused rivalries in Paris, Moscow, Vienna, and Berlin that manifested themselves in the Great War.

As far as the continent's imperial structures are concerned, French ambitions played an eminent role from the seventeenth century onward. True – France's kingship was not in a position to step into the Roman–Caesarian line occupied by the Habsburg Empire; it succeeded, however, in developing a highly energetic profile of expansive imperial power in the succession of the biblical kingship of David, first through Louis IX in the thirteenth century, then through Philippe IV, Henri IV, and the great cardinals of the seventeenth century, and finally through the Sun King,

Louis XIV. Louis XIV's solar program can be traced back to the radiant crown of Constantine the Great, which adorned his statue, consecrated in May 330, in the Forum of Constantine in the city of Nova Roma in Byzantium; its rays, as legend would have it, contained nails from the cross of Christ.

After the events of 1789, the *nation soleil*, the nation of the sun, incorporated a program of dominion from a shining center into its understanding of its global mission. When the National Convention proclaimed on September 25, 1792, that the French Republic was a political entity *une et indivisible*, the inner imperiality of the nation conquered by the kings and condensed in Versailles was brought back to Paris. What would one day be called *le mal français* – the French ailment – became ever more conspicuous with each passing decade after the "transfer of empire" from Versailles to the metropolis. Paris inherited from the kings not only the banalization of the nobility, but also the debilitation of the regions, for which, to this day, no proper recompense has been made.

Napoleon Bonaparte finally consummated the conversion from biblical monarchy to Roman-style Caesarism when, at his coronation in Notre-Dame de Paris on December 2, 1804, he hastened to exchange the pious crown for a pre-Christian laurel wreath; to similar effect, by decree of February 1806, he promised the victorious army of Austerlitz a return to Paris beneath an Arc de Triomphe. Having married Marie Louise, the Holy Roman Emperor's daughter, Napoleon wanted to make his son, born in 1811, a "King of Rome" – though this fact remained a marginal detail in view of the later course of events.

As regards Moscow, it was drawn to the notion, floated in the sixteenth century by the monk Philotheus of Pskov, that it might epitomize a "Third Rome." If initially it displayed religious overtones, it was soon driven solely by the compulsive drive for the creation of a great empire as excessive as it was crude. With about 150 subjugated tribes and nationalities, the imperial imperative could only be asserted through the means of forced Russification. In the west, the reach of the Muscovite central power extended as far as Finland, Poland, and the Baltic lands; in the east, after a continuous expansion that began with the founding of the western Siberian city of Tyumen in 1586, it reached as far as the city of Vladivostok ("Ruler of the East"), founded in 1860 and located nine thousand kilometers from Moscow, which would one day become the terminus of the Trans-Siberian Railway. If Karl Kraus could designate the Austria of his day as an "experimental station for the end of the world," the whole of Russia in the period from Peter the Great to Putin could be taken as an experiment in escaping from ungovernability into despotism.

Even smaller countries, like Belgium, which was created in 1830, could hardly content themselves with playing mere minor roles in the drama of empire-formation in the mode of later translations. Now, as ever, the projects of the Belgian crown in the Congo remain among the darkest chapters of European colonial practice. In Italy, since the fifth century, the spirit of centralized empire-formation had given way to the pluralism of urban cultures; finally, however, Italy too reasserted its right to expansion, as if at the last minute, with claims upon Libya for example, until under Mussolini even distant Ethiopia was to be incorporated into *Italia Imperiale*.[22]

Finally, as concerns the ominous national socialism of the Germans, which from 1933 to 1945 sought to realize the long-lost dream of the "Reich," it was not only use of the ordinal "Third" that aroused suspicions. The hollow new structure was severed by the course of events after 1806 from the line of authentic imperial history based on Rome. Its ideologues, Hitler and Rosenberg in particular, were all the more willfully determined to reinterpret European antiquity as a whole in the spirit of Aryanism. This demonstrated that not only individual works but sometimes entire civilizations fall into the hands of counterfeiters. And, although elements of haphazard appropriation were hardly lacking in earlier translations of the Reich, it was only when National Socialism came to power that it proved that determined annexationists were capable of distorting an entire antiquity.[23]

If one turns to still acute phenomena in the chain of *translationes imperii*, it becomes entirely clear that classical Europe represented neither a territory nor an effective faith community, and certainly not the often maliciously termed "Christian club." The question of its borders is therefore almost as far off-track as the question of its "identity." In each case, only the most current supporter of the aforementioned political–dramaturgical program can be understood as the real Europe in power-political terms. Each time, the Europeans on duty were represented by different players, calling themselves, variously, Ambrose of Milan, Charles Martel, or Charlemagne; in later times, their names were Otto II, Pope Gregory VII, Charles V, Oliver Cromwell, and Louis XIV. The names of Napoleon I and Queen Victoria also entered the list – the latter after 1876 as "Empress of India," as if British Caesarism, bypassing overcrowded continental Europe, had at a late hour favored skipping over to Asia.[24]

Since the start of the twentieth century, the current staging of the play has been taken over by a player who emerged from an offshoot of the British dominion: the United States of America. Without the script's inherent propensity for detaching itself from the place of its first performance, this process would have remained impossible. The dramaturgical evidence leaves no room for doubt: anyone who considers the city of Washington D.C. from the perspective of political urbanism will right away recognize the extent to which the proper style of old European imperial classicism was in evidence there too, culminating in the construction of the Capitol dome, completed in 1863. The various state capitals vied with Washington, often erecting their own capitol-shaped statehouses. Already in 1782, on the Great Seal of the United States, one finds once again the figure of the eagle, which has symbolized imperial sovereignty since ancient times. It was sacred to the Romans as the bird of Jupiter, armed with the lightning and thunderbolts of supernal force and power, which, according to Montesquieu, should be called the executive. The Roman legions marched beneath Aquila standards and swore their oaths by them. In the seated statue of the Lincoln Memorial, created and built between 1915 and 1922, the glorified president rests his hands, to his left and to his right, on two Roman bundles of rods (*fasces*), which from time immemorial have served as a symbol of executive power. By erecting this monument in the shadow of the First World War, the notables of the American capital announced that they were now ready to assume the role of a fourth Rome. There is no doubt that the foreign policy of the United States – a country that was rightly characterized as an *île-continent* – took on imperialist traits over the course of the twentieth century, whereas in the nineteenth century its script was still largely determined by its westward expansion. The seemingly uninhabited expanse, which stretched to the Pacific Ocean, served the inhabitants of the founding states and the streams of newcomers from the Old World as a space of colonization in an internal outside.

These deliberations, notwithstanding the rhapsody and dubious haste of their expression, call attention to an extremely ironic corollary. They have suggested that the momentum of the politically and dramaturgically conceived phenomenon of Europe has for some time now no longer been located in the geographical continent of the same name! According to the logic of its staging, since 1945, acting Europe, not to say incumbent Europe, finds itself on the other side of the Atlantic – more precisely: on the east coast of the USA. The fact that, since 1945, commands for the North Atlantic world have largely issued from a Romanized building called the "Capitol" is no mere caprice in the history of political style. It testifies to the epoch-spanning stability of imperial decorum; in it, the ancient rhetoric of the sublime state lives on in modern times.[25]

Commentators and editorialists of European origin have become accustomed to concealing the irony of this finding by resorting to the palliative term "the West" as a way to sum up the Old World and the USA in an inclusive formula. The antiquarian term "the West" (*occident*), with its pseudo-geographical connotations derived from the setting of the sun, is chosen to sustain the suggestion that Europe continues to play a leading role in the re-staging of a script inherited from Roman antiquity. However, it is easy to see that, for the inhabitants of the Old World, conditions have emerged that, in the language of theater people, are called "post-dramatic." It is not uncommon in this part of the world to go to the theater and convince oneself, under the guidance of artists such as Samuel Beckett, Robert Wilson, and Christoph Marthaler, that – in a somehow interesting way – nothing is happening any more. Great politics has brushed past the Old World. Invocations of former greatness no longer have any effect. The all-too-German expression "das Abendland," signifying the West, where the evening sun goes down, a term virulent since the days of Oswald Spengler and with an afterlife in the celebratory speeches of Christian Democrats in the 1960s and the European propaganda of Otto von Habsburg, no longer seduces anyone, not even in the reunified Federal Republic of Germany. No longer are there any imperial embers to be found glowing in their last light under European ashes. The power to stage events resides on the other side of the Atlantic. All attempts to include us, present-day Europeans, in the

"West" via NATO and with the help of free trade agreements fall into the category of "overarching structures." We've known about them since long before the anthropologist Helmuth Plessner warned they were destined to collapse.

Anyone with experience of books and states knows that irony seldom arrives unaccompanied. For a while now, it has seemed that the westward translation of the European script across the Atlantic has not been quite enough. Russia carried the Soviet agenda for almost seven decades, first with ideological seriousness and then, after Stalin's death, with a gesture of gutted grandeur; once Russia scrapped this agenda, around 1990, irony found itself activated on the eastern flank of the Old World too. Following the implosion of the conspiracy that had bloated into a confederation of states calling itself the Union of Soviet Socialist Republics, it was inevitable that, freed from its pretense to communist universalism, Moscow would pull out of the drawer its post-sixteenth-century script transferring Rome to the regions of *Rus*. Since then, the name Putin has stood for the curiosity that, in Europe's ever more distant East, a re-Russified national empire is re-emerging, which – due to translation in the succession of the Third Rome – declares its bitter opposition to the post-imperial community of states called Europe, seconded by the Patriarch of Moscow and all Rus', who, fearless of anachronism, refers to the papal function by rejecting its Roman exercise in order to reclaim it for the orthodox site of salvation, Moscow. One still awaits an adequate analysis of the lopsided front between the fake imperium of Russia and the still misunderstood post-imperial political entity in the West called the European Union.[26]

At the present time, Russian propaganda has two strategic advantages: on their side, Europe cannot yet create a leadership with a hegemonic profile, not least because of the obligatory discretion of Germany's posture; on the other side, Russian agitators can exploit the instabilities of post-imperial Europeans to reproach them with what had been their own concern more than a hundred years ago: their ostensible "decadence," currently manifest primarily in the licensing of same-sex marriages. The truth is that Russia itself has long had many reasons to see itself reflected in the so-called decadent conditions of its western neighbors. Its true situation is far worse than the arrogant actions of its government would suggest. As a result of its relapse into meaningless imperiality, it has maneuvered itself into a position where it is stamped as a pariah among nations. The attempted *retranslatio imperii* in post-Soviet Moscow imparts no luster to its dramaturges – indeed it renders them in a position of vassalage to China. In the long term, the attack on Ukraine will inflict damage on Russia's reputation – it places its self-respect ever more squarely on a foundation of deliberate self-deception. For the time being, figures like Putin, Lavrov, and the oligarchic gallery can maintain only the most squalid partnerships – names like North Korea, Syria, and Iran are exemplary. For the world as a whole, it would be calamitous if China did not keep this club of the unfrequentable at a distance.

Not only do ironies seldom arrive unaccompanied, they also sometimes generate footnotes transmitted along with the text. When, in a voluntarily called referendum, the British voted by a narrow majority to leave the European Union in June 2016, they ultimately voted not to be a member of a club that was willing to accept members like themselves. Its members on the continent were and remain clearly determined to put their imperial pasts behind them by agreeing to a new and decidedly post-imperial *modus vivendi*. The referendum on the stupid, syllable-sparing, so-called Brexit brought into visibility something that would not have become so clear without this process – namely: the British way of withdrawing from historically lapsed claims to world domination sought to distinguish itself, even retrospectively, from continental expressions of the same. Plainly, there is more than one way of processing the fact that one is no longer the master of things. When Britons resign themselves, they wish not to be confused with the losers on the continent. For, seen with the sun sinking low in the sky, what is Europe, but a club of successors to now-humbled empires? Even the *renuntiatio ab imperio* follows a script that is not tied to territories given once and for all.

Lesson one
The grande école of the world: Europe as a learning context: From the book of enhancements

Europe – where, after all, is it? And how might it understand itself if only it could follow a productive path to its own wellspring? Admittedly, what has been said so far concerns only, as it were, the grosser aspects of European culture: its historical imprint, its programs of power, its imperial frame. Or, maybe more aptly, its political exoskeleton, if one might compare empires with insects, for whom the stabilization of the animal body is imparted by its external armor. Such analogies may be of interest to political anatomists, but for theorists who inquire into a culture's *punctum saliens*, its center of vitality, for theorists attending to the affective vocabularies and formative grammars of local life, stage directions for the main actors and the state actions of rigid political hypersubjects will not suffice. If Europe were merely a program for the pursuits of giant beetles who claw into each other as empires or states, we would sooner or later be able to relinquish the subject to higher biology.

In order to talk about Europe in a way that reveals more than just the contours of an idea of power and the world, an idea emanating from Rome but realized since in multiple refractions, one must place oneself at the emotional hearth of its languages. What one airily calls Europe today – as if Europe had become in actuality the compact entity that Napoleon thought he had nearly in hand at the peak of his power – was in its early beginnings a polyphony of widely scattered local idioms that had but one trait in common: by being spoken, they demonstrated that real successes in life were achieved within language circles, whether tribes or peoples. They manifested themselves in the more or less successful transmission of complete life-form programs, alias "cultures," to subsequent generations. Nations or peoples are the sites of success for languages, and languages for their part are propagation effects that accompany speaking populations through their phases of success. In terms of systems theory, contexts of this type represent what are called "simple reproductions." Their strong feature is seen in their ability to successfully manage the three primary fields of a collective aptitude for survival – the pillars of the classically understood "reality principle," to use Sigmund Freud's term – namely nutrition, procreation, and armed self-assertion.

We know from the usual historical narratives that since Caesar's Gallic expeditions, Romance Europe has been a special site of success for Latinity in the regional language zones. This happened in more than just the areas where imported Latin mutated into Romance vernaculars with the help of substrate languages – as in Provence, Spain, Portugal, Sardinia, Romania, some Helvetic enclaves, and, above all, in the zone of the northern French *langues d'oïl*,[1] where the Romanized Gauls prevailed at the level of everyday speech against the idiom of the Frankish ruling class, to which they owe their still valid but always misleading name, as, so to speak, the "Indians" of our continent. Between Naples and the Alps, Latin disintegrated through popular intermediate stages into an idiom that, after Dante, Petrarca, and Boccaccio, came to be called Italian. Mutations of this type occurred wherever baptized princes of Germanic, Gallic, Anglo-Saxon, etc., origin were clever enough to surround themselves with an elite of Latin-proficient "ministers," subalterns who understood the empire, and organizationally gifted clerics. With the early institutions of higher learning, the *universitates studiorum*, Latinity gained an efficacy that amounted to the establishment of an empire at the level of education; the *translatio studii* lasted until the eighteenth century, when universities were conquered by local vernaculars. Yet, even into the first half of the twentieth century, one had to have learned and practiced Latin in order to be considered educated. In the early universities and cathedral schools, and in the re-established academies from the fifteenth century onward,[2] a process took place that could best be described as a first accretion of the ability to speak about

God, the world, and the rights of both spheres. In these domains, those who were able to speak and write were those who were able to acquire the elements of Latin syntax – including the energetic gerundives and absolute ablatives – as well as the vocabulary of Christianity and Roman administrative thought enriched by Stoicism and other Greek relics.

If there is a secret of Europe, it is hidden in processes that extend beyond the level of simple reproduction. In order to gain an idea of the tendencies that began in the fourteenth century and, in their sum, brought about what constitutes European empowerment and the Eurogenic process – with consequences continuing into the present day and undoubtedly beyond – one has to deal with a curious learning dynamic that gained currency in European systems of knowledge-circulation since the late Middle Ages – something beyond the well-established paths of the seven liberal arts.[3] The situation itself is absolutely astonishing and deserves to be stated in a succinct thesis: it must be accepted as a fact of the history of civilization that in Europe – and only in Europe – there began at that time a "process" (we will have to clarify this term), which must be characterized as a learning context spanning more than seven centuries, with strongly selective *and* intensely cumulative effects. It goes far beyond what the historiography of the *Annales* school had set out to study, with its focus on long-term traditions at the level of genealogical and sacred practices. With regard to its long-term learning dynamics, Europe constitutes a singularity in cognitive history – even China, the leading world power in self-stabilization through imitative learning, has nothing comparable to offer. It was Europe's discreet master thinker, the Czech reformer John Amos Comenius (1592–1670) from the Unity of the Brethren movement, who, in the middle of the seventeenth century, summed up the basic truth of this continent in one sentence: all the world's a school, and all the people in it are united through the intercourse (*coetus*) of learners and teachers.[4] The only thing missing from this dictum is a reference to the diachronic dimension of the school context – the school itself takes on the dimensions of a fabric spanning eras. Though the pattern of the weave will change and various paradigms of knowledge and ability will replace one another – and sometimes contradict one another – there persists a whole nexus of learning, testing, researching, and practicing. On this essential point, Comenius surpasses the dramatic thinker William Shakespeare when the latter has the melancholy Jaques say in *As You Like It* that all the world's a stage, and all men and women merely players.[5] No, even actors can be grasped as disguised versions of teachers and students; a society of mere mimes, role-players, and dissemblers would at best perfect the art of entertaining and deceiving each other – and not by a single step would it advance learning for an enlarged, enriched, and more deeply understood world.

We place here our first bookmark in an early chapter of the Book of Europe. To get a preliminary idea of the revolutionary learning context that made this region of the world unique, it is useful to return to Jacob Burckhardt's work *The Civilization of the Renaissance in Italy*. In a chapter entitled "Glory,"[6] Burckhardt depicts a process that, in view of its consequences, we might call the "Petrarchan paradigm." In April 1341, the poet Francesco Petrarca (1304–1374) was (nearly) the first bourgeois contemporary to be crowned *poeta laureatus* by a Roman senator on Capitoline Hill, an act sanctioned by the King of Naples, Robert of Anjou, following a ritual in the style of the Roman imperial era – and an event reproduced many times since at courts and universities up until the eighteenth century. Later, poets and virtuosi famously preferred to wear invisible crowns of genius. The Roman scene of 1341 made it manifest that an era had dawned in which the acclaimed princes of the symbolic sphere were able to take their place alongside the heads of dynasties.

From today's perspective, the extraordinary nature of the process can be appreciated in terms of systems theory: the truly modern era began, as Burckhardt demonstrated, with the modernization of celebrity. It can be grasped as the launch of a growth cycle in which startup reputational capital, however acquired, generates further reputational gains. The new stars of scholarship, poetry, rhetoric, the visual arts, and music provided the initial impetus for a context that, even seven hundred years later, is identified as a complex continuum of the European culture of individuality. Petrarca is the first modern man, as Burckhardt rightly emphasized, insofar as he was able to ride one of those waves of celebrity that are still unfolding today, often amplified, in global dimensions, more arbitrarily than ever.[7] When Charlie Chaplin would occasionally remark that his name was known in parts of the world where people had never heard of Jesus Christ, he was speaking as an heir to the Petrarca effect. The good news of the modern age is: You don't have to be of noble birth to win glory! Distinguish yourself through your talents and the things you do! Take care that you win recognition for your deeds and your writings and you will win a place for yourself in the company of kings – if not above them, who knows? When Greta Garbo, known as "The Divine," made the decision to end her career in 1941 at the age of 36, she demonstrated that the gesture of abdication was no longer reserved for crowned heads.

If anything exemplifies the change in world conditions at the dawn of the modern era, it is this Roman episode from the middle of the fourteenth century. Times in which the cards of social mobility are reshuffled and dealt anew are rightly called modern. Anyone who inquires deeply into the driving forces behind the new upheaval discovers a principle whose effectiveness has hardly yet been adequately articulated, let alone thought through to the end. The whirl of success surrounding the name of the poet Petrarca clarifies a connection to which, three centuries later, the aforementioned European educationalist Comenius would explicitly draw attention with his ontology of "being toward school" [*Sein zur Schule*]. It is based on an effect of inexhaustible scope, which underlies contemporary theories of learning and without which no plausible cultural theory would be conceivable: where what has been learned and achieved is securely embedded in the milieu of knowledge and ability, such that it can serve as an exemplar well enough known to be cited, it is obviously easier to latch onto new learning. Where an initial excellence has been achieved, further accolades can follow more effortlessly. Applied to Petrarca's experience, this means that once a sufficiently high level of celebrity success has been achieved, there is an increased likelihood of additional accolades following on from the earlier ones.

It was in the fourteenth century – with its innovative celebrity economy for the first time announcing social mobility across the boundaries of class – that discreetly revolutionary effects emerged, over the course of time, to permeate social life in all its areas or "subsystems." In a 1968 publication, the American sociologist Robert K. Merton (1910–2003) called it the Matthew Effect.[8] He was initially referring, in all apparent innocence, only to the self-reinforcing effects of citations in academic literature. Scholars whose name and works are cited more often inevitably attract still further citation, especially in their first flush of fame – one could almost speak of a comet's tail of ensuing references. Merton alludes to the Gospel of Matthew; there, in the context of the parable of the talents that precedes the threatening discourse on the judgment of the nations, Jesus is said to have made the provocative pronouncement:

> For to all those who have, more will be given, and they will have an abundance, but from those who have nothing, even what they have will be taken away. As for this worthless slave, throw him into the outer darkness, where there will be weeping and gnashing of teeth.[9]

If we leave it to the theologians to clear up any scandal caused by statements that sound somewhat "incorrect" to modern ears (and not only to them), what remains is a stimulating lesson for the religiously unbiased reader. Since Jesus will not readily be taken as a source of inspiration for neoliberal heartlessness or winner-takes-all effects, it can be assumed that he was talking about something completely different.

Indeed, it is this completely different aspect that must precede any proper understanding of recent world conditions. By emphasizing that to him who has, even more will be given, Jesus *implicitly* articulated the principle inherent in the Petrarca effect and expressed again in Comenius's strong idea of school: in the school of life as Europe organized it, ultimately only one major subject is taught; it is called "Success"; the minor subjects bear various names to denote diverse paths to titles, diplomas, and master's degrees. In substance, however, all learning here is learning for success. It often takes place as a process of learning enhancement that is traditionally rendered with words like "*askesis*," "discipline," and "exercise," and in the present day by the term "training." Where bearers of success coexist in the majority, they challenge each other to competitions from which reciprocally enhancing effects can emerge. Comenius goes so far as to say that the world as a whole "is not unjustly described as a *house of discipline*."[10] The thinker of didactic practice was the first to interpret Europe, here simply called "the world," as an echo chamber of generalized teaching and learning.

As soon as teaching success stabilizes at a higher level, the elevated position of the teacher vis-à-vis the student imparts the authority to teach through institutions called schools – originally: places of leisure. Where it is expertly practiced, educational effects emerge, and sometimes advance very far indeed. The Academy in Athens, founded by Plato, existed with brief interruptions for more than 900 years. It was closed in 529 CE due to the bigotry of the emperor Justinian I, only to be revived as a gathering place for the intelligentsia after the fall of Byzantium in the mid-fifteenth century in centers such as Rome, Florence, Naples, and Venice.

Only because Europe's institutions successfully transmitted cognitive, technical, and artistic expertise from the late Middle Ages up to the present day, was it possible for the links of tradition in this part of the world to survive major crises without ever being completely broken – even if "chain" is probably too robust a metaphor for such subtle processes. In order to fit in, novices had to be prepared to orient themselves within the state of the art and the arts. This included the imposition of being humbled by the expertise and knowledge of the masters. Where admiration outweighed the indignity, looking up to a role model became an effective incentive. One must freely admit that the figure of the master, in whom is condensed a quantum of cultural authority, with demonstrated skill and a warrant to teach, is also to be found outside of Europe in various high-cultural forms, especially in Asia, and notably in China, where teachers have traditionally been objects of veneration, and in India, where a not always discreet gurucracy has flourished since ancient times. Neither in China nor in India, however, did organisms of skill culture emerge that could compare with the permanent revolution of the critical spirit in Europe.

Europe's most important psychocultural invention is therefore not the teacher, whether this person is called *didaskalos*, *magister*, *doctor*, *maître*, *maestro*, or *professor ordinarius* – figures willing to reproduce their knowledge and expertise in their pupils – but rather the student, who succeeds in activating humility and ambition at the same time. While humility without ambition results in subalternity, ambition without humility leads cultural institutions into the kind of narcissism that was cherished in medieval times by courtly societies as exalted ensembles under the watchword of *la Joie de la cour* – "the Joy of the Court"; in early modern times, it continued in the social activities of self-enthused elites. From the *fête impériale* in the era of Napoleon III to the party culture of postmodern consumer cliques in London, New York, and Dubai, the tone in popular media is set by those circles who congratulate themselves on being as extraordinary as they believe themselves to be.

Where, however, ambition, humility, and talent converged, the "good Europeans" invoked by Nietzsche made their appearance – a minority group now as ever. They were the ones who, for more than half a millennium, undertook momentous attempts to understand how to optimize the governance of states – which, after costly trial and error with various forms of government, resulted in the endangered *Gesamtkunstwerk* of today's democratic institutional system. It was good Europeans who achieved optimizations in the production of tools and goods, yielding benefit to people beyond all calculation, whether by way of markets or through state redistribution. It was good Europeans who demonstrated how to proceed in shaping legal systems, in order to narrow the gap – long an embarrassment for sensitive intellectuals – between de facto legal power and the ideals of justice. It was good Europeans who were at work to establish the newer institutions of research and learning inspired by the idea of the Academy: like the one conceived under the name of Solomon's House in Francis Bacon's *New Atlantis* (posth. 1626), and all the others that were realized as institutions under the effort of figures like Marsilio Ficino and Leibniz. Much the same applies to the organization of general welfare, propelled by efforts to achieve the best possible for society, whether on the basis of Christian and philanthropic motives or under the impetus of socialist postulates. The good students of Europe made it a custom to absorb the customary in order to go beyond it. Even so, it must be admitted that in the dark fourteenth century[11] and in the era of conquests starting in the sixteenth century, terrible offspring of the emerging nations appeared; they produced effects that were no less cruel than those of Asian despotisms. Their ruthlessness is documented in archives affiliated with the ever-expanding "universal history of infamy." From a world-historical perspective, the atrocities of European agents on external fronts were surpassed only by the Muslim slave trade, of which the extent and routines of religiously cloaked inhumanity are still barely known in the Western hemisphere, though it lasted from the middle of the seventh century up into the early twentieth.[12]

What consistently gained the upper hand in all the widely separate spheres of the learning disciplines and their perpetuative transmissions, albeit without the actors themselves being able to grasp it, is what was, at first aphoristically and associatively, called the Matthew effect.

If one translates it from the sphere of parabolic speech into analytical discussion, the outlines of a phenomenon emerge that found its logically, technically, and process-theoretically correct definition only around the middle of the twentieth century. Since then, people have spoken of positive feedback loops, or the recursive self-improvement of processes through their own results.[13] What is generally taken as sociology, political science, economics, human sciences, and their subject matter, means, from a systemic and process-logical point of view, above all the field of studies on feedback-based circularity effects in social systems. Two hundred years ago, in Hegel's *Science of Logic* (1812–1816), a first attempt was made to get to the bottom of those processes in which effects seem to take on the role of their own causes; in Hegel's proposal, however, the extent of mystification remained too high to be generally convincing. The fruitful impulses of dialectics, which sought to translate being into expressions of becoming, were taken up by modern systems thinking, which for the time being, it seems, marks the height of the rationally possible. In this context, Marx's analysis of capital processes temporarily served as a paradigm for understanding positive feedback loops. Marxists with a sense for the systemic dynamics of capital circulation were not merely being presumptuous preceptors in the times when they enjoyed the conviction that they were one step ahead of the rest of the thinking world. They really had one of the most significant examples of feedback-driven processes in sight – because what is the "accumulation of capital," if not precisely this? However, because of their fixation on processes of the so-called economic base, they misjudged the breadth of the realms of reality in which feedback effects lead to endogenous amplifications with modernizing consequences, in particular in the spheres of state action, science, law, engineering, medicine, and the arts.

After discovery of the feedback dynamic, everything that one had been accustomed to accepting as being, reality, and the world, appeared thereafter in a radically different light. As the entirety of conditions and processes, "everything that is the case" can be broken down into three typologically distinct circuit loops in light of a generalized feedback analysis. In addition to simple cycles of self-preservation (*circuli stabilitatis*), which are commonly understood as "nature" or as self-regulating ecosystems, but which are also observed in "traditional societies" that resist the temptation of innovation over very long periods of time, two dynamics that create differences become conspicuous when studying more complex social phenomena: those that pass into virtuous cycles of self-enhancement (*circuli virtuosi*) and those that lapse into vicious cycles of self-harm (*circuli vitiosi*). They are responsible for the process-theoretical – methodologically amoralistic – interpretation of tendencies of enhancement and deterioration in cultural complexes. In this field, the voices of Nietzsche and Luhmann converge; they are accompanied by overtones from the instruments of Hegel and his successors, supplemented by the logical apparatus that, since Norbert Wiener's and John von Neumann's trailblazing studies, has been called cybernetics, or the science of self-regulating mechanisms.[14]

Connections such as these would be more familiar to educated Europeans today had it not been for a dissident student of Hegel who, in the mid-nineteenth century, weighed in on the continent's intellectual history with an intervention that, despite its genius, and seen as a whole, resulted in more emotionally charged confusion, dogmatic short-circuits, and political distortions than in lasting results. Initially, Karl Marx had followed the rebellious accusations of the early French socialists, according to whom modern manufacturing and factory systems had brought about little more, in sum, than a structural transformation of slavery, as if the direct exploitation of serfs under the dictates of manorial lords were ultimately replaced only by the direct exploitation of proletarian labor in the wage system. Thereafter, the thinker succeeded in demonstrating how the dynamics of recent European civilization were increasingly determined by the laws governing the self-reinforcing economic processes he preferred to study. Marx described it as the circulation of capital, by no means irresistible and sometimes critically faltering, but which, through its metamorphoses into the form of money, commodities, knowledges, and machines, aims at the self-valorization of value.

Marx remained so absorbed by the loops, amplifications, and crises of these processes that he contented himself with applying the schema of positive feedback loops – the reconversion of effects into second-order causes – exclusively to the circulation of capital investment in the industrial system. This brought to light important insights, not least with regard to the "organic composition" of capital, in which large-scale machinery and the qualification of "skilled labor" play an increasingly important role. Indeed, the dynamics of capital circulation, especially after the Industrial Revolution of the late eighteenth century, had effects that can justly be described as "earthshaking." Above all, the close connection between the British coal-mining industry and the national textile industry with its power looms and machine technology – something that had been underway for more than a hundred years and was nevertheless formulated in the *Communist Manifesto* of 1848 in prophetic tones – had brought about an emergency in "social change," of a type not infrequently supplying the raw material for revolutions. The systemically sophisticated, albeit highly problematic thesis from the first volume of *Das Kapital* (1867), according to which capitalized money, once translated into commodity form, circulates like an "automatic subject" and in doing so sweeps the "relations of production" along with it, made an impression through a kind of plausibility-at-first-glance.[15] It is imperative to bookmark this momentous passage in the Book of Europe. Over 150 years ago, the reading of this passage divided the minds of socialism and liberalism. In its own circulation, the ominous "automatic subject" brought about its progressive "disembedding" from the givens of lifeworlds and it demonstrated a propensity to ruthlessly assert its own will against older relations of "class and standing."[16] But, while the liberal side defended the belief that the unfettered "subject" could be guided by the power of entrepreneurial will, the socialist camp professed its intention to bend it to the primacy of the party, which is always right.

It is in the nature of the modern "condition of the world" – to take up Hegel's deceptively harmless expression – that the most abstract ideas resonate in the most concrete inventions: in September 1867, the same month and year in which the first volume of Marx's *Kapital* was published by the Hamburg publisher Otto Meissner, Alfred Nobel patented a newly developed nitroglycerin product in Sweden. It was cleverly marketed under the reassuring name of "Nobel's Safety Powder." On the road to fame, the inventor had remained close enough to the sphere of humanistic affectation, and, as a brand manager, he was sufficiently agile in his own interests to attach the Hellenizing name of *dynamite* to the promising new substance. Demand showed that the invention was "timely" in every sense of the word. All of a sudden, an explosive substance – a "means of production," a hyperenergetic agent – appeared in the world, bringing an end to the late medieval regime of gunpowder. From then on, the course of historically turbulent times belonged to substances with intensified explosive power; at first, they were deployed primarily in diamond mining and alpine tunnel excavation. In Switzerland, in the late nineteenth century, anarchist assassins were awarded the no-nonsense name *dinamitardi*; and, when Nietzsche wrote in *Ecce Homo* (1889; Why I am a Destiny §1), "I am no man, I am dynamite," he drew the metaphorically inevitable corollary from the new explosive. After 1887, Nobel's patented Ballistite likewise revolutionized firearms, artillery, and, by extension, warfare as a whole, by placing into the hands of states a means of destruction with an effectiveness hitherto unknown. With this, modern technology experienced the definitive realization of its magical core. Since ancient times, magic has been practiced as a ceaseless juxtaposition of conjuring up and conjuring away. Nobel's inventions brought about a breakthrough in the broad field of magicking unwanted objects into thin air. While in archaic times magic was practiced as a method of mental telemalignancy, i.e. as the working of the will to harm someone from a distance (for example, by fatally cursing, by hexing, by killing someone in effigy), in modern weapons systems magic is operationalized as exploding, poisoning, irradiating, etc., from a distance.

As Minerva's owl flies over Europe, a rugged terrain comes into view, with forces driving progress and forces holding it back. It was inevitable that the synergistic effects of the Industrial and French Revolutions since the late eighteenth century would provoke a wave of "reactions" from the now so-called "establishment." They unfailingly put Newton's third law to the test: *actio est reactio* – for every action, there is an equal and opposite reaction. They converged in the paradoxically modern political movement that came to be called "conservatism" after the publication of Edmund Burke's *Reflections on the Revolution in France* (1790). Ever-erupting conservative impulses testify to the permanent revolution on the *actio* side – indeed, conservatisms have been accumulating their defeats for more than two hundred years. The question of what it means to be conservative has been answered, more or less originally, in every decade since Burke's day. Taken together, the proposals reveal how "reaction" tends to take shape as a response to the thrust of an action: it reluctantly adapts to new circumstances in order to preserve as much of the old as possible, but nowhere is it able to keep pace with the forces of innovation in the long run. Europe could be defined as the place in the world where the disequilibrium between driving and inhibiting forces was first intensified into a fundamental condition. It was no coincidence that it was in the late eighteenth century that the term and concept of "evolution" entered into use, suitable as it was for giving cognitive form to insight into the dynamics of asymmetrical new developments.

The exploitative circulation of competing capital funds would surely have come to a standstill after a few cycles had they not been continually restimulated by a steady stream of inventions, each with a tendency toward increased efficiency, on the part of what are now called the "means of production." From the seventeenth century onward, following a brilliant prelude in the Renaissance (keyword: Leonardo da Vinci), it was modern engineering that set in motion an unforeseeable surge of self-enhancing practices in the world. The invention of the art of invention as a regular discipline, thanks to the collaboration of geniuses and engineers, generated a king tide of innovations, some of patentable quality, some not. In the flood of fancies, countless products without practical use drifted intermittently by – as if they were *moments musicaux* of a mechanical imagination celebrating itself, exemplified by early automata like Jacques de Vaucanson's Digesting Duck in 1739. Some contemporaries at the dawn of the engineering age arrived at the cheerful conclusion that invention and civilization had always been synonymous. Between 1805 and 1822, a progress-happy Protestant pastor named Gabriel Busch (1759–1823) published a twelve-volume handbook of inventions in Eisenach and Vienna, in which humanity was celebrated as a godlike species of inventive creatures.

This undertaking was based on a little-noticed shift in emphasis that had taken place in the doctrine of the holy trinity. While late medieval Christianity had taught the *imitatio Christi* – not least as a result of a devotional book of the same name compiled by Thomas à Kempis around 1418 – and thus also the art of suffering as the highest quality of human existence, more recent centuries saw the beginning of a learning cycle for virtues of a more active orientation, culminating in the imitation of creative power – one might almost speak of an *imitatio patris*. Didn't Leibniz remark that to write a "beautiful novel" was to imitate the Creator on an earthly level? Imitators beyond count had no need to be told twice. By the twentieth century, even tailors had become godlike enough to present their new collections as "creations," and inventive chefs were not far behind.

Those who wanted to grant a higher consecration to modern creativity declared – following the Calabrian theologian Joachim of Fiore (1135–1202) – that the modern and contemporary era as a whole was the Age of the Holy Spirit, a spirit that, especially after the French Revolution, might prefer to speak under secular pseudonyms. From the eighteenth century onward, organized research and the modern discipline of invention and inventiveness combined to produce what historian Peter Burke recently pronounced a "knowledge explosion."[17]

Beyond modern invention, one hyper-innovation, introduced in the seventeenth century and utterly unexpected at the time, propelled modern conditions to a new dynamism. With the intensified mining of bituminous coal in deep pits – and fueled by a new imperative to conserve wood[18] – the vanguard of industrializing civilizations began a grandiose and fatal affair with what would later be called "fossil fuels." Even with the highest admiration for the great sociologist, it can hardly be claimed that the "Protestant ethic" invoked by Max Weber for the previous century played a role in this. Two years before the publication of the first volume of Marx's *Das Kapital*, the British economist William Stanley Jevons triumphantly proclaimed the dawning of the Age of Coal in his treatise *The Coal Question* (1865) – while at the same time warning of its possible end.[19] He suspected that, in the long run, it would not be enough for England to "be an island and have coal" in order to withstand continental competition, especially from the methodically organized Germans.[20] And yet, for Jevons, coal was the true sovereign of modern life – such that it kicked even the "automatic subject" of Marx's analysis down to the second rank. Without it, "humanity" would immediately fall back into a state of archaic wretchedness – an early instance of the rhetoric of imminent regression to which advocates of the status quo have regularly resorted in the years since. But, whereas the analysis of capital highlighted the special position of the "labor power commodity" in value creation, Jevons's reflections drew attention to one culturally revolutionary oddity of "coal as a commodity." Coal yielded a miraculous surplus of "extra energy" – an expression absent from the literature of the time. In fact, reckoning on huge and ever-growing quantities of available extra energy has dominated the economic, technical, and cultural scene since the late eighteenth century. The fact of "exploitation" – which, since the spread of social–egalitarian ideas, had become as visible as it was outrageous – was initially recognized only in relation to the unpaid labor of serfs and slaves, and shortly thereafter in the often-underpaid human labor force in the factory system. Leaving aside Jevons's memorandum, which was scarcely considered on the continent, hardly any attention remained to weigh up the massive exploitation of what later became known as "sources of energy," but which might have been better called "sources of extra energy." Without the constant expansion of extra-energy effects, however, the course of world history since the late seventeenth century would be completely unthinkable, especially given the introduction of machine power in factories and the transition in seafaring from wind power to coal engines.[21] While restless capital, organized in such a way that it revolves around itself, kept bourgeois society in motion as its "automatic subject," coal, as the efficient energetic subject of the modern age – supplemented after 1900 by oil and after 1950 by natural gas – lent its tireless driving force to power production in the spheres of manufacturing, consumption, and transport. If aggressive modernity was able to speak the language of optimism, progress, confidence in growth, and abolition with regard to the undignified living conditions of slaves, non-aristocratic women, Jews, and foreigners, it was only because, all things considered, the influx of anonymous forces from the depths of the earth's past gave such demands a growing plausibility – and, indeed, a prospect of realization.

From early on, the energetic subject of modernity – like the "automatic subject" – came to exhibit titanic traits. It manifested itself in giant ships, bombastic world expositions, and hyperbolic towers. Taken all together, non-human sources of motion ushered in a pyromaniac age, which rushes on from one dissolution of boundaries to the next. The secret of its expansion lay in the abrupt development of the earth's "subterranean forest":[22] through it, the modern world tapped into an almost measureless immensity of energy reserves from the far geological past. Only then was it possible to break decisively through the barrier of natural scarcity that had determined and delimited an older principle of reality: whereas the irremediable slowness of wood growth had ensured that a branch or a log could be burned only once,[23] it suddenly became possible to burn a piece of wood millions of times over, if it were transformed into coal and extracted from the depths of time, since its "next generation" seemed always readily obtainable. The novel experiences of disinhibition and a dissolution of boundaries evoked a previously unknown sense of the uncanny in civilization and were cautiously designated as an "excess."

Elsewhere, there was talk of the return of the Titans, that pre-dynamic race of mighty gods, full of strength and violence. Sensitive contemporaries were seized with the fear that a time had begun in which human Dasein would come to resemble a dreamlike ride on the back of a dragon.

The proletariat has been consistently overestimated, and often cultishly courted and exalted in the traditions of the left from Babeuf to Lenin and Mao, but it had, in the 1848 *Manifesto* and from the outset, been content with its role as more or less poorly nourished assistants to coal-fired machines. With a calmer perspective, this would have been plain from the beginning – but over a long period, emphasis was placed so resolutely on political–economic phenomena that basic eco-energetic insights receded almost entirely into the background. Apart from that, one hardly needed to wait for Marx-inspired analysts of political economy in order to understand that there was a recursively self-intensifying discipline of invention and inventiveness underway that, together with the engine-powered economy it inspired, had radically changed the face of the world since the eighteenth century. The art of invention would perpetuate itself through the academic institutions it created, such as the École polytechnique in Paris in 1794, and technical universities in Germany, such as what is now the Karlsruhe Institute of Technology in 1825 and in the USA, with the Massachusetts Institute of Technology in 1861.

The discipline of invention and inventiveness had functioned autonomously since the seventeenth century. When Marxist theorists attempted to include it as "intellectual labor" under the category of the "proletariat," they betrayed their inability or unwillingness to grasp, beyond the sphere of the circulation of capital, the inherent laws of self-reinforcing processes of the cognitive and technical domination of nature. When, on the other hand, there was occasional talk of an "intellectual proletariat," this was usually in reference to academics, whose studies gave them no place in the labor market, and who were seeking a basic income in political agencies. In short, the evaporation proclaimed in the *Communist Manifesto* (1848) of "everything that would exist in stasis and everything of the order of social standing" was by no means due solely to the repercussions of disembedded monetary flows on the economic life of their host societies. Moreover, when conditions evaporated, this happened first in the "language games" of literature, in the "discourses" of the tribunes of the people, and in the futuristic fantasies of utopians.

As the Petrarca phenomenon had shown, the reputation economy of the late Middle Ages had already developed a dynamic that cannot be understood without local Matthew Effects. In similar fashion, the modern discipline of invention and inventiveness developed a thoroughly idiosyncratic, self-reinforcing dynamic. Much the same applies to any number of modern practices and disciplines, in which implementation is consistently subject to protocols of self-intensification – above all to the organized sciences, the medical system, and the arts, but also to relatively recent phenomena such as tourism; it applies above all to sport, which became endemic in Europe after 1900 and which, through its dual orientation toward peak performance and mass appeal, remains particularly committed to the spirit of recursive self-intensification.

Despite all these indications, one might conjecture that the significance of phenomena determined by positive feedback loops will reveal itself most fully only in the extended present. Since the mid-twentieth century, processes of great consequence have been taking place in the spheres of physics and cybernetics and transitioning into applied artificial intelligence, such that one cannot avoid speaking of an integral civilizational revolution. One must be prepared for it to surpass even the most dramatic effects of the Gutenberg era. It transforms feedback-fueled learning processes, previously the domain of humans, into the autodidacticism of machines. The process as a whole could be interpreted as a temporally condensed mirror image of European learning processes at an advanced school for devices engaged in study. With it, there emerges a second-order uncanniness. It is no longer only by the ghosts of the dead that the human world feels itself haunted; in times to come, it will be unsettled even more by a noospheric haunting and the roamings of self-programming spirits without pre-existence. The non-graves of tomorrow will open wider than any graves of the past. The haunting of the future could show how the spirit of the not-yet is taking on meanings that are more dystopian than eutopian.

As regards the dimension of self-reinforcing systemic effects in the political sphere, the statism of the Western world – after its preliminary developments in the "autumn of the Middle Ages" – has asserted itself as a massive entity in its own right since the mid-seventeenth century. From the days of so-called absolutism, through far-reaching fiscal practices and expanding legislative regulations – not least in the areas of measurement, weights, currencies, fees, and fines, as well as civil status and names – the emerging modern states promoted a multitude of self-reinforcing effects from which emerged the bureaucracy, the school system, the judicial system, the transport system, regional administrations, and the multi-faceted archipelago of so-called infrastructures, right down to polyclinics and municipal social services. The fact that the state has functioned, since the twentieth century, as the largest employer in the economic domain illustrates how, in this field too, rewards are given to those who already have. In Germany, government agencies are currently far in the lead with nearly 5.3 million employees, 1.7 million of whom are civil servants (figures from June 2023); in France, one in five workers – a total of 5.6 million – is on the republic's payroll. The thesis circulated by vulgarized Marxism, notably by Lenin, whereby the modern state is ultimately just the executive organ of the capital-owning class, provides nothing more than a shallow excuse for the inability of dogmatically stupefied intellectuals to assess the stubborn self-reinforcing recursions of feedback-fueled social systems. This deficiency persists as long as one adheres to the intellectually ruinous schema according to which the phenomena of the "superstructure" are explained by the structures of the "base." As the driving force behind a movement that sought nothing less than world revolution, the half-truths of Marxism not only inspired the crimes against humanity committed by Lenin, Stalin, and the Maoists, they also proved to be an epistemological catastrophe – they promoted the seizure of power by a half-knowledge that wanted to pass itself off as the whole.

One of the animating principles in the sphere of the modern state was formulated as early as 1863 by Adolf Wagner, when he established his law of increasing state activity and its finances, though this would have to be supplemented by a law of the corrupting effect of a self-serving, entrenched party system. It should be emphasized, in this regard, that corruption typically reaches its nadir in systems with one-party rule. For a century, Marx-inspired intellectuals derided Wagner's realism (as mere "academic socialism") on the question of the state, though they could counter it with nothing better than foolishness about the state's supposed eventual withering away.

To characterize the "eurogenic process" of the modern era, or, more precisely, European empowerment as a centuries-spanning learning context, requires one to elucidate a structural change in learning that took place in a lengthy and largely unprogrammed curriculum. A dramaturgical mechanism was set in motion in this field that altered the relationship between the teaching and learning generations in Europe. From the perspective of cultural dynamics, what is commonly called modernization denotes a progressive shift from learning through the imitation of the old and the aged to learning through an imitation of the recent and the new. While the first mode could be denoted with the term "tradition" – the passing on of the tried and tested – for the second, one might use the term "mode" or "fashion." This of course recalls the etymological relationship between mode and modernity, but it also provides an opportunity to emphasize the fashionable nature of imitative behavior in the contemporary world in general. The broader concept of fashion encompasses more than just processes that affect the self-design of modern individuals – their apparel and general bearing, for example; it refers to everything that concerns how they present themselves: vocabulary, beliefs, reading habits, listening habits, taste preferences, and attributes of personal enhancement. In a certain sense, the "cultural history of the modern age," as a whole, is a single *querelle des anciens et des modernes*, a quarrel of the ancients and the moderns – not merely in the sense of a dispute over the primacy of ancient masters over contemporary authors, as sparked around 1700 by

French critics who, as proud contemporaries of the Sun King, no longer wished to bow before the classical writers of Greece and Rome. There is a constant friction produced between learning from proven models of the past and an orientation toward the new, which, not having been historically certified, makes its impression precisely through its novelty – and through the promise of improvement or increased vitality that it contains. For this reason, the process of modernity as a whole cannot be understood without the dynamics of learning through an engagement with novelty. By the end of the eighteenth century, fashion had already attained the prestige of an inescapable authority; even Kant concluded that it was better to be a fool in fashion than a fool out of fashion.[24] Indeed, since criteria such as originality, entertainment value, surprise factor, and increased profitability have come to the fore, novelty as such has gained a privileged status. Neophilia has become the defining habitus of the educated – people sense "revolution" everywhere and often welcome it uncritically as a refreshing change. Since the 1920s, even conservatives have presented themselves as revolutionaries so as not to miss the train of the times. Cicero's maxim declaring that *historia magistra vitae est* – history is the schoolmistress of life[25] – has lost its force due not only to an increasing valorization of the present and the cult celebrating innovations of the day, but also from cultural and learning-system factors; the pedagogy of the tried and tested has been subject to a progressive weakening ever since.[26] There are practically no adherents left for the belief that historical knowledge can impart wisdom without causing harm. Indeed, who today seriously still believes that "history" is nothing other than a collection of examples worthy of either imitation or censure?

The process can be elucidated through the example of modern surgery's rediscovery of anesthesia: after the first operation under general anesthesia was successfully performed with ether at Massachusetts General Hospital in Boston on October 16, 1848 – a true October Revolution and with irreversible effects – within mere months knowledge of the new procedure was disseminated and incorporated into the practice of many hospitals around the world. The advent of anesthetization not only gave rise to an extensive surgical practice, it also inaugurated a new mode of patienthood. Like almost no other feature, it shapes the modern *conditio humana*. An awareness of operability or tolerable treatability in conditions of physical crisis fundamentally changes the human experience of being in the world. No other innovation demonstrates so emphatically the conversion of modern life to learning from contemporaneous developments. The sudden emergence of the art of anesthesia attests to the triumph of "fashion." Considered, then, in terms of its contribution to cultural learning, what is called mode or fashion appears as a sorting process that, out of a thousand experiments, eliminates nine hundred and ninety in order to retain ten; from a functional perspective, it is a method of arriving at new classics. Ether and chloroform became chemical classics until they were succeeded in turn when new substances came on the scene, such as ketamine, propofol, and so on. Even from the turns of the fashion clothing carousel, individual products came off and became iconic; ten thousand designs were proposed, forgotten, and eventually recycled; jeans and the little black dress became ubiquitous archetypes. Where seasonal fashions turn their backs on study and learning, as in couture, cosmetics, and pop culture, they celebrate variation for variation's sake. This is inherent in the willingness of the many to follow rapid change.

The emergence of almost everything into fashion is fundamentally related to the acceleration of historical events felt everywhere in the years since 1789. Of course, where fashion, as an imitation of the new and the unheard-of, sought to become political, it propagated the illusion that the events in France between 1789 and 1793 could be replicated soon enough in other European settings too – and why not in South America or anywhere else where emancipation from obsolete powers appeared on the agenda? It would turn out that even among Europeans, a full century would pass before the taste for republic and democracy became popular; indeed even France took its time, enduring four relapses into monarchy before its republican stage assumed more stable form with the Constitution of 1875. One is constrained to admit that the triumph of mode or fashion over tradition, so characteristic of the modern world, is forcefully moderated in the political domain by the inertia of reality. When monarchical traditions do make an appearance today, they are often more fashionably decked out as a dictatorship.

To understand what is meant here by "Eurogenesis," it is necessary to interpret the circumstance that, according to statistics on religion,

Europe is the most "unbelieving" region in the world. There is no lack of evidence for this conclusion. The literature on topics such as secularization, loss of faith, the triumph of the scientific worldview, the individualization and spiritualization of religion, laicism, and active and passive atheism, fills libraries; with each new decade, countless meters of shelf space must be added to accommodate it all. Whatever is added, there are likely to be few statements not overshadowed by the theses articulated in Nietzsche's "Lenzerheide Fragment" of June 10, 1887.[27] If we refrain from placing a bookmark in this document, it is because the catchphrase that appears in it – "European nihilism" – contains an impulse that exceeds the scope of the considerations undertaken here. It opens out into a boundless cultural–critical polemic, in which the dividing line between European self-diagnosis and anti-European hate rhetoric becomes blurred.

It suffices here to point out that a comprehensive learning context, such as the one suggested so far, can be understood only as, at the same time, the silent drama of a great, complementary unlearning. Alongside the mass of elements acquired and retained – whether one calls them "objective spirit" with Hegel, defines them as the mass of "culture" with Simmel, or describes them as "archives" with Foucault and Derrida – there are revealed in this drama vast fields in which things have been cleared away, overcome, finished, lost, and forgotten – or however one might describe the state of cultural relics that have fallen into disuse. Europe is, among many other things, the world's market for exquisite antiquities, complemented by underworlds of bric-à-brac, junk, and the air of ruins. As Walter Benjamin once remarked, there is no testimony to culture that is not also a testimony to barbarism. One might add that there are no current achievements, no virtuosities, no refinements, that are not counterbalanced by a loss of form, desublimation, a breakdown of habitus, and decivilization. What is called cultural pessimism is the conviction that, as developments progress, the losses outweigh the gains. To weigh things up in such a manner is wrong, as one-sidedness tends to be; even so, it has many arguments in its favor. The modern world has spun the wheel of fortune thousands of times over, often distributing its rises and falls in unpredictable ways. Within it, spins the great wheel of a mental shift, re-dating contemporaries within their era.

To describe Europe as the stronghold of unbelief in the world – in a neutral tone, it goes without saying – implies the assertion that there are forms of unlearning and disenchantment that can be counted as gains. To put it bluntly: Europe's most significant, albeit risky, achievement in the history of civilization consists in having freed individuals from a state of total membership in closed cult and faith communities. This issue has been discussed since the days of the early Enlightenment under the banner of "religious freedom." As a result of its banalization, this expression has become too impoverished to give a proper idea of the range of its meanings.[28] Not only does it express the freedom of "confession" enjoyed by individuals in liberal states, it is preceded by the modern fiction that one can subsequently choose or reject the faith in which one was raised – to be more precise, not merely that one can overwrite or deactivate early engrams, but that one can efface them completely – which is an impossibility. Over and above that, it denotes – and this is its far greater significance – the release of religion as such from its age-old function of holding together a given group of people in a compulsory communal synthesis. If Europe has accomplished one feat that will remain part of any universally applicable program of civilization, it is the progressive liberation of religions as such – however one defines them – from the task of securing the cohesion of ethnic and political ensembles through symbolically coded psychological and social constraints. In our part of the world, the function of cultivating cohesion between members of the same nation who do not know each other has long since been transferred to non-religious cultural agencies – first and foremost, state schools, the free press, the legal system, universities, and literature; entertainment media, insurance companies, pension funds, concert halls, museums, and the pluriverse of associations, also play a role here. They relieve what is called faith of the task of unduly homogenizing social ensembles. The young Marx was right when he claimed that all critique begins with the critique of religion; the critique of religion, for its part, begins with the rejection of total communitization. Its first success is the decriminalization of apostasy.

One could almost describe free Europe as a union of unperturbed apostates. "Unbelievers" need no longer fear persecution within it; believers can turn away from the peloton of unbelievers without risking more than a certain smile. Where else in the world are the phenomena of a non-totalitarian, non-integralist community formation so fruitful, so diverse, and so intractably developed? What would "societies" be without communities? What would a "citizenry" be without associations, clubs, choirs, and neighborhoods? These allow a flourishing "freedom of communities within communities."[29] It should be noted at this point that so-called "laicism" in France is a misnomer for the emancipation of individuals from religiously codified compulsory membership – French laicity, born of anti-Catholic pathos, tends to take on the characteristics of a community that, if not coercive, is at least oppressive. Forced laicism is the unconscious negative image of the 1685 revocation of the Edict of Nantes, with which Louis XIV had revoked sectarian toleration and abetted *le mal français*. Properly understood, laicity is not expressed in the rejection of religious creeds; it is realized as an insight into the poetic character of religious teachings. It proves its worth when it prevents the club of a dead prophet from becoming a forced community of his believers.

If one were to describe in a simple phrase the most important gain from the processes of the European Enlightenment, one would initially arrive at a negatively formulated statement: it consists in the progressive unlearning of obsequiousness. Monsieur Teste would say: *La subalternité n'est pas mon fort – Subalternity is not my strong point.* Put positively and translated into Spinoza's language, this means that enlightened Europe will survive as long as creative passions keep those of *ressentiment* in check.

Lesson two
Out of Revolution: How a German historian writes Europeans' autobiography

The Book of Europe – how can we assure ourselves of its legibility? How can we persuade ourselves that this "continent without qualities," is – despite its elusive character – not altogether lacking in recognizability and may even enjoy a degree of narratability? Where is one to begin in order to grasp the amorphous quasi-object "Europe" under the light of its presentability – whether lit from an external source, or from a luminosity inherent in the object itself?

In the pages to come, I would like to assume the role of the odd foreigner from Jorge Luis Borges' story "The Book of Sand," who knocked at the door of a bibliophile in Buenos Aires and presented himself as a seller of rare Bibles. His *Book of Sand*, however, was the negation of the possibility of forming a coherent story. It imparted, *eo ipso*, the message that, as a reader of this diabolical work, you could not locate yourself at any place within it; you could never find again a passage that had once attracted your attention – supposing it had ever existed – and so you would never be able to reassess whether it really had anything to say to you. Reading in the infinite is the impossibility of being affected by a story. The salesman in Buenos Aires describes the dilemma precisely:

> If space is infinite, we may be at any point in space. If time is infinite, we may be at any point in time.

The book that I carry with me in my bookseller's suitcase and am now offering to the public for purchase, albeit initially only for a brief review, is the perfect anti-*Book of Sand*. It represents the most vehement protest formulated in recent times against the blurring of human Dasein into Infinity – and its little sister, Indifference. Indeed, it opens upon the utmost urgency, not to say officiousness, with which a book can communicate with a reader. From those who take it up, this book reserves the right to demand a receptivity, even a willingness to learn and suffer to the extreme – and far beyond what the operas of Wagner and Stockhausen demand of their listeners.

The discussion here concerns the voluminous work *Out of Revolution*, written by the historian and language theorist Eugen Rosenstock-Huessy, published in 1938 by Wipf & Stock in Eugene, Oregon, USA, and bearing the somewhat bizarre but resounding subtitle: *Autobiography of Western Man*.[1] Upon cracking it open, the reader is greeted by Horace's motto: *De te fabula narratur* – "The story is about you." We note in passing that Karl Marx availed himself of this same formula to save German readers of his work *Das Kapital* from falling into the fallacy that everything treated there concerned only the English – because No, to the contrary, it also concerned readers on the continent, and the Germans in particular.[2]

Autobiography of Western Man – the very phrase is apt to arouse disconcertment in several respects. For one thing, the term "Western man" has become problematic for today's ears; there is hardly a European today who would unreservedly identify as belonging to a collective of "the people of the West," even though "identitarian," communitarian, and regionalist movements are currently experiencing a boom. This is in part because a great majority are currently dominated by anti-collectivist motives; but some hesitation in embracing the expression also comes from the fact that many members of Euro-American civilization have begun to regard themselves as reflected through the global East, the global South, and global indigeneity such that their appetite for self-affirmation has altogether withered away.

Still more disconcerting is the genre designation "autobiography." As is well known, one of the discoveries of European antiquity was that individual human beings are worthy and capable of being biographed – the *bioi paralleloi*, the *Parallel Lives*, of the great Greeks and Romans, written by Plutarch in the second century CE, documented this fact with long-lasting effects. From the late Middle Ages onward, a phenomenon emerged in European cultural practice that could be described as a democratization of biography. Life stories worthy of being passed down to the memory of posterity are no longer restricted to just those of saints, princes, generals, and resplendent women.[3] The biographical turn reached its first point of maturity when sixteenth-century humanism proclaimed the virtual equation of individuality and life narrative.[4] Modern European anthropology summed it up in the presumption that human beings are not only living creatures whose existence deserves a depiction – they are also ones capable of telling their story themselves. When Wilhelm Dilthey, in an analogy with Kant's efforts to explain the possibility of the natural sciences, wanted to establish the categorical foundations of the humanities, it was the autobiographical competence of the European individual that remained at the center of the schema for orienting the possibility of history and historiography.[5] Without the autobiographical nucleus, any more far-reaching history would remain either a mere collection of examples from the lives of others, of vague existential value, or a veritable nobody's story, recounting the succession of past circumstances without personal reference. But, since the history of a nation, a sect, or an institution spans many generations and thus goes beyond the "self-understanding" experience of the individual, a mature historiography must be able to show how the "sources," the documents, the scriptural and material testimonies of the past, can be woven together into a narrative in such a way that they do not completely lose their connection to what has been remembered and experienced. At the same time, they should shed light on "coherent wholes" that no one person "experienced as such."[6] Since the nineteenth century, with the golden age of historicism, this occurred largely by training individuals to embrace an affiliation with their nation: with the nationalization of their selves, they acquired the ability to consummate themselves in a convergence with the past fates of their "people," their "nation," their "culture," as if these past dramas were something that, with a grain of salt, could be of continuing existential concern for them. It was in the tendency of historicism, however, – and what Nietzsche called its "antiquarian" attitude – to blot out the autobiographical and memorial core of the larger narratives, with the result that individuals themselves feel ever more like flotsam in stories belonging to no one.

These cues should suffice to illustrate the unusual nature of Rosenstock-Huessy's undertaking. The author wanted to conceive a narrative collective-self capable of recapitulating the history of Europe from the eleventh century to the present day as if it were the novel of its own life. To illustrate the extravagance of the project, one would have to imagine that Aurelius Augustinus, the master of Christian autobiography, had not recounted his *Confessions*, completed in 401, as a sequence of his own questionable actions, but had conceived them as the true history of Christianity as a whole. He would have presented it as the evolution of a messianic sect from the province of Judaea; he would have given an account of the stages of the Church – persecuted, struggling, and triumphant – as if they were part of the course of his own life; he would have continued to speak about the heretical crises up to the great turning point under Constantine, the Christian Caesar, and the elevation of Christianity to the imperial religion under the Emperor Theodosius in 393, as if reporting events from his own years; he would have done all this under the premise that he had been granted privileged insight into God's script – and that he had recognized that his own appearance was foreseen in a late section of the great exposé. It had really been predetermined that a tiny group of Nazarenes in the 30s and 40s of the first century CE would be called upon to conquer the "world circle," i.e., the Roman Empire. On top of that, he, Aurelius himself, would have been truly ordained to describe the external calamities and internal crises of the Church over a period of 350 years, as if he had suffered them *in persona* – hence, he would be the authorized heir and proclaimer of the knowledge revealed thus far concerning God's plans for the world.

As is well known, the vision at Ostia forms the turning point of Augustine's "conversion."[7] As for Rosenstock-Huessy, he left his readers in no doubt as to where and how the turning point came to him: he claimed to have had a kind of "vision" in the midst of the "storm of steel" at the Battle of Verdun in 1916. Under the unremitting grip of the fear of death, the insight crystallized within him that this European war, which had become a real world war, would necessarily bring with it a revolutionary uprooting of all life as it had existed to that point – and, even more than that, that no return to a new civility would be possible until all the consequences of this incommensurable experience had been drawn.

The question underlying Rosenstock-Huessy's book, which is enormous in every sense, is this: how is a return from world war possible? Somewhat more formally: how might one determine the conditions for the possibility of demobilization? Rosenstock-Huessy shares the pathos of this question in common with a number of his contemporaries, who were desperate for an interpretation of the catastrophe then facing humanity. He shares it with Karl Barth, whose radical new interpretation of Paul's Epistle to the Romans in 1922[8] caused a theological sensation; he shares it with Hugo Ball, co-initiator of Zurich Dadaism, who, after the end of the war, made a turn toward early Christian modes of thought;[9] he shares it with Ernst Bloch, who, in the two versions of his early work *The Spirit of Utopia*,[10] proclaimed a revolutionary gnosis born from a spirit of anticipating a better life; he shares it with Paul Valéry, who, in his essay *La Crise de l'esprit*, written and published in 1919, expressed his shock at the fragility of the highest achievements of culture: "We later civilizations … we too now know that we are mortal";[11] he shares it with Lenin, who with grandiose cynicism recognized the collapse of the tsarist regime in Russia as a singular opportunity for the Bolsheviks to seize power; he shares it with Martin Heidegger, who, with his analysis of finitude, or rather his interpretation of Dasein as "thrownness" and "being-towards-death," linked philosophical thinking to the mood of irreversible mobilization; he shares it with Benito Mussolini, who repudiated a return to civil peace by lecturing that fascism was the horror of a comfortable life. He shares it with Adolf Hitler, who expressed his refusal to accept defeat with the famous words from *Mein Kampf*: "I, for my part, decided to go into politics."[12] He shares it with the novelist Hermann Broch, who, in the final part of his trilogy *The Sleepwalkers*, has a wounded man in a field hospital say to his nurse: "none of us will ever really get home again."[13] He shares it especially with Franz Rosenzweig, who, in his work *The Star of Redemption* (1921), turned away from all traditions of theoretical philosophizing in order to accept only a "new" form of thinking, one "contaminated" by real existence: a thoroughly de-eternalized reflection on the premises of unredeemed life, thoroughly exposed to temporality.[14]

Rosenstock-Huessy's autobiography of Western man must therefore be understood as a document of the delayed return from the World War. While returning fighters of fascist tendencies on both the right and the left committed themselves to a continuation of the struggle under new slogans of the postwar period, disdaining any thought of demobilization,[15] Rosenstock-Huessy resolved to remain under arms in a different way: he did not want to demobilize until the whole truth about the catastrophe of European civilization had been pronounced and a new mission for the coming times had come into view.

It would take until the publication of *Out of Revolution* (and its earlier version published by Diederichs Verlag in 1931)[16] before the author saw that the moment had come to exercise his right to demobilize. One could go so far as to say that the book we are bookmarking here in its entirety is actually a field-post letter delivered twenty years after the end of the war to puzzled readers on American soil – a delay not due to an error on the part of the military mail, but because the author simply took so long to organize his addenda, excursuses, and postscripts.

We have not yet clarified the motif that confers upon the book its invasive pathos. What was it that allowed the author to presume to tell the story of a millennium as if occupying the position of a subject who could encompass the sum of its chapters as a series of contexts he himself had experienced? As the author himself emphasizes, this is a sequence of no fewer than twenty-seven generations. Supposing that individuals possess the ability to incorporate, with some lucidity, three generations of average duration into the bounds of their experience, nine-tenths of Rosenstock-Huessy's series would remain outside the individual's own time span as far as macro-autobiography is concerned.

The riddle resolves itself as soon as we take a closer look at the basic operation of Rosenstock-Huessy's narrative technique. It can be deciphered by reference to the motto *de te fabula narratur*, which is also activated here. The former soldier at Verdun referred to an experience that can only be described as a giant leap into the position of a purely mediumistic authorship. As the medium of his ecstatic experience, he offered assurances that, in the face of unremitting extremity, there had been a falling away of all the masks with which individuals in normal times will customarily disguise themselves as players of social roles. He had been suddenly uprooted from everything in bourgeois life that fosters pretention, routine, self-satisfaction, and vanity. Only when humans are stripped down to pure mortality does it become possible to pose the essential question: what actually and ultimately constitutes life in the *conditio humana*? Rosenstock-Huessy's answer was this: it is allowing oneself to be seized by an idea to which the individual can devote their entire existence. This leads to a second question: how is life to be continued in the harsh light of the incommensurable experience of war? Before any more concrete answer appears, it is only the postulate of a rebirth that is plain to see: the Dantean motto *incipit vita nova* – "thus begins a new life" – becomes the banner under which the word "postwar" will henceforth signify as it does. The total reduction that emerged for the author from the condensation of Dasein into bare existentiality was concentrated into a quintessential concept: "the revolution." After 1918, no authentic life was possible any more that did not take place under the sign of "revolution." The new life demands a "new learning" and a "new teaching" – and, consequently, the fundamentally changed use of a lifetime. The author interpreted this as a mandate to explain, in stages, to his fellow citizens, who had been spared to one degree or another, how war, revolution, and truth intertwine in "real history," that is, in the sequence of life-giving inspirations from the preceding millennium. There have been petty revolutions often enough at other times and in other places: palace revolutions, overthrown governments, changes of dynasty – the Book of History is little more than a collection of examples illustrating the phrase: *plus ça change, plus c'est la même chose* – the more things change, the more they remain the same. This time, however, the future of the world as a whole was at stake – for here and now would be decided the future fate of freedom, the one that Europeans have fought over for the past thousand years. The World War, as it was understood, demanded a "world biography" for the use of its survivors; it could not be content with a mosaic composed haphazardly from local fragments of memory.[17] Only an author audacious enough to narrate Europe's fate from the perspective of its freedom-creating revolutions could become a world biographer. Those who speak of "revolution" are reaching for the whole; those who believe they are participating in it want nothing less than to change the world and everything in it. The years after 1918 were a time of grand words; for people in those days, expressive, even all-encompassing verbal gestures rolled easily off the tongue.

Proceeding from evidence gained during the war, Rosenstock-Huessy spent the years thereafter studying European legal and state history from the Middle Ages onward as a sequence of moments in which authentic revolutionaries – comparable to Hegel's "world-historical individuals" – stood before their peers to rebel with absolute authenticity and death-defying single-mindedness against the intolerability of the confused and unjust conditions of the state and society, despite the fact that, in every age and in most parts of the world, the vast majority of people, due to inertia, despondency, and immersion in base everydayness, somehow tolerate the chronically intolerable. Rosenstock-Huessy's array of exemplary revolutionaries is as limited as it is unambiguous: it embraces the names of Pope Gregory VII, Luther, Cromwell, Robespierre, and Lenin. The first name stands for what Rosenstock-Huessy calls the "papal revolution" of the eleventh century: this unusual designation amounted to more than just an incisive reinterpretation of the so-called Investiture Controversy between the papacy and the empire; it also contained a discovery with far-reaching consequences for the understanding of church and statehood in Europe.[18] The other names indicate historical watersheds commonly referred to as the Reformation – referred to by our author as the "German Revolution" – as well as the Glorious Revolution in England (which put an end to the years of Puritan dictatorship[19] and might better have been called the "Glorious Restoration"), then the French and finally the Russian Revolutions – the latter two, of course, remain present in public consciousness today under their usual names.

In sum, the phrase "Out of Revolution" amounts to a call: "People of the West, listen up! A returnee from the utmost extremity speaks to you now!" The belated field-post letter is directed primarily at the decadent Christianity of Europe and its enlightened epigones, including their atheistic descendants. The label "decadent" was fully appropriate for the European churches, since it was, predominantly, the baptized members of several formally Christian nations,[20] who could be persuaded to kill each other by the millions. Quite obviously, the motif of *imperium* that occupied modern nations had carried off the victory over the trans-national idea of *ecclesia*. The young Rosenstock (he took his wife Margrit Huessy's surname in 1925), who was born in 1888 into a Jewish family, who joined the Evangelical Lutheran Church in Berlin at the age of seventeen, and who took his conversion seriously, must have been struck by this fact as a disaster in the history of religion, indeed as the manifest bankruptcy of Christianized civilization. The author wanted to give this dumbfounded old world a moment of truth in the baptismal font of extremity.

> In the white heat of revolution, a society reaches the height of its sincerity, penetration and clairvoyance into its own self. In the same way there exist in the life of every living soul one or two solemn moments when he speaks the full truth about himself.[21]

Full of the conviction that his wartime experience had made him "congenial" with respect to all the real revolutions of the "continent,"[22] the man who had returned from a baptism by fire claimed the prerogative of interpreting, if not justifying, the violent excesses of great upheavals. Those who present revolutions as creeds also confess their acts of violence as if they were inevitable. The author was aware that, as a rule, only military force is capable of drawing new borders – and, when the time comes to redraw them, revolutionary force will claim its own legitimacy. Rosenstock-Huessy had, of course, understood that as an individual he could not be the legitimate author of an autobiography of Europeans – but he believed he was called upon to serve as a medium for the "real" Author of this inspired book. Only the "spirit of revolution" as such would be qualified for this function, inasmuch as one might postulate its existence. The author left his readers in no doubt as to the Christian identity of the revolutionary spirit. It was characteristic of the postwar atmosphere that, open to all forms of extremism as it was, it tended to equate the spirit of the times with the spirit of the world – and also that it did not bar identification of revolutionary spirit with the Holy Spirit. The reader of this strongly assertive book would take note, at the very least, that the Holy Spirit was no pacifist.

The war had exposed the extent to which nationalities had dismembered Christian universalism; almost everywhere, the churches had become concierges to powerful states. Max Weber was right to speak of the "world dominion of unbrotherliness,"[23] against which the Protestant message was as ineffective in the modern world as it had been in the medieval one of petty princes, robber barons, and warlords. From the tenth century onward, their predecessors had been taught, with difficulty, to refrain from slaughter in the name of God on the holy days of the week, from Friday to Sunday.[24] At the conclusion of the World War, a moment seemed to have arrived that made it necessary once again to assist the free spirit as it blew across a landscape of total confusion – though of course there could be no talk of a "Peace of God" in view of the newly forming power blocs and the battle formations they were moving into place.

It speaks volumes about Rosenstock-Huessy's spiritual recklessness, not to say unscrupulousness, that he so much wished to see a timely storm inflamed by the Holy Spirit in the then still ongoing Russian Revolution, even though questions about the true inspiration behind the events in the USSR must have arisen as early as 1931 – and, at the latest, by the height of the terror in 1938. Certainly, Lenin had conceded defeat on the Russian side in the Treaty of Brest-Litovsk in March 1918 and relinquished some territories in the west in order to gain the *unum necessarium*, the "one thing necessary": the chance for socialist world renewal. Rosenstock-Huessy trusted that the Bolshevik leader had followed a credible calling; he stood by the notion that Lenin had not merely acted out his obsession with a baseless theory. With Lenin's death and Stalin's rise, there was more than one reason to doubt the bold Christian hermeneutics of the revolution – and likewise the doctrine that "deeply religious" imperatives were ultimately being realized in Eastern Europe, albeit under worldly and violent auspices.[25] It should have become evident, by the Moscow Trials of 1936 to 1938 at the very latest, that the "dictatorship of the proletariat" was more of a sham, designed to seduce intellectuals and spokespeople for the voiceless classes, than a figure of speech for a Holy Spirit who might pursue godly goals with aplomb, even under an atheistic pseudonym.[26]

In pointing to the idea of the necessary pseudonymity of Christian impulses, we touch on the logical core of Rosenstock-Huessy's thinking, then and later, in which center stage was held by "the language of the human race" and the coexistence of people under the pressure of a multi-dimensional reality demanding answers. His most important intuition was expressed in his assertion that, in the future, it would be important to think the truth under conditions of multilingualism – a challenge that implied more than the peaceful or unpeaceful coexistence of national and ethnic idioms.

Wherever the dictates of multilingualism assert themselves, what is called truth – especially in religious matters and apart from anything else it might mean – has always been the product of a struggle between the translatable and the untranslatable. The "spirit" functions as both translator and critic, preserving the untranslatable from the falsification unavoidable in translation. The necessity of translation is the *conditio sine qua non* of the historical world. Indeed, "truth" itself, and Christian truth above all, seems from the outset to be governed by the principle of allowing itself to be falsified in order to be disseminated in a way befitting its expansive nature. What has been called the miracle of Pentecost[27] refers not only to the experience of a collective enthusiasm beyond languages; it likewise implies an impetus toward border-transgressing imprecision. The Pentecost event proved, in the first instance, to be a *protestantisme sans frontières*, a Protestantism without borders.

The process of pseudonymization has been identical with Christianity and its linguistic vestment from the very beginning. It began with the fact that the Hebrew term *maschiach*, Aramaic *mschicho*, transliterated into Greek as *messias*, was translated into the expression *christós* – with the result that Christians, to this day, are the people who stubbornly mispronounce the name of their savior. It continued with the circumstance that the letters of Paul and the four canonical Gospels were available exclusively in Greek, so that hardly an original word of the Aramaic-speaking preacher Joshua could penetrate the semi-transparent veil of the Grecophone world. With the Latinization of Christianity, there followed a second stage of alienation through translation until, finally, from the late fourteenth century onward, popularizations in the vernacular began to appear – Wycliffe's Bible of 1395, the Old Czech Olomouc Bible of 1417, Mentelin's print of a German Bible in 1466, the Luther Bibles of 1522 and 1534, Olivétan's French Bible published at Neuchâtel in 1535, and its optimization in the Geneva Bible of 1557, which served as a source of inspiration for the Huguenots. None of them would be conceivable without belief in the possibility and reality of a *translatio veritatis*. When Protestant pathos was condensed into the slogan *sola scriptura* – by scripture alone – this necessarily also meant *sola translatione* – by translation alone.

At the next stage, however, on the threshold of the Enlightenment, when it was necessary to move from the third to the fourth translations,

Rosenstock-Huessy recognized the need to bracket the entire system of traditional theology and *religio* – as life in the monasteries had been traditionally called – in order to assert with renewed emphasis the principle now called Protestant, the right to directly access the Holy Scriptures, after one and a half thousand years of church history. Unlike Luther, who translated both backward and forward, rendering the New Testament from Greek and the Old Testament from Hebrew into a German language that was then emerging in the process, Rosenstock-Huessy, an enlightened philologist, attempted to explain why, how, and by what right the British jurists of the seventeenth century, the French Enlightenment thinkers of the eighteenth century, the German idealists of the early nineteenth century, the Russian anarchists of the late nineteenth century, and, finally, even the Bolsheviks of the twentieth century translated essential elements of the Gospel into profane languages, often in open rejection of the founding texts and sometimes even under the banner of atheism. In his eyes, Christianity – insofar as it had avoided becoming entrenched in traditionalism – had existed under the law of forward translation since at least the days of the French Revolution. It called for mediations with the worldly, scientific, and aesthetic idioms of an age that had only one thing in common with religious antiquity: namely, that people faced with situations of great extremity are capable of reflecting on things of great compass, things worth risking their lives for. With this clause, the author preserved himself from converting transposable Christianity into a spiritual effervescent tablet that dissolves within a secular global ethic or becomes blurred in the formalism of a doctrine of communicative competence.

The most consequential forward translation took the form of the *Declaration of the Rights of Man and of the Citizen*, adopted by the French National Constituent Assembly on August 26, 1789, and accepted by Louis XVI. From the outset, there was no doubt about its religious character. Early illustrations of the solemn declaration show the seventeen articles and their preamble inscribed on two tablets of the law, in a visual analogy with the Ten Commandments. One might have thought the deputies had troubled themselves to climb Mount Sinai to have the articles inscribed in clay by the finger of God and then brought his statutes down to Paris, where they were adopted after numerous amendments. Above the two tablets hovers the all-seeing eye of God in an equilateral triangle, the meaning of which could not have been unclear to anyone at that time.

If Rosenstock-Huessy has earned a place in the European history of ideas outside of philosophy departments, it is because he took the Hegelian figure of the cunning of reason, and he succeeded in surpassing it with the cunning of the Holy Spirit – or, rather, he succeeded in proving that Hegel's concept of the processual idea or world spirit had never meant anything other than the product of a theoretical neutralization of the third person of the Trinity on its journey through time.[28]

It is not hard to see that Rosenstock-Huessy develops his message – first to postwar Europeans in 1931, then to Americans in 1938 – in dialogue with Nietzsche's destruction of metaphysics through a relentless "genealogy of morals." Meanwhile, he is also certain that the high-sounding metaphysical fabrications of old Europe have perished in a severe test of their logical and practical validity. Nevertheless, he believed that, in his own case, he would pass the genealogical test – the examination of whether his motives were born of good parents. He saw himself as a combatant, who had stood naked before death and emerged transformed from the ordeal. Those who returned "home" from the war, shaken but lucid, belonged, as the author asserted, to a new kind of aristocracy, a nobility of authenticity – as also expressed somewhat later, and in different form, by Albert Camus. It was from this code that there emerged a vocation for his task in the times to come – as it would turn out, a service on behalf of peace without borders.[29]

In the postwar years, Rosenstock-Huessy became ever clearer in his conviction that the truth that matters does not depend on "another world." It is nourished on the future of this world. The gentility of the coming age would not invoke their origins and ancestry; they would legitimize themselves through their readiness for the future, carried by a dedication to the new and the necessary. At the same time, in accordance with the double meaning of *revolutio*, something original is restored within the new:

> All the revolutions of Europe share this same heroic rallying of past and future against a rotten present.[30]

For this author, the true name of the other world is thus no longer "the beyond" or "the hereafter." Access to it is not pioneered through philosophical "transcendence." Instead of transcending into post-mortal spheres, he looks to revolutionary change. Revolution is a force both spiritual and physical and it engenders a nobility of its own. Returning from Verdun like Jesus after forty days in the desert, the author addressed himself in 1931 to his contemporaries within and beyond the German-speaking world, then he did it again in 1938, when Europe was temporarily lost, to the English-speaking public; his aim was to involve them in his authoritative vision of the coherence of revolutionary upheavals in the design of a broader, freer, richer world.

It cannot be said that Rosenstock-Huessy's achievements ever suffered from under-exposure. And yet, with both publications, he did suffer what can only be described as a writer's bad break. Hitler's rise to power in early 1933 had rendered his reinterpretation of Europe's polyvalent revolutionary history obsolete – the Nazi movement opposed the ideas of 1789 and the Christian ethos encoded in them with a "national revolution" – that was more of a neo-pagan revolt. And then, by the end of the 1930s, the imminent entanglement of the United States in a renewed World War deprived the voice of a German émigré of the resonance needed for its reception. Even so, there is an argument to be made that Rosenstock-Huessy is one of those authors whose later reputation was saved by an earlier lack of success. His misjudgments about the world situation in the 1930s were so wildly wrong that he was lucky they went initially unnoticed. Thus, as late as 1938, he still attributed sincere pacifist intentions to Hitler,[31] and described him, somewhat condescendingly, as resembling a "peasant pope";[32] he preached that a major new war was quite impossible, since modern weapons condemned it to absurdity. He wished to believe that the original communist program for the withering away of the state was taken seriously in Stalin's universe; rather curious too was his bold thesis that Freudian psychoanalysis, which made sense to the puritanically inhibited Americans, was superfluous in France because the philosophy of the sensualists had long since preempted it. In close proximity to vigorous misinterpretations of all kinds, one finds lucid statements such as the claim that Hitler was actually the unknown soldier from the ordinary people; that he represented a figure typical of the era *before* the Reformation, and that the dictator from the Viennese lower depths was openly speculating that the German people, weary of lackluster Protestantism, finally wanted to see a leader, a *Führer*, who acted as if under direct divine inspiration.[33] Which showed: theocracy may have been officially finished and the princes chased out the door by the grace of God, but they were climbing back in through the windows, dressed as dictators.

Rosenstock-Huessy's methodological weaknesses are abundantly evident in his misjudgments; their flip side is a plethora of brilliant insights. The author's vulnerable point lies in the axiomatic realm: his conviction that human history as a whole, and European history of the last millennium in particular, can be understood only through the movement of passions, creeds, and inspirations, brings him the embarrassment of having to distinguish between different enthusiasms, without being able to provide any criteria. Rosenstock-Huessy shares with some recent media theorists and historians of revolution a failure to distinguish between noble enthusiasms and eruptions of mass delusion.[34]

Rosenstock-Huessy decided not to observe the spirit of the revolution where it had already been effectively theatricalized and theorized by the actors themselves, as happened in its appearances after 1789. The author's unexpected coup was articulated in his thesis that, from the High Middle Ages onward, the wind of intellectual and political awakenings blew through the powerful nations – beginning in Italy, passing through Germany, to England and France, and finally providing for the transformation of conditions in Russia too. For him, the chain of revolutions was a quasi-sacramental reality, indeed a necessary sequence of advances toward a generalized freedom among the peoples of the Old World. All Europeans are its heirs, even if only passively so. Most of them live without any insight into the historical sources of current conditions. But every individual in this corner of the world ought to understand that if they claim to be free and to possess inalienable rights, they can do so only because they, like the rest of their fellow citizens, were baptized in the font of revolution. Of course, the vast majority of Europeans are revolutionaries only nominally – baptismal-certificate revolutionaries as it were. This was true in 1938 and it remains true in 2024. People go through existence without proper consideration for what is owed to the struggles and sufferings of previous generations.

As Europeans, the author states, we all exhibit the same revolutionary pedigree on our mental birth certificates and we are related like cousins to the heirs of revolutions in other countries.[35] To be sure, every people undergoes only one revolution and is permanently marked by its outcome; "every (subsequent) revolution, however, is set aflame by the land of the old revolution."[36] The subsequent revolutions, in their turn, cast their light back upon past upheavals. Tellingly, countries that have undergone an earlier revolution tend to be less susceptible to the impulses of future ones. This fact pattern can be seen with special clarity in the case of England: by the time Louis XVI met his end under the guillotine, England's regicidal phase lay almost 150 years in the past. The British Isles were somewhat open to the ideas of 1789, even as they remained immune to those of 1793; they had already taken up essential elements of the French advance into their own concepts of liberalism, notably with the Bill of Rights of 1689 – albeit with the qualification emphasized by Edmund Burke, that he did not demand his rights as a "human being" but as an Englishman. According to Rosenstock-Huessy, the continuing influence and habitual legacy of earlier revolutionary experiences can also be seen in the fact that Germany, as the motherland of the Reformation, which he treats under the name of "the German Revolution," took a very lively interest in the events in France, but did not allow itself to be carried away in the undertow of radicalized republicanism; when events among their neighbors to the west were reported in Germany, the situation was further complicated by the fact that it was not only the news of the Parisian terror that aroused abhorrence. Napoleon's campaigns came to leave countless contemporaries with additional deep aversions to influences from across the Rhine.

On the "family tree of revolutions," the Russian Revolution was the only one that was clearly aware of its derivation from one of the preceding revolutions – the French; it explicitly figured itself as the consummation of what had remained only a sketch in France. Throughout its entire structure, there seemed to awaken an epochal feeling of the insufficiency of all previous political upheavals: undeniably, earlier struggles had achieved progress in the field of freedoms, both religious and civil, but they had shied away from the material, not just formal and legal, realization of the principle of equality. Hadn't Marx already explained that socialism was the "declaration of the permanence of the revolution"? It was Lenin's demonism, or, as some believed, his genius, that, instructed by his reading of Marx, he seized upon the gap between the promises and the realization of the French Revolution in order to project it onto Russian conditions. This, of course, was not a gap that could be closed merely by way of reform. In Russia, a chasm opened up between promises and reality, one that even the most extreme measures would hardly have sufficed to bridge. Nowhere else in Europe were the subtly demoralized elites so far removed from the grossly demoralizing realities of life in villages and small towns as in Russia, and nowhere was the necessity of a radical change invoked with such vehemence by a small elite. In Lenin's eyes, such circumstances provided the ideal starting point for the revolutionary determination to try to divert the course of the world away from the "bourgeois" primacy of freedom and to force it into a more egalitarian channel. The leaders of the uprising appointed the "proletariat" as the subject of radical egalitarianism, without regard for the fact that, quantitatively, the working class in pre-industrial Russia had almost no significant profile as compared to its vast peasantry. Nonetheless, the Communist Party asserted its claim to be the lucid head of the proletariat – even if the latter required some bulking up in order to be presented as an appreciable factor.

The effective linkage between the Russian and French Revolutions came to pass because Lenin had learned from the failure of the Jacobin Terror: when, in the summer of 1794, a few moderate parliamentarians – later known as the "Men of Thermidor" – got rid of Robespierre and put an end to the Reign of Terror, this effort could only succeed because there were still a handful of opposition figures who did not yield to intimidations from the regime of the guillotine and who, in any case, wanted to forestall their own liquidation in the furies of politicized morality. For Lenin, from very early on, one thing was utterly certain: after the Bolshevik Revolution, if it were to succeed, there could no longer be any such figures. The secret police force known as the Cheka, founded already in December 1917, would ensure that equality before the terror was achieved overnight; Lenin's September 1918 decree "On Red Terror" had the advantage of clarity on this point. The equality enforced from the outset under the deadly accusation of counterrevolutionary sentiment was supplemented under Stalin by equality under the five-year plan, which resulted in the sorting of Russian society and its satellites into either smoothly functioning comrades or else saboteurs. In its convergence with a utopia emancipated from all friction, the figure of *Homo sovieticus* took shape. The fact that the prohibition against friction infringed likewise upon intellectuals in the West, and how this happened, forms a dark chapter in the history of European ideas, which was to last until the start of the 1970s.

Relative to the 1931 draft of his book on European revolutions, Rosenstock-Huessy was already, in the 1938 revision, somewhat less confident in his forced salvation–historical interpretation of the Russian Revolution. Nevertheless, he could still astonish his readers with unusual theses. In his diagnosis, the young Russian revolutionaries of the late nineteenth century were fundamentally "disappointed Europeans"; they had realized that the West would always be ahead of them in everything, with one exception: their readiness to go to the extreme in a selfless struggle against the status quo. They would get to the top through a quality of which Westerners had previously only known the name, but not the substance: through that radicalism that knew how to escalate into relentlessness. In 1938, Rosenstock-Huessy remained unshaken in his view that the young revolutionaries who had prepared the events of 1917 since the late nineteenth century were, even as avowed nihilists, authentic martyrs of an anonymous faith, activists of self-sacrifice, such as even the Jesuits and Trappists had hardly been in their heyday.[37] For them, the renunciation of personal happiness translated into an unprecedented aptitude for political cruelty. For them, walking over corpses grew into a spiritual discipline. In Rosenstock-Huessy's eyes, Lenin's biography spontaneously gives rise to the legend of a martyr of action. In his interpretation, the whole history of the Russian Revolution, from the fatally failed Decembrist revolt of 1825 to 1938, fitted into the schema of a progressive teleology: through early defeats to final victory. At long last, even the most unfree of Europeans could partake in the blessings of the Western European history of freedom – even if at the price of a still deeper enslavement, which one might try to justify by declaring it a merely provisional measure. With questionable magnanimity, the interpreter empathized with Lenin's perception of the situation: what was Russia in 1917 but a corpse it was necessary to electrify?[38] The Spirit blows where it will and it spurns no pseudonym, not even *pyatiletka* – "Five-year plan." Rosenstock-Huessy had heard nothing – or wanted to hear nothing – about the slave camps created by Trotsky after 1922 and the Gulag officially established after 1930. And, although he was not one of those apologists who were determined to remain silent or prevaricate into the 1950s and 1960s, he could not and would not do without the revolution in Russia for his grand narrative of the march of the Spirit across the stage of world history.

In his books of 1931 and 1938, the author's prejudiced view of events in Russia reflects the widespread desire among European intellectuals of those years to keep Russia, as a latecomer to the Western family of nations and cultures, as close as possible to themselves, notwithstanding the centrifugal forces that were pulling it toward "the barbaric," even "the Asiatic." They endeavored by all means possible to accommodate the Russian "Westward Drive," which had been virulent since Peter the Great – and, more than that, they cherished the pleasing illusion that Russia, notwithstanding its monstrous eastward expansion, constituted an admittedly alienated but not entirely lost part of the Western family of nations, due particularly to its proximity to the Hellenic, pre-Latin paradigm of Christianity.[39]

Toward the end of the nineteenth century, the Vatican under Pope Leo XIII (1878–1903) proved to be a stronghold for courting Russia: the power-conscious hegemon of the Catholic Church dreamed insistently of reconciling Russia and the West, as the Protestant historian Theodor von Sickel attested in his report on an audience: a reclaimed Russia could even dictate peace in Europe and "establish social order" there – a strong dose of tsarism would do the restless West some good; and once the Eastern influence had gotten the chance, the Protestants of Europe would certainly "follow the example of the Russians."[40] Needless to say, neither the Tsar nor the Patriarch of Moscow were willing to submit to the late-resurfaced claim of the Roman Curia to spiritual world domination. These events demonstrated how, around 1890, the Holy See still knew how to give weight to its far-reaching expertise in matters of imperiality – with Rome, not unwillingly, falling for the rhetoric of Joseph de Maistre, the Savoyard ideologue of the papacy.[41] If Western intellectuals made little sign of submitting to Russian rulers, with all their fuss about Russia's inalienable "freedom" of faith, quite a few them after 1918 nonetheless submitted to Moscow's claim to be recognized as the center of the Bolshevik world dominion to come.

When Rosenstock-Huessy all too hastily integrated the Russian Revolution into his intellectual history of revolutionary upheavals, he succumbed to suggestions of a Franco-Russian connection as maintained by the Marxist school. Before 1914, and even more so afterward, their lecturers wanted to make the world believe that the flame of 1789 and 1793 had been passed on, via the stages of 1830, 1848, 1870, and 1905, to the key players of October 1917. Hadn't the young Ernst Bloch, in a moment of defiant naivety, even declared: *Ubi Lenin, ibi Jerusalem* – where one finds Lenin, there one finds the new Jerusalem? Oswald Spengler's early judgments on the Russian Revolution showed a higher degree of clairvoyance when he remarked that Bolshevism would remain nothing more than an import of Western ideas that could never really take root in Russian soil.

Rosenstock-Huessy set aside such concerns, so as not to disrupt his grand narrative about the peregrinations of the Spirit of Revolution through the countries of Europe. Much to the contrary of tendencies in conventional historiography, he began his long ramble, his *Grande Randonnée*, in the High Middle Ages: in his account, it began with the "monk" Hildebrand – a subdeacon and later archdeacon by status, born in the Tuscan village of Sovana – who assumed the name Gregory VII upon his election as Pope in 1073. Gregory VII came to the finding that the German Emperor's supremacy over the Church, as expressed in his right to appoint bishops, was incompatible with the true meaning of the all-encompassing Catholic Church. Shortly after his election by acclamation, Gregory VII proved himself to be a power-seizing fanatic with great combative energy. In his Olympian solitude as pope, separated from the rest of humanity through his obligations as the indivisible proxy for the Absolute, he had to decide whether the emperor should continue to be granted his hitherto existing privilege or whether there were grounds to refuse it to him. Here, the primal scene of sovereignty in "the West" emerges before the eyes of contemporary observers: sovereignty does not lie with those who decide on states of emergency, as was later argued by an eager lawyer for the German dictatorship; to begin with, the only true sovereign is the one who decides from the highest office for guiding souls and consciences in Christian communities, in this case through the appointment of bishops. Gregory VII voted that power-seekers, members of clans, and lackeys of worldly powers should not be allowed to attain high ecclesiastical position through imperial vote; these should be reserved for more spiritually suitable individuals, who could be referred to, somewhat anachronistically, as "clerics" (*clercs*). Their appointment was exclusively a matter for the Holy See. Furthermore, in the future, strict adherence to celibacy was to be enforced among clergy in order to estrange priests from their worldly ties and orient them solely toward Rome. Gregory VII is often portrayed as a prematurely aged ascetic, but, by asserting himself and his extremely pointed postulates – the unprecedented 27 principles of the *dictatus papae* of 1075 proclaimed the supremacy of the papacy over all secular authority and led to the humiliation of Emperor Henry IV at Canossa in January 1077 – his dramatic power struggle against the King of Germany and Holy Roman Emperor initiated a development that Rosenstock-Huessy unreservedly calls the "papal revolution."[42] It resulted in the emancipation of the Church from the clannism of feudal society. The first meritocracy in Europe formed in the Roman Curia, where proven talent and genuine vocation countered the protectionism of local interest groups. The papal curia grew into the prototype of an administrative apparatus that could be described, with a somewhat polemically tinged expression from the eighteenth century, as a "bureaucracy."[43] The power-conscious pope made his mark in the history of European revolutions as the first proponent of a new kind of freedom, when he demarcated a sphere for the faithful to which the organs of worldly power were to have no access. The author went so far as to claim that it was only the dualism of spiritual and temporal power – which Gregory VII enforced with institutional effectiveness, and which was a major motif of great politics up until the Reformation – that became constitutive for the European understanding of freedom, far beyond the binary of *civitas Dei* and *civitas terrena* taught by Augustine. By placing conscience between two imperatives, basic dualism emancipated it from subjection to a single master; Rosenstock-Huessy made no secret of his conviction that every monism, whether grounded metaphysically or naturalistically, sooner or later opens out into tyranny; what is called democracy likewise remained an unsecured pledge, insofar as even popular governments had inherent monocratic tendencies.[44] It was certainly no coincidence that Rousseau, too, had suspected Christianity of being a political nuisance; he wanted to believe that his notion of the *volonté générale*, the general will of the people, would be better suited to a religion like Islam, which tended to efface self-will.

In the author's interpretation, the cultural and historical consequences of the "Papal Revolution" can still be felt in Italy today; it is not least because of this that the country became the graceful garden of Europe and developed into the matrix of a Catholic-curated *bene vivere*. In the territories influenced by the Guelphs, the extension of civil rights from the cities to their rural surroundings gave rise to that Italy of cultivated landscapes and microcosmically perfect city-states that still attracts pilgrims from all over the world to these strongholds of art – quintessentially condensed in the archetypal Italian image of the "Madonna in the Landscape."

With the terms and provisions of the Russian Revolution of the twentieth century and the Italian (or more precisely, the Papal-Guelph) Revolution of the eleventh and twelfth centuries, the author marked the basic points of orientation for his *Autobiography of Western Man*. The middle section consists of the three events that brought Germany in the sixteenth century, England in the seventeenth, and France in the eighteenth, into the world cultural heritage of revolution. In detailed and knowledgeable chapters, Rosenstock-Huessy corrects the generally accepted notion that it was "the people" who qualified as subjects of revolutions because of their revolt against those in power. On the contrary, it was only ever small groups of highly motivated actors who, through their actions, and when the time was "ripe," dared to bring about radical change and leave an enduring stamp on the character of their nations.[45] In the case of the "German Revolution," it was the princes of the smaller and larger states – the crowned heads in the territory of the Old Empire numbered around three hundred – who initially formed a clear majority in taking up the anti-Roman and anti-centralist impulses of Luther's teachings. They were supported in this by their reformed doctors, whose powers of theological discernment supported their princes' exercise of the *ius reformandi* in their territories – in accordance with the formula of the Peace of Augsburg of 1555: *cuius regio, eius religio* – essentially, "in the prince's realm, the prince's religion." In order to determine as political sovereigns how people should believe in their territories, the princes leaned on their theologians, who often lectured at the newly established state universities. Only legitimate experts of exegesis (from 1513 on, Luther held the professorship for the interpretation of scripture at the University of Wittenberg, founded in 1502) could assure them of their right to rule over citizens who, as individuals with immediate access to God – and as literate recipients of Holy Scripture – were themselves entitled to a sort of sovereignty.

In the case of England, it was the members of the rural nobility, the gentry, those five thousand families inspired by their old English rights and freedoms, who served as a focal point for the conservative and rebellious energies of their nation. In January 1649, after decades of quarrels between the crown and the parliament, they overthrew and executed King Charles I (1600–1649) on charges of high treason, with the ironic result that they soon found themselves under the dictatorship of the Puritan military commander Oliver Cromwell, until, toward the end of the century, they were able to celebrate the restoration of a now domesticated monarchy under the paradoxical banner of "the Glorious Revolution." In its English shade of meaning, the word "liberal" is still hard to separate from its landed-gentry connotations. Thanks to deeply liberal influences, the life script of the typical British entrepreneur remained set: he assured his spiritual election by earning £5 million as a capitalist and then donating £4 million of this to philanthropic causes as a Christian gentleman.

As far as France was concerned, it was numerically insignificant portions of the literate and cultured bourgeoisie who, influenced by the ideas of Voltaire, Montesquieu, and Rousseau, took the gamble of Jacobin escalation after 1789 and, with the execution of the king in January 1793, took an irreversible step toward republican concepts of government. The active bourgeois elites, who – alongside the masses in the capital – conferred momentum upon the revolution, were probably not much more numerous than the members of the first and second estates (the clergy and the nobility), who together numbered around 250,000 out of a total population of 27 million. It is plausible to suppose that, if a general election were to have been held in 1793 – had such a thing been at all conceivable at the time – the Jacobins would have won little more than five percent of the vote. Among other effects, the French Revolution gave rise to the quasi-immortal characters of the rentier and the tribune of the people – the latter mutating into the public intellectual in the late nineteenth century.

What is common to the three middle revolutions – together with their pre- and post-history – is a strongly pronounced religious–political pole. In each case, the relationship between states and Christian tradition was redefined in its own unique way: out of the German Reformation came the concept of denominations in the territorial principalities; the English Revolution and its prelude under Henry VIII gave rise to the para-Catholic Anglican state church, which for a time had great trouble keeping the later Anglo-Israelite zealotry of the Puritans under control. As for the French Revolution, it resulted in the sudden disempowerment of the Catholic Church and the unceremonious expropriation of its property; under Napoleon, it was relegated to the rank of a concordat partner, tolerated like a foreign power, and acknowledged with pragmatic irony as the civil–religious binding force of the people, until, under the law of laicity in 1905, it was completely degraded to the status of a bystander in the secular republic.

As for the human significance of the events, their long-term consequences were evident, both at the cultural level and in concepts of character formation. With respect to Germany, Rosenstock-Huessy highlighted three phenomena that left their stamp on the national character: the German civil service, which was devoted to the state and admired even by Lenin; the German university with its secular cult of the professorship; and German music, which, inspired by Luther's chorales, gained world renown from Johann Sebastian Bach and Handel, through to Beethoven, Wagner, and Schoenberg; it hardly needs to be said that Weimar Classicism and the philosophy of German idealism were Protestantism through and through, albeit in a different register.

As a legal historian, Rosenstock-Huessy placed a vital cultural–typological emphasis on the observation that, after the "glorious return to the old liberties," case law, with its agile conservatism, became more formative than ever on the British way of life; the post-revolutionary gentry internalized the principle of the right to resist princely repression to such an extent that the fiction of the monarch's integration into the House of Commons under the concept of the King-in-Parliament seemed to them like the natural order of things. Above all, however, it was the figure of the "gentleman" that gave rise to a post-revolutionary

British cultural character of cosmopolitan charm. The gentry ideal of an effortless access to attitudes of unstrained superiority manifested itself in the gentleman's methodical understatement and stoic reserve. Those who suppose that such things are easy to achieve should let the experts correct them: "it takes three generations to make a gentleman," according to an adage recorded in the *Oxford Dictionary of Proverbs*. A man of this style would, if necessary, be impressed by captains, jockeys, and older members of the House of Lords, but not by priests and professors; certainly, butlers were not forbidden to read books, but the gentleman himself kept his distance from anything that seemed intellectual and bookish. After his translation into the figure of the sportsman, the quiet nobility of fair play grew into an element in the popular "global ethic"; in it, from 1900 onward, the English idea of sport (derived from the Old French expression *se desporter*: "to relax," "to enjoy oneself") celebrated its deserved, if not always quiet, victory over German notions of prowess and efficiency through gymnastics and physical training. The fact that today's top athletes are hardly the most relaxed people reveals that in the world of competition, work and pleasure switch places.

As for the global consequences of the French Revolution, they are indeed still on everyone's lips; the collapse of communism in 1990, however, has retrospectively inflicted severe damage upon their authority. Anyone with imitators like the Soviets no longer needs critics of their own. The traditional cultivation of Franco-Russian amity, without which the French Left was previously unthinkable, has become an embarrassment, since Putin's desire for the destruction of Ukraine became nakedly apparent, and only a few actors are still willing to stoop to it.[46] Moreover, the course of things had revealed why the naturalization of Jews in France – often held up as the crown jewel of Gallic universalism – had been only halfway successful; civil equality had been granted to them as children of Adam, not as unwavering descendants of Abraham. As soon as the Abrahamic element proved more tenacious than anticipated, an anti-Jewish unease arose even among French advocates of universal human nature. Rosenstock-Huessy's diagnosis is clear: "The French could not bear that any nation should be more messianic than their own."[47]

If French ideas remained politically and morally vibrant, it was thanks especially to the aura of the Declaration of Human Rights, initially interpreted mainly as men's rights but revised repeatedly in the years between 1789 and 1948. From there, principles such as the separation of powers, universal suffrage, and freedom of expression gained acceptance worldwide, if not universally. It cannot be denied that the exuberance of French universalism suffered severe mortifications early on – and not only on account of the revolutionary calendar proclaimed in 1792, with its rationally conceived ten-day week, the failure of which drove Napoleon to reinstate the Gregorian calendar in January 1806. The messianic element of the message of freedom *à la française* was undermined, particularly by the flood wave of aggressive nationalism that swept across Europe in the wake of the bourgeois revolution. In the land of revolution itself, it appeared in a patriotic major key, but almost everywhere else, where France's neighbors near and far suffered the deployment of Napoleon's armies, it surfaced with distinctly Francophobic tones. A man like Georges Clemenceau was caught up in the wave of Gallic patriotism when he declared that "humanity" was a beautiful word, but "France" was even more beautiful.

All of these sweeping processes share a common trait, with regard to the individual, that can be described as a radical promotion of human being. It affects, from the ground up, being-in-the-world for members of the species *Homo sapiens*. Its effect is a profound suspension of slavery that preempts all abolitionism. To date, it has not been replicated in Asia, the Arab and Muslim world, or the nations of the Global South, which is why people there like to emphasize – in order to legitimize venerable forms of repression in line with patriarchal structures – that there are a number of independent civilizations, and that the pathos of universal human dignity and female equality is therefore nothing more than a Eurocentrism, to which one should be wary of giving credit.

The revolutionary promotions of the *conditio humana*, as the author summarizes them, have hardly been fully thought through to this day. They suspended all forms of old nobility by defining human beings per se as creatures that cannot be non-noble. By creating what Rosenstock-Huessy calls "laity sanctified,"[48] the Reformation made every human being a creature with priestly competence – since faith can no longer be confined to a church, each individual is now immediately connected to the infinite. The English Revolution made every gentleman a peer of the king; the French Revolution made every person of talent and good will a member of the new meritocratic nobility with traits of Adamic popular appeal. The generalized forms of address – Herr, Sir, monsieur, madam, madame – were intended to make it clear that the purpose of revolutionary movements ultimately lies not in improved social services, but in a general ennoblement.

Modern mass cultures, viewed against this backdrop, follow regressive motifs almost entirely, since they speak to people in their pre-reformation, unrevolutionary ordinariness; they appeal to a hereditary vulgarity that refuses to acknowledge a commitment to serving the common good and knows nothing of culture-sustaining care for the life chances of one's grandchildren. Wherever autocracies, dictatorships, and populisms are at work, the assumption is made and confirmed that in political matters, only base emotions such as fear, greed, and vindictiveness can be relied upon. Russia has broken away from Europe through its commitment to baseness; it has returned to the stage of pre-reformation submission.

As an anthropologist of European revolutions, Rosenstock-Huessy subscribes to the notion that human beings are creatures who, in order to flourish, need uprooting from where and what they come. He believes that humans must be repotted, as it were, and transplanted from present into future conditions, because they easily dwindle and decline in their hard-packed home soil. He thus raises a basic objection to any form of nativism. He has nothing more than silent skepticism for the cult surrounding indigenous cultures – though he is ready to listen to what foreign voices have to say as soon as they speak up for themselves. It was not for nothing that Rosenstock-Huessy summed up his philosophy of language (ignored to this day among academic specialists) in the maxim: *respondeo etsi mutabor*: "I respond, even if I am transformed."[49] Those who remain where they happened to have come into the world and who comport themselves in all matters as mere children of their time and place, without hearing a call from somewhere up ahead, from an omega point in history however vague – these people lapse into the parochialism and stupidity of what used to be called local demons. Any uprooting from an exhausted birthright, however, must be matched by an inauguration into a legitimate new source of ardor, so that individuals in the post-revolutionary space do not fall into disorientation; in the lull following times of struggle, they sink too easily into a dull sense of not knowing what to do next. The same could even be said – *entre nous*

– of today's Europeans, who often look to Brussels in bewilderment, not knowing whether it is really the better angels of our nature that are taking care of what happens there.

With considerations of this sort, our author has earned the right to address himself not only to American readers of 1938, but also to citizens of today's Europe. For those among you who wish to know more details, we have placed a somewhat broader bookmark here, albeit in a place virtually unknown to the general public. Quite a few Europeans today need, it would seem, a kind of inner mission, albeit less in the sense of re-Christianization than in the sense of a reflection on the historical sources of their civility. Like their forebears in the 1920s, they hardly know where they come from, let alone where their journey will take them next.

Lesson three
History *a priori*:
The book of endgames – Spengler's prophecy and how it came to be fulfilled

If the First World War became a key event in raising questions about the nature, fate, and future of Europe, it was for one reason above all: soon after the war's conclusion in November 1918, the feeling spread across the entire continent that, in the end, only losers had emerged from it – notwithstanding the peace treaties of Versailles and Saint-Germain, signed in June and September 1919. Their wording was tantamount to a *Diktat* imposed by the victorious powers; their effects contributed to the general dejection; the hustle and bustle of the recovery years, which gave rise to the myth of the Roaring Twenties, was able to mask the clouded circumstances with only the greatest of trouble. Even the United States of America was among the losers, in part anyway, once it became clear that only a fraction of the war loans it had issued to Great Britain would be repaid. Nevertheless, with their entrance into the European war in April 1917, they gained a global political hegemony that they would not relinquish for the next hundred years.

Starting in the spring of 1918, the Spanish flu virus unleashed a pandemic whose number of victims worldwide far exceeded that of the war. The sense of the value of human life underwent an almost unprecedented decline. If the world of yesterday, in Stefan Zweig's nostalgic account, had lived in an "age of security,"[1] then, with the capitulation of Germany and Austria, a new psychopolitical era was dawning, aptly coined by the hybrid neo-German noun "Verunsicherung" – a term renderable only inadequately by the English "uncertainty" or the French "incertitude." "Verunsichert" was the Dasein of Europeans who found themselves "exposed" in a postwar world of uncertain rules. A prescient reflection of the new situation was evident in the literary prototypes of "existentialism" – not least in the novels of the poet-aviator Antoine de Saint-Exupéry *Southern Mail* (1929) and *Night Flight* (1931), and of the young adventurer André Malraux – the latter had presented, with *La condition humaine* in 1933, a manifesto, as it were, of the new mood of being-in-the-world, oscillating between the ecstasy of the struggle for power and the vacancy of an opium rapture.

The night-flight quality of human existence in the postwar era was conceptualized on German soil most notably by Martin Heidegger, when he lectured in his inaugural address at the University of Freiburg on July 24, 1929, entitled "What is Metaphysics?": "The nothing is the complete negation of the totality of beings. [...] Anxiety makes manifest the nothing. [...] In anxiety beings as a whole become superfluous." Dasein itself means being "held out into the nothing." "Being held out into the nothing – as Dasein is – on the ground of concealed anxiety makes man a placeholder of the nothing." Hence, it is through anxiety that the "total strangeness of beings can overwhelm us."[2] With quiet fortitude, Saint-Exupéry had countered statements of this kind in advance. He wished to believe that, in the shadow of war, a new elite was forming among pilots and others, a group of men without insignia who felt themselves to be "brothers in arms" in the struggle against sinking into a diminishing and dehumanizing everydayness. Hadn't existence always meant flying through thunderstorms?[3]

To diagnose these times within a restricted frame, as if the whole course of events were merely the reversal of bourgeois security as it lapsed into a gloomy mood among the losers, would fail to give the proper measure of those years. A significant part of the postwar atmosphere was already evident in impulses that announced themselves during the last two years of the war – one might describe them as a tendency to take flight into illusion. Indeed, the disposition to flee into postures of a defiant misrecognition of reality became itself reality-determining. It was in the nature of things that such tendencies were evident first and foremost among the eventual losers. The expression "der Krieg nach dem Krieg" – the war after the war – which Oswald Spengler claimed to have had in his head since the summer of 1918,[4] suggested that nothing would be achieved through armistice alone. To be sure, the "fight goes on" syndrome marked most profoundly the Bolshevik and national-revolutionary – alias "fascist" – reactions to the war's outcome, but it also encompassed a wide spectrum of willful poses ranging from Zurich Dadaism and its aftermath in Surrealism to the pathos of the struggle with the absurd; it escalated from neo-Catholic gestures of seeking refuge in the saints to the cynicism of ostentatious imposture. A prelude to all of this, which did not bode well, played out in the spring of 1917, when General Erich Ludendorff (1865–1937), Germany's *de facto* military dictator, despite being convinced as early as December 1916 that the war could not be won, fixated on at least wresting a peace on terms favorable to the German Reich – which is why, against the dissuasive urging of Walther Rathenau, he declared unrestricted submarine warfare in January 1917, at the risk of provoking the United States's entrance into the war. Relying on a defiant emotional judgment, he wanted to bet everything on a single card and to put into play the "machine god of the U-boat," a *Neptunus ex machina*.[5] Even before the end of the armed conflict, when the American President Woodrow Wilson declared war in April 1917, and when the Bolsheviks seized power in Russia in October of that year (or, if one prefers, in January 1918), installing under the loftiest promises a regime based on illusions and terror, the bipolarity of the world powers began to make its mark – a development that would shape the twentieth century up until the implosion of the Soviet Union. For the German Reich, under the aegis of Wilhelm II from 1888 to 1918, the political *summum malum*, the greatest evil, that Bismarck had feared as the nightmare coalition against Germany, had materialized in the Great War – and not least because of a monarch's defiant posturing.

A political and cultural climate had arisen, with a confused mixture of anxiety, defiance, and bitterness, in which Europe had to be re-explained to Europeans. Everywhere throughout the Old World, an imperative to diagnose the times was asserting itself. Beginning in 1808 with Fichte's *Addresses to the German Nation*, Germany increasingly assigned therapeutic, political–psychagogic, and national–pedagogical tasks to traditional philosophy, alongside its contemplative and analytical functions. Rosenstock-Huessy's writings from 1931 and 1938 can, for their part, be understood only as a response to the imperative to "grasp one's time in thought" – certainly not in a Hegelian sense, but rather in the sense that diagnoses of the actual state of affairs should serve as practical inspiration and orientation amid a confusing situation. Rosenstock-Huessy had translated the imperative to diagnose his times into an autobiographical impulse and, legitimized by the mandate of the crisis and stimulated by his forcefully aired lay-theological enthusiasms, he came up with a hyper-autobiography from out of the spirit of revolutionary successions: *Ecce Homo occidentalis!* Behold the man of the west! For him, it seemed evident that history as a whole could not represent a mere pretext for "giving meaning to the meaningless," as the philosopher Theodor Lessing (1872–1933) had claimed in his well-known book;[6] nor did he wish to content himself with the fiction of a progress-as-if, by which some liberal skeptics attempted to extricate themselves from the European debacle. Since Rosenstock-Huessy was not a Hegelian, that is to say, because for him the self-realization of the idea in the course of time was an empty theorem, he could lay his theological cards freely on the table; he suggested that the historical process was a continuation, on a vast scale, of the Acts of the Apostles, using global political and secular means – why not a kind of "telephone game" for adults? One warning was to be heeded, however: those who whisper the sentence "You shall love your neighbor as yourself!" into their neighbor's ear at the beginning of the transmissions must reckon with the risk that, after a long chain of forwarding, the phrase would re-emerge as "Destroy the class enemy!"

Rosenstock-Huessy's ambition to re-explain Europe to the Europeans and his procedure of tracing its decline back through a series of revolutions that have shaped "us" into what we can and should be, would not have taken the form they did had they not been anticipated by a book that caused a furor throughout the German-speaking world, from the moment it was published in early autumn 1918 (by the renowned Viennese academic publisher Braumüller): Oswald Spengler's *The Decline of the West* – a book presented to the public with the intimidating subtitle: *Outlines of a Morphology of World History*.[7] If it had come down to the subtitle alone, the work would never have transcended a small circle of professional historians. The main title, by contrast, had an instant potency that can hardly be interpreted as anything other than the luminosity of an archetypal message. Europe had never been closer to the motif of Apocalypse Now than at this moment. Spengler's book title bore rich overtones in the German word *Untergang*, a decline or sinking that applies to suns, ships, dynasties, peoples, and civilizations – while French requires three different verbs to denote the setting of the sun, the sinking of a ship, and the decline of a culture, and English distinguishes among sunset, shipwreck, fall, doom, and decline. Moreover, Spengler's phrase "Untergang des Abendlandes" – the decline of the West – is heliologically overdetermined: the term *Abendland* presents an ideologically charged Germanization of the Latin word *occidens*, which naturally has the word *oriens* as its counterpart. If the *Abendland* – the West, but literally "the evening lands" – were to go down, this would signify, to a German ear, that the part of the world where the sun sets would likewise perish. Hence, there were also cosmological resonances at work that accommodated the darkening Zeitgeist of the historical moment. Two months after the book was published, on November 11, 1918, the head of the German delegation, Matthias Erzberger of the German Centre Party (born in 1875, assassinated in the summer of 1921), signed the armistice agreement in the Compiègne Forest, in which the German Empire was forced to admit its defeat in the World War.

Hence, the next bookmark in the Book of Europe is placed into a work whose title swiftly became proverbial and traversed the entire twentieth century, even if knowledge of its contents declined sharply soon after its publication; the second volume, subtitled *Perspectives of World-History* and published in 1922, surpasses the first in originality and audacity but was received with only weary interest. When the era of the Golden Twenties began with its breakthroughs in "New Objectivity" and its strained frivolity, only to end with the Great Depression in 1930, the coinage "the decline of the West" was already a hackneyed cliché; it circulated in the linguistic games of vulgar pessimism that united the inflation-impoverished bourgeoisie with the masses of the new white-collar civilization. The fact that, at that time, Spengler's book was found in every German household with any remaining reading culture speaks to the virulence of its initial success. The English translation appeared in 1926 under the title *The Decline of the West*, the French, with significant delay, in October 1931 as *Le Déclin de l'occident*, and the Spanish under the title *La Decadencia de Occidente* in 1932, with a foreword by José Ortega y Gasset.

Spengler's work is by no means a belated field-post letter. Around 1915, its author had been deemed unfit for military service due to his nervous constitution; he spent the war years in relative safety, living the life of a gentleman scholar with no professional obligations in Munich's bohemian district of Schwabing – not far from the house where, around 1901, Lenin had brooded over plans for a revolution in Russia. So, it was not on account of any direct, personal experience of the war that Spengler was one of the first who sought to clarify the position, with respect to world processes, of those who live in the *Abendland*, the "Western world" on which the sun was setting. His affinity with the public mood in the Autumn of 1918 was the consequence of an unexpected coincidence, perhaps secretly desired by only the author himself. Up until the summer of 1918, he believed that German arms would at long last prevail; his book, then, was to be read as an appeal to the fortitude of the eventual victor, in the face of tasks to come in the winter of Faustian culture.

As a diagnostician of the European crisis before the First World War, Spengler had acquired a keen sense for the lines of conflict along which potentials pent up over decades were pressing for discharge. Amid a climate of prospering *Lebensphilosophies*, it was not only among European youth that an awareness of the intensifying technologization of Dasein had arisen; everyone was talking about the social alienation of individuals, about the hectic pace of life in the big cities, and about the spiraling transience of relationships between and among uprooted people. The typical traits of decadence that Nietzsche claimed to perceive in Wagner's art – the brutal, the artificial, and the idiotic, with which exhausted subjects allow themselves to simulate a dying sense of interest – were ubiquitous in literature, on the theater stage, and in the daily press. An association between ideas of decadence and recent culture was in the air and on the streets; Spengler could have picked it up anywhere, even if he hadn't chanced upon a volume of classical historian Otto Seeck's history of the decline of the ancient world, *Geschichte des Untergangs der antiken Welt* (1895–1920). Seeck was a student of Mommsen and taught in Münster; Spengler carefully avoided mentioning Seeck's name in his otherwise extensive references but, from that point on, as Spengler explained later, the title of his work had been decided.

The misery of Germany's defeat did indeed provide an ideal breeding ground for the reception of a work that seemed to offer nothing less than a hermeneutics of gloom grounded in world history. Indeed, didn't it virtually provide instructions for dealing with a fate at once difficult to accept, yet impossible to avoid? With its Goethean concept of form and its Nietzschean style, Spengler's book represented something like a belatedly delivered *Untimely Meditation*. Thanks to its unique context, it proved to be the most timely of all possible publications. At the very moment of its fiercest misunderstanding, it was delivered to the public like tidings from the cool heights of Sils-Maria or from the austere seclusion of Weimar. It is easy to see why Spengler's protest against the supposedly illegitimate "pessimistic" interpretation of his book had no effect.

Naturally, for its part, Spengler's writing also had a strong *de te fabula narratur* to it – something Rosenstock-Huessy misjudged when he later reproached the author for writing history in a way that had no connection to people's living memories, indeed charging that Spengler wrote only for people weary of their own memories.[8] Martin Heidegger likewise misjudged the matter when, near the start of his Freiburg lectures on *The Fundamental Concepts of Metaphysics* in the winter semester of 1929–1930, he suggested that readers of cultural diagnoses were Spenglerians once more – people who had become so bored with themselves that they were willing to play extras in a world-historical swords-and-sandals movie.[9] In truth, the exciting aspect of Spengler's deliberations on the situation of "the West" lies in the fact that it is precisely *our* decline, and *your* decline within it, that was being depicted here in such sweeping strokes. More than a decade later, Rosenstock-Huessy countered this suggestion with an equally expansive vision of *our* revolutions, and *eo ipso* an evocation of *your* participation in the upheavals and convulsions of broader history. His exposé of a chain of revolutions from the late eleventh century to the early twentieth century is, plainly, laid out in parallel with Spengler's time frame for the Faustian culture of the West, thereby arousing suspicions that the author wanted to ensure that his exposé eliminated from its treatment all traces of history as a history of decline. Anyone who, a good decade after Spengler, would claim to explicate historical and then-contemporary Europe to the Europeans of that era, and sought to do so freshly and in terms of a general theory of revolution, understandably did not want to talk about processes of senile torpor, sclerosis, divestment, and the impoverishment of individual identity within the mass. For Rosenstock-Huessy, the true and real history of our world is the history of people's exaltation through the Gospel message; this inevitably implies its translation into the incognito of secular humanism and thus into a multiplicity of political, moral, therapeutic, and aesthetic idioms.

In Rosenstock-Huessy's confrontation with Spengler, an advocate of negentropic process logic clashes hard against an apologist for civilizational entropy. In other terms, one could speak of the collision of utopianism and pragmatism – or, to recall Musil's now classic distinction, of the unfathomable opposition between the sense of possibility and the sense of reality.

Spengler's powerful aspiration declares itself in his claim to have discovered a "logic of history" that prevails beyond the local, the random, and the singular; it is a logic, or rather a schema, that can be read in the destinies of cultures, as if they too were subject to universally valid biographical laws. The adventurous nature of the Spenglerian enterprise is clearly evident in his suggestive thesis: the author earnestly believed that he had discovered a new species, a para-biological entity even – called "cultures," or more precisely, "advanced cultures." He wanted to use the growth of this species to display the laws of a biographically and biogrammatically representable transformation of form. This, he argued, takes place with sublime and universal regularity under the dual demands of growth and entropy. Spengler insisted on identifying eight such super-entities that emerged in full independence from each other. His list includes ancient Babylonian, Egyptian, Indian, Chinese, Central American, Neo-Babylonian-magical, classical, and Western European cultures – although it is only to the last three that he brings any notable clarity. Based on his qualifications as a meta-botanist, Spengler claimed that, guided by Goethe's morphological thinking and by analogy with the biographies of individual human beings, he was able to define the laws that govern the life cycle of his super-plants. He developed the conviction that his research had taken him from the study of oracles and religious divination to a scientifically based form of prophecy, indeed to a precise theory of collective destiny. The first sentence of the introduction to *The Decline of the West* leaves no doubt about this:

> In this book is attempted for the first time the venture of predetermining history, of following the still untraveled stages in the destiny of a Culture,

> and specifically of the only Culture of our time and on our planet which is actually in the phase of fulfillment – the West-European-American.[10]

Anyone who sorts through the vocabulary of this preamble – history, destiny, culture, planet, stages, fulfillment – already holds in hand the essential articles of Spengler's historiosophical grammar. These are expressions that fit into a metabiological and metabiographical register, and, within certain limits, also into a cosmological one. At first glance, there is little to be discovered in them that would entice a reader out of the stance of well-tempered indifference with which, given sufficient theoretical education, one would be accustomed to receiving discourses of a "world-historical reflections" type, *à la* Jacob Burckhardt. Indeed, even Hegel's reasoning in his *Lectures on the Philosophy of World History* (1822) could be comprehended through this attitude of unruffled observation. Mention of "West-European-American," however, a proper noun here used as an adjective, is apt to break any spell of virtual theoretical indifference. For the attentive reader, this naming of names evokes an inescapable sense of *tua res agitur* – this also concerns *you*. Its impetus is conveyed at the moment when readers grasp that the culture described here, later explicated as "Faustian" or as Gothic Catholicism, with its obsessive, floating motif of exposure within a boundless space pulsating with varied forces, is none other than the culture to which they themselves belong, like it or not – and not as mere observers and witnesses from the sidelines, but as partners in destiny and fellow sufferers.

The reader's act of self-inclusion within the aforementioned culture and its fate through time does not occur without a tangle with complex consequences. What at first glance might be perceived as an intoxicating ride together on the omnibus of "great history" proves, on closer inspection of the theorem, to be the imposition of seeing oneself as a *compagnon de route* of a comprehensive fatality. Spengler is tactful enough, anyway, to replace the word "decline" with "fulfillment" in his opening sentence. Nevertheless, it should be clear that the author's vision of the "fulfillment of the West" seeks to involve the reader in an endgame that allows for no merely contemplative participation. On the contrary: it delivers a summons to accept a partnership of fate. It is not for nothing that the author invokes Nietzsche's motto of *amor fati*, which belongs to a tragic conception of the world. Just as Leonardo da

Vinci had dispensed the motto typical of the Renaissance: *chi non può ciò che vuole ciò che può*, "As you cannot do what you want, want what you can do," Spengler issues the Prussian-Neo-Stoic maxim: "Those who understand that reality does not ask for their wishes should want what they must." If you cannot bring yourself to want what you are capable of, you will sink into anonymity without a trace; if you do not have the strength to want what you must, events will pass you by without taking any notice of your existence.

Spengler's pretensions aim to liquidate the difference between philosophy and a situational briefing in order to arrive at a new form of forward-looking historiography. He means nothing other than this when he writes of the already perceived, yet "still untraveled stages" of the fateful event. Spengler expresses his conviction that future history can be developed from the spirit of the not-yet – he does this, however, not in the sense of the utopian thinking conceived by Ernst Bloch, as it was expounded in his early major work, *The Spirit of Utopia*, and published in the summer of 1918.[11] While the young ecstatic Bloch attempted to merge the darkness of the expanding self into the latent potentials of the illuminating world in order to unleash the powers of creative anticipation, Spengler undertook the task of projecting the apparent or real evidence of a morphological–biographical schema, proceeding from childhood and youth through maturity to old age, onto processes of an openly unfolding history – and this with the autosuggestive certainty of having revealed, once and for all, the principle of things to come. Spengler's "not-yet" ("still untraveled") bears upon things to come, whose paths can be determined in advance through clear knowledge of the laws of entropy. In fact, the author took up the second law of thermodynamics, in which he sought to discern the scientific version of the mythical teaching of the twilight of the gods.[12] Because cultures, like plants of the highest order, are subject to aging and they build up to what Spengler calls the stage of "civilization," that is, final infecundity, imperialistic externalization, and Alexandrian self-citation, an anticipatory insight into future history is possible before it becomes reality, or rather, before its inevitable self-realization. Accordingly, the author wanted to bring forth into the world nothing less than a scientific theory of the fate that shapes history, even if in the form of an objective declinism, which could equally well be denoted a fatal perfectivism.

With this, Spengler enters onto much the same terrain as that where Immanuel Kant had stepped foot a century and a half earlier, when, with due caution, he extended his central question about the possibility of *a priori* knowledge to historical objects – anticipating in some respects Wilhelm Dilthey's efforts to develop a theory of knowledge for the historical world, also known as a "critique of historical reason." In his late work of popular philosophy, *The Conflict of the Faculties*, published in 1798, Kant posed the question in a rather casual tone: "But how is a history *a priori* possible?" and he answered it succinctly: "if the diviner himself creates and contrives the events which he announces in advance."[13]

Kant's inquiry is subtly ironic; it suggests that, for the most part, it is the prophets of doom themselves who actively contribute to the realization of their own predictions. Making history *a priori* – history according to plan – is most surely achieved by persons careless of humanity's corruption or destruction. The Königsberg philosopher seems not far here from discovering a schema of the self-fulfilling prophecy. Admittedly, he cannot yet cite any examples of a prophecy that came true in the strict sense – unless one were to take in this way his laudatory remarks about the enthusiasm initially aroused by the proclamations of the French Revolution. But it was precisely the course of this revolution that became paradigmatic for the experience that shaped modern historical consciousness, according to which the unpredictable obstinacy of the real series of events will always prevail over the purposes of soothsayers, ideologues, and political planners. Indeed, the insight that things always turn out differently from what was expected belongs to the essential fund of recent historical experience.

It can be professed without further ado that it was the course of the French Revolution that allowed the concept of fate, from the early nineteenth century onward, once again to contest the primacy of the figuration of history as a project.[14] If, in a happy turn of phrase, one could define the Enlightenment as an attempt to "sabotage fate,"[15] it should be added that fate often became operative through the self-sabotage of the Enlightenment – or, rather, as a result of the unfolding of its inherent paradoxes. Among these, the incompatibility of its postulates of freedom and equality plays a corrosive role. To this must be added the experience that efforts to realize a rule of the many, one that would "emanate" from the people, instead regularly result in something quite different: the rule of the few (*oligoi*) "from politics and economics" – and this for a systemically obvious reason: the most important modern nation states, often emerging from an overextension of the monarchies that preceded them, are far too large, too cumbersome, and too dependent on bureaucratic and fiscal procedures to be truly shaped by their active citizens, the much-vaunted *citoyens*.[16]

If history were possible *a priori*, in Spengler's mode, it could not take effect as a self-fulfilling prophecy of doom; it would have to be based on laws of process that assert themselves independently of projects and prognoses. On this point, Spengler was ahead of the author of *The Conflict of the Faculties* with a term that – alongside the concept of entropy – came into maturity over the course of the nineteenth century: "development." Spengler used it to interpret, in a "morphological" or hyper-biographical way, the transition from a mature culture to an aging, graying civilization that was essential to his diagnosis of the times. While working on the first volume of his opus between 1912 and 1917, he was, as a participant and biographer of his own culture, condemned to write a latently autobiographical document: indeed, he could not help but integrate himself into the very "process of civilization" that he was trying to grasp; he had to admit that the now well-advanced stage of decrepitude in West-European-American culture, which he called a "civilizational climacteric," affected him deeply. At this stage, cultured individuals have no choice but to submit to the imperative of their times, adopt a Stoic attitude, perhaps a Prussian attitude (why not?), and carry out their duty, like that sentry at Pompeii whom no one had thought to relieve when the volcano was erupting and who was discovered by excavators, still at his post, almost two thousand years later.

Notwithstanding his panoramic view of different cultures, Spengler proved unable to forsake his Eurocentric perspective. He was unable even to seriously desire anything else, though he attempted, with varying degrees of felicity, to apprehend particular Chinese, Egyptian, and Neo-Babylonian cultural processes by way of analogy. He saw himself as someone who was not allowed to step out of his own late-Faustian skin. The compliments that people wanted to give the author for his relinquishment of Eurocentrism and his culturally relativist theses came to nothing: Spengler remained captivated within his identification with the late stages of Faustian civilization, but, despite the military defeat, he also held fast to the notion – presented as a warning – that only a coherent Western policy of the grand, imperial style would be capable of thwarting a perilous alliance between the two threatening "world revolutions," that of Bolshevism and that of "colored" peoples. Needless to say, he still harbored some hopes for Germany's key role in the "hour of decision." The declaration that "We cannot permit ourselves to be tired"[17] was a word of self-admonition. The proposition "Caesar's legions are returning to consciousness"[18] made plain the extent to which Spengler remained dominated by the idea that a final battle for earth and world domination was impending; only a resolute militarism on the part of the West would be able to assert itself on the field. The idea that a global division of power could ever come about – as it did thanks to the "balance of terror" during the Cold War era after 1946 – lay completely beyond his monopolar, hegemonic imagination.

In the preface to the revised edition of *The Decline of the West*, published in 1922, Spengler conceded that he had written a work entirely bound to the spirit of the age. Like Rosenstock-Huessy's *Autobiography of Western Man*, it could equally have been called *Ecce Homo occidentalis!* – "Behold the man of the west!" – but it could also very plausibly have been classed as a confession.

> A thinker [...] has no choice; he thinks as he has to think. Truth in the long run is to him the picture of the world which was born at his birth. It is that which he does not invent but rather discovers within himself. It is himself over again; his being expressed in words; the meaning of his personality formed into a doctrine [...].[19]

Spengler's editor and biographer, Anton Mirko Koktanek, honed statements like this into psychological diagnoses. He has quoted from Spengler's diaries, in which the young author accused himself of poetic incapacity. "I can only plan, only draft and complete things in my head. Execution appalls me. I cannot bring myself to begin."[20] A dozen literary sketches and a few draft plays remained unfinished, including notes for a play about Tiberius and a suggestive character study of the megalomaniac arsonist Herostratus.

> For this deep-rooted poetic impotence, he [...] finds, through projection, a rationalizing explanation: it is not he who is infertile, incapable of procreation, merely pseudo-pregnant – it is his age, his era, the all-encompassing, the very ground, the superego. This transition to civilization is the climacteric of culture.[21]

Through its hyper-autobiographical implications, Spengler's book makes its readers fellow sufferers in the embarrassment of a Dasein that has come too late for great art and real creativity; it invites them to become partners in heroic sterility. Only as accomplices in fidelity to an ultimately lost cause, he believes, will people in the final stages of their culture gain the opportunity to demonstrate a kind of ultimate greatness.

Such impositions would surely have met with even fiercer resistance than they faced in the actual event, except that the author's remarks on the cultural and political situation of the time were so rich in apt and suggestive observation. Despite its manifest weaknesses, its one-sidedness, and its strained constructs, it remained an impressive, not to say titanic undertaking to depict the transition of late Faustian culture into the stage of its globe-spanning civilization. What Spengler was able to evoke so suggestively in this context were powerful, reality-shaping entities such as large-scale machine technology, invasive financial capital, an arrogant press, the metamorphosis of politics into party strife, expansive bureaucracy, and the libidinous life of large cities. In Spengler's description, the physiognomy of the late cultural world, set against a flattened Faustian backdrop, also included the excess of the museum enterprise, the ubiquity of arts and crafts, and the all-devouring effects of newspaper journalism. Spengler offered highly lucid statements on phenomena such as "Second Religiousness" and the syncretism of worldviews, in which one cobbles together traditional cults and beliefs as one sees fit. It is no surprise that the author noted the feminism of his time and the early signs of mass tourism and saw them as harbingers of a self-congratulatory decay. For him, with the limitless proliferation of secondary literature, the era of authentic art and poetry had come to its conclusion. What remained were catalogues and composites. When words have all become sales pitches, brisk and blasphemous tones will prevail. Theodor W. Adorno's 1949 judgment that, in his time, the author of *The Decline* had "found hardly an adversary who was his equal," is a tribute to the often-impressive empirical plausibility and the elitist sharpness of Spengler's observations[22] – besides which, Spengler's and Adorno's views on the tendencies of the culture industry and the internal contradictions of the Age of Enlightenment were much less divergent than many admirers of Adorno and many detractors of Spengler were inclined to admit.

Of all the diagnostic and prognostic propositions derivable from Spengler's hyper-biographical–morphological scheme and his classical models, those of truly risky significance, from the perspective of the history of political ideas, were above all those bearing upon the fatality of the transition from republican to Caesarian-monocratic forms of government. Next to no one has pointed out the profound irony of Spengler's "applied morphology," according to which it is precisely the late phases of cultures which, in their final flickering out, see the ascendency of Caesarian centralism, militarism, soldiers aspiring to the imperial throne, and the hollow deification of incidental rulers. Spengler's "cultures," superplants of the highest type, do not wither away in their later stages; they disintegrate into mutually incompatible tendencies: here, the over-refinement of later "nervous art" and relativistic epistemologies; there, the over-brutalization of neo-barbaric mass phenomena. The cultural–geriatric system of the great bricoleur did not envisage a phase of well-earned dotage for the globalized sphere of the Faustian soul supposedly withering away around 1900; it insisted that the current bearers of Faustian civilization, though sickened through their drive for the infinite – led by the expansionist British, but including partly also the Romance peoples and above all the Germans, the mother nation of Faustianism – must rise up with fateful necessity in a surge of imperialistic old-age fury, indeed must make a late, decisive grab for undivided world power.

There is no doubt that Spengler succumbs here, as in many other places, to the élan of the grand analogy. When it came to the question of "decline," for the author of this inspired book as for modern Europeans more broadly, there could naturally be only one paradigm: the Western Roman Empire. Edward Gibbon had already set the tone, at the height of the Enlightenment, with his magnum opus, *The History of the Decline and Fall of the Roman Empire* in six volumes, with the first volume appearing in 1776 and the last in 1789. German scholars such as Theodor Mommsen and Otto Seeck methodically elaborated further on this enormous subject material. If there was any plausibility in speaking of a decline of the West, it was to be won especially through the exploitation of analogies between late Roman and late Western European data and trends. Spengler's work confirmed this assumption across the board. He found his material, especially in the first volume, mostly by juxtaposing features of Apollonian–classical with Faustian–West-European culture. In doing so, he came up with many ingenious analogies. In this context, it is easy to grasp why Spengler saw Napoleon's rise under the clear afternoon sky of mature European culture as announcing the dawn of the late Caesarian phase – after all, according to the schema, the endgame of civilization was supposed to span a good two hundred years – which implied that the appearance of the new Caesar would be imminent in 1918. In the eyes of the Munich seer, the nineteenth century meant little more than a phase in the contenders' advance to the final struggle for world power – a struggle that was to remain an intra-European or Western drama, with less than fleeting involvement for "the rest of the world." Fixated on his morphological hypotheses, Spengler remained unamenable to the critical argument that, from a dramaturgical perspective, the Roman Empire never "declined" or fell but was instead re-enacted in multiple metamorphoses and translations. The captivation of his gaze by the late stage of Western European culture and his conviction that a Caesarean-monopolistic conglomerate of power would imminently emerge blinkered his view of the irrepressible pluralism of the political and cultural systems of action that gave the modernizing world its dynamism on all continents.

Spengler's most important and, at the same time, least correctable error in reasoning was reflected in his assumption that the world at the time of the First World War could, as a whole, be interpreted as if it were little more than a surface for projecting and enacting its Faustian finale. Spengler's doctrine of the endgame of the Faustian sphere was something that he associated far too closely with the narcissistic overextension of the Western European "cultural soul," which he wanted to believe was manifesting its heroic agony in his own person. The internal dynamics of the sphere that Hegel defined as the realm of "objective spirit" thus escaped Spengler. In truth, by that time, disciplines such as the European natural sciences, European engineering, European factory systems, European property law, European medical procedures, European concepts in art, and European constitutional theory had already become widespread and detached from their origins – supposing they had ever really been conditioned by "Faustian" dispositions and the demonic pull of infinite space. They formed themselves into universally accessible, relatively easily transferable, fundamentally replicable, locally adaptable corpora of concepts, rules, and procedures – all without relevant copyright protection. If in actuality there were such copyright constraints, one couldn't help but describe a large-scale political and technical construct such as Maoist China and its filiations in the twenty-first century as a single, colossal plagiarism of Europe, since it "borrowed" virtually everything from the West that constitutes its current strength, albeit minus the idea of human dignity and the post-1945 turn to a culture of post-imperial self-reflection. Any attempt to relativize Europe's scientific, technical, artistic, and political–moral diffusions, in terms of a Faustian stage of old age or as if they were bound to the soil of the Old World, would amount to a senseless re-provincialization of interculturally established universals. One fears that Spengler, who as a philosopher stood on a "German path to pragmatism" according to which "what is true is what works," massively underestimated the universalism of the positive validity of European ideas and procedures, insofar as he coupled them too strictly to the expanded endgame of West-European–American culture. He never succeeded in dispassionately considering the transcultural intrinsic values of the "technical age." Undoubtedly, this was also attributable to the methodological poverty of his conceptual apparatus. Beyond the overused concepts of development and entropy, what was missing from this was the crucial process-theoretical idea of positive feedback.[23] Its effects can induce dynamisms and capricious growth phenomena, whose graphing no longer has the least thing to do with biographical patterns and organic transformations – or any other figure from the world of narrative. Feedback logic allows for much more coherent and conclusive explanation than one gets with vacuous notions of an extensive cultural dotage. Moreover, even with Spengler himself, one cannot be sure whether he was not simply using morphological pretexts to recirculate the classical idea of *senectus mundi*, the senectitude of the world, enriched with an added value of Caesarist fantasies and anti-democratic posturing.

More than a hundred years after the publication of the two volumes of *The Decline of the West*, the question of whether Spengler wasn't "right after all" has answered itself. If the word "decline" meant Western Europe's entry into an age of dictatorships, then Spengler's prophecy would have been temporarily fulfilled – even if the "Führer" Adolf Hitler was too pathetic, too deplorable in the eyes of his herald, to justify expectations of a new Caesar or someone like a Tiberius. Spengler did not live long enough to form an opinion about figures such as Stalin and Mao Zedong. When, in a 1936 lecture at the Société française de philosophie, the French scholar Élie Halévy rendered part of Spengler's findings into the formula *L'Ère des tyrannies*, the Era of Tyrannies, he laid out the source common to Bolshevism and right-wing extremist dictatorships in their shared strategies of terror-based conspiracy government; Halévy's remarks culminated in the assessment that Sovietism, due to its conspiratorial structure, constituted fascism in the strict sense.[24] In light of Halévy's diagnosis, the ideological battles between fascism and anti-fascism were nothing more than demons conjured up in the air – show fights of a politically draped ideological monstrosity with itself. What was later called "totalitarianism" in the wake of the studies by Franz Borkenau and Hannah Arendt[25] was in fact a misnomer for the conspiracy system created by Lenin, which sought to control entire states and societies and to generalize war.[26]

As concerns Spengler's Caesarist predictions for the lands of today's "West," they have long since been definitively dismissed – except that they are now returning from Europe's lost Far East as a Muscovite specter. Indeed, it was precisely the fact that Europe possessed neither the means nor the will to exercise global hegemony that constituted its charm and its virtue up until the beginning of the twenty-first century. It also turns out to be its conscious weakness, not to say its amiable shame and disgrace, that it has for too long committed itself to a pseudo-Kantian illusion of perpetual peace and neglected its self-assertion in an unpeaceful world.

If, on the other hand, the term "decline" were used to describe the circumstance that the Western European sphere had been displaced from the center of world power by the course and consequences of the Second World War, then at least the weaker half of Spengler's predictions would have come true – though they did not anticipate the momentous locking-in of the bipolar "world order" between 1945 and 1990, to say nothing of the neo-imperial ambitions of China, Russia, Iran, and Turkey, which have little in common with each other apart from their shared motif of revenge against the West. If the word "decline" means the withdrawal of a once highly cultured and vibrant region of the world from real history and its regression to a condition of post-historical fatigue and ahistorical indifference, it would hardly be appropriate to apply it to the events and conditions in Western and Central Europe in the three-quarters of a century from 1945 to 2024. Spengler had deduced the idea of fellahdom (from the Arabic word *fallāḥ*, meaning "plowman") from conditions in Egypt in the post-pharaonic and post-Roman periods and declared that it embodied the futureless future of burnt-out advanced civilizations; it was, he thought, the fate of their populations to revert to the *modus vivendi* of a primitive peasantry.[27] Now, one need not hold the dominant lifestyles of today's European bourgeoisie in high moral regard; it might be supposed that for the vast majority of them, their *modus vivendi* means little more than the promise of an existence within the horizons of liberal consumerism. This is realized in a rather favorable, though not unproblematic, way among the broad middle classes, where a certain democratization of luxury is gaining ground; among the less fortunate, it secures, through social transfers, a sluggish subalternity that rarely erupts in protest but during elections easily rallies around platforms for right-wing, radically coded discontent. One might regret that for most inhabitants of this part of the world, the word "Europe" does not represent a slogan or a rallying cry under which one would ride into battle, panache aflutter in the breeze. Objections in this tone, however, do not suffice to validate those prognoses of fellahization projected by strict interpreters of history as the inevitable fate of cultures after the end of their thousand-year cycle of existence. In place of a monotonous fellahin peasantry, the lands of Western and Central Europe have seen the flourishing, in less than a century, of an incalculable wealth of lifestyles, arts, and literature, as well as a wealth of mobility, creativity, and sensibilities that, by their very existence, belie all sweeping cultural pessimism, even if there is no shortage of phenomena that deserve to be registered as "decadent." But then, perhaps *decadence* is simply an inadequate word to describe the bizarre and desperate notions with which people will defend themselves against the sense of their own insignificance.

Those wishing to consult Spengler's work in order to discharge the necessary task, renewed after 1945, of once again explaining Europe to Europeans, would find there much that is well suited for making past catastrophes more comprehensible, but they would find hardly a handful of sentences that could be meaningfully applied to the historically and politologically unprecedented construct that is the European Union. If it seemed advisable to pull a bookmark from Spengler's magnum opus and place it here into the Book of Europe, this was primarily to call attention to the dubiousness of a consultation in the spirit of Lebensphilosophical fatalism, something which seems to have been gaining ground again for some time – appearing half decked out in neo-Stoic robes and half draped with infamous analogies to late Roman conditions. Readers of Spengler today who would have him interpret Europe's situation for them risk falling into an exogenous depression even more acute than was the case with readers in the 1920s. It is even less likely today that a clear impetus for action can be extracted by reading this ominous book. If Spengler can be profitably read today, it is only by those who intend to enlighten themselves about the risks of declinism, whether written in a heroic or a defeatist tone. As a political consultant, Spengler belonged in his day to the camp of national-conservative hawks; he would have no advice for a structure such as the European Union, since it is located so completely outside his conceptual world, and beyond even his dreams and interests. No doubt, he would have despised the new construct. It has bound itself to an ethos that grants preference to mediocre conditions over provocative extremes; it is steeped in compromise and shies away from anything that demands decision and sharp red lines. Contemporary Europe has completely flipped the concept of civilization into something positive – with the nuance that this is no longer presented with attributes of a domineering, sterile old age, but rather with adult maturity, even relaxed mediocrity, as expressed by both sexes and their variants. This is the basis for the unconcerned assent among most people today to Jacob Burckhardt's judicious note that "we cannot fathom the economy of world history."[28] One contemporary historian of religion, Linus Hauser, has outlined the spiritual findings of the current majorities in our part of the world and captures them in his apt description of a culture of "finitude becalmed."[29]

Only this much remains certain: decline is not for the faint of heart. Those who traffic in declinist sentiments should be aware that they thereby increase two risks: the conventional talk of decline tends, on the one hand, to grow into a self-fulfilling prophecy; on the other hand, it provokes mental reflexes in the form of defiant optimism, which can lead to the misjudgment of real crises. The years following 1918 showed how easily anti-declinist reaction, inflamed by feelings of doom, could devolve into a broad stance of anti-relativism, as when incensed possessors of healthy common sense mobbed in protest against the abstruse theories of the Jewish physicist Albert Einstein. In either case, declinism is grist for the mill of false prophecy. One might confidently advise historians, politicians, and interested citizens in our time, and urge them to study the past century as if it were a prophetological laboratory conducting tests to determine which rescue measures would be most suitable for which crises. From such studies, one should not expect definitive results. Be that as it may, one preliminary recommendation becomes apparent: it is always well to be wary of saviors whose aid services turn out to be worse than the problems they propose to solve. It is not yet possible to say with certainty whether the greatest injury lies with the myth of decline and doom, the myth of the final decisive battle, or the myth of the savior. At the present time, one can venture to predict that Europe's future will remain more or less out of harm's way, even in the face of multiple crises, as long as its citizens manage to resist the pull of mythical solutions promised by national-conservative "gatherings," fictitious "brotherhoods," and bogus "alternatives."

Lesson four
Dire vrai sur soi-même – Speaking the truth about oneself[1] The European book of confessions

The preceding retrospections on the work of Eugen Rosenstock-Huessy and Oswald Spengler have acquainted or reacquainted us with authors whose works, as presented here, can be grasped only as metastases of an exuberant autobiographical passion. Their authors deemed it necessary to depict an entire millennium in order to introduce their contemporaries to their diagnosis of the present and to mark their own position in the tableau. The two books can thus be read, without undue force, as extended confessions. Rosenstock-Huessy presented himself to the world and to his contemporaries as a key witness to European history from the eleventh century onward: his conscience was heavy with the legacy of the history of freedom in the European millennium – but, at the same time, it inspired him to issue a kind of *admonitio generalis* to inhabitants of the Old World and their North American cousins. On the verge of the abyss that had opened up in Europe with the almost simultaneous seizures of power by red, black, and brown fascisms, he wanted, from the transatlantic shore in 1938, to recall "Westerners" *en bloc* to their authentic political and spiritual history. If he occasionally struck the tone of a military chaplain, he did so with appreciation for the fact that he must not leave his readers in the dark about the struggles that lay ahead. The situational report took precedence over the theory.

Spengler's fatal work likewise possessed a scarcely concealed confessional core – its author included himself, with the pathos of a wakefulness without illusion, in the collective dynamic of a Faustian cultural finale. He engaged the fate of a final philosophy for his own position in the grand course of events – one marked by a proud sterility of retrospection and an archival spirit that is in its element when compiling typologies and conceiving analogies. Spengler thrived on the suggestion that he was congenial to his era, since he felt in himself its tendencies to torpor and decay. Convinced that he was arriving too late, that he was a laggard, indeed the last of the last, he developed his basic mood with a certain sad pedantry in every detail, as if only in bidding farewell to the era of abundance could a brittle final ingenuity demonstrate itself.

It accords with the psychological and biographical interpretation of Spengler's book that the author left behind a collection of handwritten notes, presumably compiled between 1913 and 1919, under the headings *Eis heauton* and *Ego* and based on the *Meditations* of Marcus Aurelius. These were transcribed after his death by his sister Hildegard Kornhardt (1885–1942) and published in 2007 under the confessional title *Ich beneide jeden, der lebt* [I envy everyone who lives]. They suggest the portrait of a man, fearful of life, whose existence consisted of a continuous flight into grand poses. From Spengler's self-portrait in about 140 fragments, sections 61, 67, and 68 are especially revealing:

> My boundless anxiety as a child facing the world and the future. How gladly would I have died from horror in the face of life [...]. Life thus stood before me as a penitential pilgrimage, something like a desolate trek through the desert [...].
>
> I remember so clearly those afternoons I secretly spent [...] as a third-year student at the University Library. The first book was Renan's *Life of Jesus*. At that time, I felt a deep happiness that was too beautiful to share with anyone. I felt wings growing on me – a new country: I knew that I myself could be something there [...]. This good fortune has recurred only now, in the years 1912–13, when the philosophy I had sought since my youth finally became clear to me. [...]
>
> When I set out to recount my life, or rather the bitter piece of consciousness that could have and should have been a life, I do not know how this narrative will differ from any other biography [...] It is not "fortune" that I have lacked; I would be grateful for any great misfortune that might have befallen me, if only it had been life. But, to this day, I can speak not of friends, nor of experiences, nor of deeds, nor of joys and sorrows, but only

> of the "I, I, I" encysted within myself, as if in a dungeon, bitterly aware of its confinement, tormenting itself without ever finding a connection to the outside world. My biography is a description of this state of affairs, nothing more. I envy everyone who lives. I have just brooded, and when an opportunity to really live came my way, I withdrew, let it pass by, and as soon as it was too late, I was seized by the most bitter regret.[2]

What follows is not an effort to pit Spengler's intimate fragments against his publications, in which he presented himself as a teacher full of fortitude in the face of fate and its rigors, a defender of stoic Prussianism and a steely herald of quasi-apocalyptic wars. The case of Spengler is of interest to us only insofar as it illustrates the insight that one was obliged to speak more than one language when attempting to explain Europe to Europeans of the early twentieth century. The thesis that *The Decline of the West* concealed a nucleus of autobiographical self-statement – presented in the mode of a general confession of late-period decadence *pro domo et mundo* – requires no further evidence after what has been said. Even more plainly than in his confessions of a personal involvement in the suffering of his times, one hears Spengler's *confiteor* in that passage of his work where he expresses the Faustian soul's sense of the world, together with its pathological core:

> An Ego lost in Infinity, an Ego that was all force, but a force negligibly weak in an infinity of greater forces; that was all will, but a will full of fear for its freedom. [...] Every limitation upon freedom was felt as a chain that had to be dragged along through life, and life in turn was felt as a living death. And if so – why? For *what*?[3]

What interests us here is a phenomenon referred to as the "second confession." The expression stands for the language of private candor, used to put into words what usually resonates only indirectly when presenting an idea or concern in the public sphere. In a sense, those who speak publicly are always confessing by revealing what, in their view, should be said about this or that matter. By contrast, what is referred to here as a "second confession" – one could also say, an additional and explicit confession – implies a form of truth-telling that cannot be conceived without the use of the first-person singular pronoun. To explain the changed world to Europeans in the postwar period – whether in the years after 1918 or in the years after 1945 – demands a minimal level of bilingualism in every local language.

If one were to adopt Spengler's speculative view of the European disposition with respect to "speaking the truth about oneself," then the later disciplines of investigative historiography and biography would have developed from a spirit of Stoic self-examination and Christian confession. They were certainly already prepared in early Christian rituals[4] and established in the semi-modern sacrament of penance, which was made binding throughout Europe after the Fourth Council of the Lateran in 1215. The notorious Canon 21 required every adult European to pronounce, at least once per year, the whole and intimate truth of their way of life. Spengler claimed outright that this decree represented the original sacrament of Gothic Catholicism. When he ventured to claim that "every confession is an autobiography,"[5] he was in truth already aiming at the inverse of this thesis, according to which, all higher forms of self-expression in modern humans tend to transform into media for self-accusation, admission, and "unbounded confession"[6] – and why not also the demand to be acquitted or absolved? Jean Delumeau (1923–2020), the scholar of sin and fear in the Western world, who lectured at the Collège de France, also believed that we, as Europeans, even in our less religious times, remain marked by "this incessant invitation" to confession and "this vast contribution to self-knowledge" that the Catholic apparatus of forgiveness brought about at the height of its efficacy.[7] And although the *mea culpa* originated in the penitential ritual of the medieval Church before its split, Protestantism would offer some of the most fertile grounds for Western confessionalism; indeed even the Communist Party of Russia, the occult arm of ageless Eastern Orthodoxy, offered comrades who had strayed from the path the sometimes life-saving sacrament of "self-criticism."

Wherever the autobiographical impulse asserted itself among European authors, the contemporary world, posterity, and psychology were called upon to provide a substitute for the fading priestly power of absolution. Indeed, one could claim that the habitus of "telling the truth" in the mode of confession, admission, and entering into the spotlight of intimate self-examination had detached itself, on European soil, from its origins in Christian confessional practice, without losing any of its defining influence; it became a formative aspect of the "inner sense," the "conscience," the "consciousness" of European subjects in the centuries of the modern era. It is reasonable to assume that, in early Christian times, it was above all the confident expectation of forgiveness that made it easier for individuals who were prepared to repent, whether male or female, to confess their transgressions, whether in the "inner forum" or in open manifestation. From the eighteenth century onward, the disposition to confess as such became more prevalent than ever before, even as the hope of absolution faded – arguably, with the publication of Rousseau's posthumous *Confessions* at the latest, there developed a literary genre of self-exposure whose authors were not seeking the indulgence of the public, let alone its forgiveness. They could already count on the historical or biographical interest of the public sphere; indeed, they were increasingly willing to serve as psychological or anthropological specimens, even as sensational case histories, in the growing pathographic and criminological archives of bourgeois society.

What one has been accustomed to calling the "public sphere" since the eighteenth century by no means indicates the simple restitution of the ancient agora with help from the press at the national level. "Public sphere" implies the conversion of a religious community, something primarily listening and singing, into a reading public; indeed, it often promotes the opening of the confessional booth onto the marketplace and the transfer of auricular confession, which had been disestablished in Protestantism, into the register of literature.[8] Educated readers develop the ear of a priestly confessor, when necessary, which, even if it has no forgiveness to extend, can open itself to intimate revelations in a discreet and sympathetic manner.

Anyone who comes across statements such as the one in Charles Baudelaire's notes, written between 1852 and 1866 and published under the title *My Heart Laid Bare*,

> A sense of *solitude*, from childhood onward. Despite my family – and especially among my schoolmates – a sense that it was my fate to be forever alone.[9]

is immediately thrust into the position of a psychologist or a literary critic pursuing an intimate clue for understanding an opaque work of art. When one finds the same author musing that "It might be pleasant to be by turns victim and executioner,"[10] one must decide for oneself whether one wishes to follow the author in his game of role reversal, be it political, criminal, or sexual in tone. The modern reader is free to choose between empathy with the torturer and empathy with the tortured. As for writers of confessions in modern times, they benefit from the license to skirt around the reader's readiness to empathize without disavowing their own will for truth. Their sovereignty is indicated in the way they indulge in rebellious speculation in the silence of written soliloquies – as Baudelaire did when he wrote the following reflection in theologically discredited terms:

> What is the fall?
>
> If it is unity become duality, then it is God who fell.
>
> At least he might have recognized in this location a bit of mischief or a satire on the part of Providence against love – and, in the world of progeneration, a sign of original sin. It's a fact: we can only make love with our organs of excretion.
>
> In other terms, would not Creation entail the fall of God?[11]

It was left to the refined hypocrite, who refrained from passing judgment, to grasp that, in Baudelaire's inner monologue, late symptoms of entropy had become visible in the once painstakingly constructed edifice of Catholicism. New flowers of evil were growing on terrain that had been only superficially cleared and levelled in late antiquity with the victory of true doctrine over the dualistic heresy of Gnosticism. The poet's "heart laid bare" attested to his irredeemable doubts with respect to the fictions that the theological central committee of the Church had devised in the third and fourth centuries – for its own salvation and to sedate the faithful.

An urge to speak the truth from afar, and from out of the depths of intimate memory, must also have been at the heart of the confession of the Chilean poet Pablo Neruda (1904–1973), who claimed that while serving as a young Chilean consul in Ceylon in 1929, he had compelled a local chambermaid, a young Tamil woman of regal beauty, who would carry away the contents of his toilet, into acquiescing to his desires. In the fourth chapter of his *Memoirs*, entitled "Luminous Solitude," there is a passage whose confessional quality leaves no room for doubt.

> One morning, I decided to go all the way. I got a strong grip on her wrist and stared into her eyes. There was no language I could talk with her. Unsmiling, she let herself be led away and was soon naked in my bed. Her waist, so very slim, her full hips, the brimming cups of her breasts made her like one of the thousand-year-old sculptures from the south of India. It was the coming together of a man and a statue. She kept her eyes wide open all the while, completely unresponsive. She was right to despise me. The experience was never repeated.[12]

A note like this would be hard to imagine outside the sphere of Latin Europe, the South American echo of which has given rise to great literature and provided significant additions to the library of confessed truths. In Neruda's lines, written four decades after the incident, there reverberates not only the confession of the beauty of sin – in distant correspondence with Baudelaire's language of exposure; even more clearly audible is the unspoken word of the priestly confessor, whom the reader is to represent: the one who confesses will be granted absolution from the guilt of his deed if, supposing contrition and insight, he solemnly vows not to commit it again. By calling up this dark episode from the distant past, the author consolidated the crypto-Catholic verb in the Spanish title of his memoirs: *Confieso*, "I confess." Let us note that this episode, published in 1974 in the confessional of the literary public, already seems a world away from the organized mercilessness of the present day, in which public accusations almost mechanically entail pronouncements of guilt, often followed by summary excommunication. If it happens that the accused denies the charge, this is construed in most cases as a confession against the grain.[13]

Considerations such as these serve to consolidate the thesis that, in topological terms, Europe is something quite different from a mere geographical entity. It is a cultural phenomenon that, to borrow a

Marxian phrase, could be said to have some "metaphysical quirks"; it forms a holographic body in which surface appearances and examinations into its depths blend into each other in an intricate way. Thanks to its archives of speaking subjectivities, in which one could place bookmarks beyond reckoning, and beyond its existence as a territory and theater of political and state operations, Europe proves itself to be a zone of linguistically accessible interior space and sensible participation – Rainer Maria Rilke's neologism *Weltinnenraum* "the inner space of the world," coined in Autumn 1914, could be applied here, with "world" understood as an inwardly focused sphere of objects of possible concern:

> Oh house, oh sloping meadow, oh evening light
> [...]
> I worry, and inside me stands the house.[14]

Beyond question, Rilke's use of language represents a subtle Europeanism – in it, the gesture of confession dissolves into an unforced self-expression of momentary feeling; one could almost say that inner-world consciousness has reached a state in which articulated feelings merge into confession without any elements of guilt coming into play – except perhaps for the quiet, resonant suggestion in Rilke's poem that contemporary people are too preoccupied and too numb in their everyday lives to understand that the images of the external world want to find peace within them.

Apart from that, the suspicion cannot be dismissed that even in Heraclitus' semi-archaic concept of the soul, a distant prefiguration of inner-worldliness already glimmered, as when the thinker stressed that

> You will not find the boundaries of soul by travelling in any direction, so deep is the measure of it.[15]

What one is dealing with here is a dictum articulated from a position prior to the distinction between inside and out that would later become binding in Europe. In the Heraclitean precept, the magnitude of the soul (*psyche*) entered into discussion in order to emphasize its co-immensity, indeed its co-immeasurability, with respect to the expanse of the cosmos.

Aurelius Augustinus, by contrast, founder of the literary genre of the confession in the West and a Latin-speaking author who drew upon Platonic and Neoplatonic concepts, underwent a process of internalization – attended by a devaluation of the external – that was so far advanced that he could apply the gesture of confession to all objects related to a sinfully straying existence in the "external world." Going beyond the early Christian practices of confession and penance, Augustine gave a new stamp to the gesture of confession by placing his life-long search under the sign of error. This resulted in the principle of presentation that governs the first nine books of the *Confessiones*. It might read something like this: "From one error that pleased me, I moved on to the next." This schema reverberates through European intellectual history, with the author – through the presentation of his own case – seeking to expose any kind of extroverted search for happiness, salvation, or God as doomed to failure. The world, as an externality, could be nothing other than the epitome of illusions that divert the individual from the One that is essential. If his own wanderings, his own errancy, didn't lead to perdition, this was because the hand of Providence ever and again snatched him back from the abyss. In spiritual biographies of Asian masters, it would probably be said that the seeker was saved by favorable karma from losing himself in the "red mist of affections" and the haze of "attachments."

In his unprecedented self-presentation, Augustine turned out to be a purveyor of what has recently been called the "biographical illusion"; it manifests itself as the compulsive proclivity of the individual to interpret his existence in time as a coherent, even purposive movement, notwithstanding its detours and periods of idleness.[16] The author straightened out the waviness of his life's wandering into a purposeful line that could be read from left to right – as if anticipating the proverb cited by Paul Claudel that God writes straight with crooked lines. At the same time, Augustine performed pioneering work in analyzing the interior space of Western subjects by using a wealth of spatial metaphors to make the case for the habitability of the "house of the soul." The inner house would be *augusta* (venerable) if God were to inhabit it; it is *ruinosa* (ruinous) so long as the high vistant remains a stranger.[17] Here, Augustine distanced himself greatly from the classical equation between *oikos* and *kosmos*, house and universe, which Hegel had praised in Greek thought for having made the spirit at home in the world.[18] As the philosopher would have it, it is thanks to the Greek miracle that the infinite has found an earthly address – which is why German thought immediately feels at home with the Greeks; Catholic Christians, however, as more recent tenants of the ancient cosmos, have often been the somewhat ungrateful inhabitants of the earthly realm, inclined as they are to flee the world.

In addition to the suggestive word "house," Augustine deployed spatial expressions such as *aula*, *campi*, *antra*, *prata*, *cavernae*, *recessus*, *penetralia*, *domicilium*, and others to emphasize the postulate of an inner world. Its urgency followed from the metaphysically based assumption that "the truth" is found within and nowhere else, other than in the Holy Scriptures. Hence the imperative formulated by Augustine in 390, three years after his conversion:

> Do not go outside; return within yourself; the truth dwells within the inner person![19]

With spatial images such as these, *Homo occidentalis* is marked as the living being who has the ability for inward "contemplation" (*recueillement*, *Einkehr*, *raccoglimento*, *examen de conciencia*) as the first sign of emancipation from the banality of the external world.

Large sections of Augustine's confessions read as if the author wanted to anticipate the Last Judgment in his own conscience. For nine years, he had wallowed in "deep mire" (*limo profundi*)[20] and had allowed false teachers to serve him the "wine of error." Indeed, during the months of his immense grief over the loss of a childhood friend, he even found a perverse "quiet in that bitterness."[21] He had been late in loving the truth (*sero te amavi*), and for far too long had cultivated a friendship with the world (*amicitia mundi*), a friendly intercourse that ultimately amounted to whorish fornication (*fornicatio*).[22]

It is almost impossible to overstate the importance of Augustinianism for the history of European subject formation. A provisional note must suffice that the Lutheran Reformation – or, as Rosenstock-Huessy would have it, "the German Revolution" – like the global impulses of Calvinism, can be grasped only as neo-Augustinian renaissances within Latin European and Anglo-European Christianity and its social expressions. It is associated with the ubiquity of crypto-Platonic figures of thought, which ensured that the natural light of reason, celebrated since the eighteenth century as that of the Enlightenment, remained coupled with a supernatural light.

Its radiance implies lighting conditions for an interior space, as indicated by the terms *memoria* and *conscientia*. Through the prefix *con-*, the latter expression indicates that the subject's self-perception includes a concomitant knowledge, thus a "co-knowledge," that was initially believed to be explicable only in terms of a discrete alliance between God and the soul. If Europeans believe they have something they call conscience, it is because, from a Platonic or crypto-Platonic perspective, their existence can only be understood through the facts of the observing and observed consciousness. The subject thus always exists under the light of theoscopy – and is defenseless in its transparency to the divine eye, for which the difference between *intus* and *extra* means nothing. From the perspective of light theory, what is called *peccatum originale*, original sin, refers to the tenacious, lived-out fantasy of the isolated subject – ultimately, that is, a subject who could turn away from the absolute observer. As such, it imagines that it can at any moment withdraw into unobserved-existence and do things that escape the eye of others – whether human or divine. The postulation of absolute observation requires the metaphysically taxing assumption that God is not only omnipotent and omniscient; but, even more than that, that he possesses an ever-present and all-attentive presence, the mostly unnoticed extensions of which reach into my pre-personal consciousness. Divine memory is aided by a continuous, otherworldly accounting of all deeds, good or evil – prototypes of such records date back to dire Egyptian notions concerning the judgment of the dead. Thus, divine hyper-attentiveness permeates not only the external course of the world, which remains obscure to human understanding, it also illuminates the world of human interiority – and, as Nicholas of Cusa attempted to show in his treatise *De visione Dei* (1453), this applies not merely to selected individuals, but to all mortals all at once. The *democratia christiana* – the mental prelude of modernity – begins with the conviction that an intelligence from on high and from within can entirely exhaust human inner worlds, however much one might wish to fence them off as a zone of private and unfathomable darkness. Which is why the ostensible "discovery of the unconscious" in modern depth psychologies brought about not merely the "insult" that Freud emphasized, but also opened up new avenues of retreat for self-illusion. European humanity exists, as it were, under the regime of a divine facial recognition – more precisely, under an inner world illuminated from on high and from within, as per the Augustinian address to the Most High: *interior intimo meo, superior summo meo* ("more inward than my most inward part; and superior then, unto my supremest").[23] My interiority, as it is accessible to me, represents an extimacy from the perspective of the utterly innermost: I am monitored not only from without, but also seen through from within. Seen from within, I am not close to myself. It was not until the dawn of the nineteenth century that the thought asserted itself with Schelling, Schopenhauer, Nietzsche, and Freud, that there was an opaque layer of unconscious processes within human interior life that could not be reached by the conscious ego and whose illumination, if not impossible, remained precarious.[24]

Let us content ourselves here with the remark that the theoscopic structure of human self-perception, or rather the acquaintance of Dasein with itself, was only made explicit in the culmination of German idealism with Johann Gottlieb Fichte: by disclosing the underivable preliminary of self-consciousness before all reflections in others, he made manifest the condition of possibility for telling the truth about oneself – even in the absence of religious and literary confessionals, never mind the legal and policial instruments of confession. The eye, the vital self-implantation, is designated by Fichte as a Uranian organ – in honor of the muse of astronomy. The thinker summed up his system in a few lines of verse: the bright eye of Urania that I once gazed into, "now sees in my seeing, lives in my living." There exists an anonymous intelligence that, in me and through me, sees what it sees.[25] In his 1936 essay on the transcendence of the ego, the young Jean-Paul Sartre noted something similar, in a sober tone and without any theological exaltation of the pre-personal consciousness.[26]

The psycho-historical consequences of these early dispositions have manifested themselves in many ways over the course of the last millennium and a half and more. Nine hundred and fifty years separate the writing of Augustine's *Confessions* from Francesco Petrarca's confessional opus *Secretum*[27] – a book whose importance for the early modern culture of self-examination and self-accusation can hardly be overstated. This work of piercing, public self-examination invokes the Church Father Augustine as a priestly confessor, an inquisitor of conscience, to assist the author – who was then around 45 or 50 years old, past middle age and showing his first gray hairs. The text's point of departure is provided by the author's confession that, despite all his worldly successes, he is still an unhappy person: *ego sum miser*. Together, the confessor and his charge work through the grounds for the latter's persisting misery. When Augustine ventures a guess that Francesco had not familiarized himself sufficiently with the fact of his mortality, Francesco can reply that he had meditated on his death so intensively in advance that he had at times buckled under the brunt of the terror.[28] One may even admit that Martin Heidegger's remarks on "being-toward-death" in *Being and Time*[29] gave little more, on the whole, than phenomenological objectifications of Petrarca's testimony, which, for its part, was based on monastic psychological exercises. It remains a revealing circumstance that returning from the anticipation of death to the lived Now brings only indirect consequences for both authors: for Heidegger, Dasein should derive its impulse toward "resoluteness" from the anticipation of death, but without anything more specific ensuing from this; Petrarca concedes that such exercises have indeed made him more serious, but finds he is as far removed from the experience of happy security as he has ever been.

In later parts of the three-part dialogue, Augustine, the priestly confessor, questions his examinee on the classic, seven-part catalogue of grave sins: as concerns *gula*, boundless gluttony, Francesco has little to confess, though he knows what it means to indulge overmuch now and again; in the matter of wrath, *ira*, he has no more to admit than the usual. Next comes *luxuria*, sexual compulsion, against which the confessant offers assurance that he has mounted a righteous defense – one hears no particulars of any possible defeats. Inquiries into envy (*invidia*) and greed (*avaritia*) yield nothing noteworthy. For further examination, this leaves only the dangerous affliction of the soul, *aegritudo* or *acedia* – often translated as "sloth," for which the quasi-meteorological term "depression" has been introduced in modern times, in order to remove it as far as possible, in the name of secular therapeutic interest, from the zone of the morally reprehensible. The interlocutors' analysis makes no inroads into the operative causes of Petrarca's spiritual drought, insofar as he may have been aware of any.

Finally, the investigation turns to the queen of vices, pride, *superbia*, an evil which theologians considered to have been brought into the world by the angel Satan's revolt against his Creator. It is *superbia* with which the confessant must grapple in the final and most rigorous stage of examination; only by confessing it and contritely renouncing it can the spiritual exercise of the confession come to its successful completion.

Hence, in the third part of the *Secretum*, Augustine presses the intimidated Francesco, arguing with the ferocity required by the facts of the matter, and confronting him and reproaching him for the most deeply ingrained evil. Here, the inquisitor deploys a most effective vise: he compels the author of the famous *Canzoniere*, which includes many sonnets and canzoni glorifying a beloved Lady whom he had met from afar in Avignon many years earlier, to confess that his love for the Lady Laura had from the outset also meant love for the fame promised in her name. His striving to become a *poeta laureatus* had from the outset tainted his supposedly selfless feeling for the noble Lady. Thus, *amor* and *gloria* had contributed the essentials to his spiritual misery – they diverted him from his proper orientation toward the highest good. Where the poet had professed to venerate a noble ideal, he succumbed, as he now admits, half unconsciously, half knowingly, to the temptation of drifting in idolatrous vanity. What was left for the confessant of such transgressions to do in the end but resign himself to the rank of ordinary sinners, even if he were reckoned as one of the most famous men of his age?

It is at this point, however, that the confessional conversation takes an unexpected turn. Francesco suddenly shows himself refractory to Augustine's admonitions – urging the poet to abandon his vain striving for fame among his contemporaries and posterity. In a nearly unrepentant tone, the poet acknowledges his longing for fame – even as his partner reminds him, fruitlessly, how unfounded such hopes are. Those who expect too much from posterity will most certainly suffer disappointment: even inscriptions on memorial stones will weather away – an eventuality tantamount to a second death. And, since the books that promise glory and honor from future generations could burn together with the libraries, one must be prepared to suffer yet a third death (*tertia mors*). The Church Father's emphatic closing words notwithstanding, Petrarca abides by his confession: "I cannot beat down that passion in my soul" (*desiderium frenare non valeo*). Thus, finally, Augustine can only express the hope that God will guide the poet's "aimless steps" (*gressus vagos*) to safety (*tutum*). From this, there emerges but one inference for the reader of our day: anyone who so openly offers resistance to the classical and medieval argument for humility in the face of mortality must be already a modern European.

After these exemplary references, it would be superfluous to present further individual cases. The autobiographical continent was at the same time a world of personally addressed letters – *le monde des lettres* – and, over the centuries, it proved its fruitfulness beyond measure. The case of Petrarca, moreover, also showed that it is but a short step from the psychology of the monastery to the psychology of genius. One of the ultimate expressions of this way of thinking was put by Goethe into the mouth of his imperiled double, Faust, as his farewell confession *in extremis*:

To the moment could I say:
Stay, you are so beautiful!
The trace of my earthly days
Would not perish into the eons.[30]

For, just as sunsets are merely the result of optical illusions experienced by those living on Earth, so too, according to the old man of Weimar in his conversation with Eckermann, the occasional obscurations of genius in posterity will remain but episodic in nature.

When it comes to the art of confession, modern Europe has, all in all, followed along Petrarca's path. Even as the aspects of contrition and penance have receded into the background, the impetus to speak the truth on one's own behalf has remained almost undiminished. In Rousseau's *Confessions* (published posthumously in 1782), the motif of contrition was already eclipsed by that of apologia. The author had in mind nothing less than an Adamic performance of disclosure, as if he were the first truly sincere human being to speak out since the expulsion from the Garden of Eden. In the memoirs of Nicolas Rétif de la Bretonne (1734–1806), a work of unrestrained licentiousness begun in

1783, and continued over decades, the apologia passed into a libertine provocation.[31] His work prompts the suspicion that the author set fire to the confessionals in order to replace confessions born of a guilty conscience with phallic picaresque novels – it is hard to avoid noticing here an early Knausgårdization of the boudoirs of Paris. In works of this kind, one sees an early tendency toward an inversion of confession, something that arrived at its fulfillment during the twentieth century in multiple psychopolitically momentous waves – in particular those that promoted erotic liberalization together with its sexological superstructures. The inverted confession steps forth as the impossibility of there being a sin. Indulging a little historical fancy, one can discern, in the Gay Pride parades held regularly in the US and Europe since 1970, burning confessionals on wheels, in which a double deliverance, from inner sin and from external discrimination, is celebrated under the open sky.

Between the late eighteenth and early twenty-first centuries, the European culture of speaking the truth about oneself, of *dire vrai sur soi-même*, unfolded in a manner unparalleled in any other civilization. At least since the publication of Goethe's *From My Life: Poetry and Truth*,[32] it has been an open secret that standing before the public and speaking the truth about oneself cannot be achieved without an added measure of fictionality. The eye of the public cannot, of course, make the same demands as the eye of God, which looks upon confessants and sees through them from within – but the regime of truth in literary confessional writing tolerates fictionalization only to the extent that the threshold of imposture is not crossed.

In the field of autobiography, the continent's multilingualism makes itself felt with exceptional richness. While the highest achievements of the genre continue to be ascribed to the Francophone sphere – from Rousseau's *Confessions* (1782) by way of Chateaubriand's *Mémoires d'outre-tombe* (1849–1850) and André Gide's *Si le grain ne meurt* (1924) to Sartre's *Les Mots* (1964) – Italian authors from Giacomo Casanova and Vittorio Alfieri to Primo Levi, Cesare Pavese, and Antonio Tabucchi have also added to its weight and luster. German contributions to the genre range from the pathographically relevant confessions of the preacher Adam Bernd (1738) to the literary heights of Johann Wolfgang Goethe (1811), Heinrich Heine (*Geständnisse*, 1854), and Friedrich Nietzsche (*Ecce Homo*, 1888); falling in beside these are high forms of literary self-description, from authors such as Ernst Toller (*Eine Jugend in Deutschland*, 1933) and Manès Sperber (*All das Vergangene*, 1973–1977). These, in turn, are joined by the writings of Elias Canetti, whose qualities include the fact that his sometimes-vicious inward gaze is surpassed in sharpness by his outward gaze. Taken together, these works challenge Albert Camus' dictum: "No man has ever dared to paint himself as he is."

If lists as a general rule have something ridiculous about them – granting exceptions like the ship catalog in the *Iliad*, which thrives on the poetry of splendid proper names – then the list presented above must be regarded as a confession of ignorance, equally in relation to Northern European and Eastern European literature and to the universe of female contributions to the patrimony or matrimony of statements of truth in the first-person.

Here, certainly, it would be appropriate to observe that, since the European Middle Ages, unburdening oneself and truth-telling from within have never been the sole domain of *pro domo* confessions. One can attest to an inclination among European speakers – since at least the seventeenth century, and even more fully since the eighteenth – not only to confess in their own name, but, in their introspective explorations, to make confessions on behalf of the whole species, as it were. The emergence of the moralists of the seventeenth and eighteenth centuries was tantamount to the establishment of an anthropological confessional. There was no airing of individual transgressions here; instead, it was nothing less than a general confession of *Homo occidentalis*, who, as so often happens, thought it was possible to speak also for "the rest of the world." If French authors were referred to as the moralists, they nonetheless argued as psychologists – from Pascal to Vauvenargues, La Rochefoucauld, and Rivarol – who, on behalf of the humanity of their time, and virtually of all time, developed that doctrine which preceded all later introspective psychologies: one knows only as much about human beings as one has grasped of the manifest and hidden stirrings of their *amour propre*, their self-esteem and vanity. From the late seventeenth century onward, after Pascal had unavailingly thrown his vote into the balance, declaring that *le moi est haïssable* – the self is detestable, European authors' reflections on inner-worldly processes gave rise to a general suspicion that human beings were creatures driven primarily by *amour propre*, however readily it might conceal itself behind idealistic and altruistic masks. It is easy to see how the worst sin in the Christian catalogue of vices (*superbia*) donned the inconspicuous guise of self-love during the transition from monastic to bourgeois society; seemingly binding on all sides, it later appeared behind the banal mask of "communicative competence"; in the terms of recent systems theory, it might be characterized as an effort to "allow oneself to be seen" by one's social world. When, at the beginning of the twentieth century, the knowledge of the moralists was recoded into the language of psychologies of the unconscious, "pride" – already neutralized earlier as *amour propre* – was further transformed as "narcissism." It is still not easy to say whether it doesn't represent a kind of constitutive ontological neurosis. It could be the *conditio sine qua non* under which individuals can bear to live within their own skin – a vaccination, as it were, with a serum of significance against the contingency of Dasein in a probably completely insignificant place in the world. In the event of misdosage, pathological reactions are known to appear.

It is easy enough to see the political implications of these characteristics of truth-telling with regard to the facts of human interior life. If modern Europeans today have increasingly agreed that they find democratic forms of life suit them best, this is not because they have selected the most appropriate form from among the six rotating forms of government that have been discussed since the days of Polybius.[33] For them, democracy emerges as the most attractive option owing to the assumption, supported by experience, that it provides the political mechanism that best regulates the sum of the stirrings of *superbia*, the expressions of *amour propre*, and the projections of both sick and healthy narcissism (to make mention once more of the three stages of "egoism" in this part of the world). As a multi-superbial, multi-self-loving, multi-narcissistic social and constitutional order, historically chastened Europe places its trust in the mutually dampening effects of a pluralism of private and collective egoisms, or rather, a pluralism of civilized hypocrisies that manifest themselves in the form of nations, parties, and corporations.

With the disclosure of a general human inclination toward *amour propre* and the consequent demand for the democratic restraint of multi-egoistic impulses, the spirit of truth-telling about oneself in this part of the world is far from exhausted. It is one of the peculiarities of European philosophy that its culmination in the early nineteenth century ushered in a self-critical turn that led to the dismantling of classical metaphysics along with its excesses: beginning in classical and medieval theories of logos and intellect, matured in the writings of Locke and Leibniz on "human understanding," and consummated in Kant's critiques and Fichte's various versions of the doctrine of science, the supreme philosophical discipline of the critique of reason turned against itself with unexpected vehemence with the Young Hegelians, with Stirner, Marx, and Kierkegaard, then also with Nietzsche and the logical empiricists of the Vienna Circle, as well as the pioneers of the linguistic turn. The philosophers' confessions went far beyond the general human confessions of *amour-propre* psychologists and theorists of narcissism. They not only reconstructed, along Nietzschean lines, the "genealogy of morals" from base urges, they exposed the provenance of technically foreshortened, "instrumental" reason in the drive to dominate nature that had come to power in Europe. In this way, the malignant narcissism of the rational animal, beyond any individual vanities, came to be unmasked and denounced as an ambivalent world power. These debunkings went beyond a critique of classical metaphysics' addiction to moonier matters; they extended to the exposure of the calamity that was being wrought – and continues to be wrought – by the global reification of being under the grip of identificatory definitions and economic valorizations. To the extent that recent philosophy presented itself as an autobiography of reason, it culminated in the admission that it had first and for the most part served the seizure of power by an imperious, anthropocentrically narrowed subjectivity. Again along Nietzschean lines, contrasting thinkers such as Martin Heidegger, Herbert Marcuse, Jacques Ellul, Theodor W. Adorno, Jacques Derrida, and others came to agree on these propositions. As diagnosticians of the pathologies of their own civilization, authors of this tendency gave more or less discreet hints as to how the maldevelopments that had come from afar could be corrected at the level of the overall culture – whether in the fatalistic tone struck by the late Heidegger when he assessed that "Only a god can save us,"[34] or in the mode of mediation between Western rationality and Eastern contemplation, as proposed by numerous thinkers from

Hermann Hesse to Raimon Panikkar, or in an activist tone, as recently adopted in subcultural circles, where people want to learn how to blow up pipelines in order to disrupt fossil-fuel civilization's butchery of the planet's ecosystems.

Among critics of the European culture of rationality who also presented themselves as therapists, the authors of the phenomenological school are of particular importance. Edmund Husserl's 1936 work on *The Crisis of European Sciences*, based on lectures given in Vienna and Prague the previous year, offered a general confession by proxy, as it were, for the maldevelopments of the European culture of rationality as a whole, exposing its destructive aberrations. In the author's view, these aberrations were driven primarily by the mathematization of the natural sciences and the boundless and misguided belief in the measurability of all things. Husserl identified a bipolar disorder in the philosophy of his time, dating back to Descartes and Locke, which manifested itself in the extreme positions of transcendental subjectivism and physicalist objectivism – both of which are complex findings that cannot be elucidated more fully here.[35] Husserl's civilizational–therapeutic reference back to what he called the "lifeworld" unmistakably brought the quintessentially European triad of confession, critique, and crisis into play, but it had to renounce the promise that every diagnosis could be assigned an effective therapy. Above all, recollection of the enlightened geocentrism of lifeworld-reason could offer no certainty that confession would be followed by absolution.

Those who would cast a glance today at the confessional mirror of old and new Europe cannot avoid answering two of the most intricate questions that must sooner or later be posed to any inhabitant of this part of the world. First, how do you reconcile the fact that this Europe is ethically founded on the Platonic–Stoic idea of self-control and religiously founded on the Christian message of peace and love, and yet it has produced an unequalled history of warlike violence and hate-driven disinhibition? There are probably few people today who still seriously believe that this problem was resolved in late antiquity with the emergence of the figure of the *miles christianus* – the baptized soldier in the imperial army who believed that it must be possible to serve, at one and the same time, under both eagle and cross. Be that as it may, Martin of Tours (316–397) – the Hungarian-born folk saint of Gaul, who cut his cloak (*cappa*) in half to help a freezing beggar – created the archetype of a mode of existence in which virility and compassion were in happy balance. Without such exemplary figures, in the positive sense of the word, one might designate Europe as little more than the homestead of an epochal schizophrenia. The diagnosis advanced by Nietzsche's Zarathustra would apply to them, albeit sounding as if it were summarizing in advance the fate of the First World War:

> Not only the reason of millennia, but their madness too, breaks out in us. It is dangerous to be an heir.[36]

The second question that no citizen of the Old World can avoid in the long run is: how do you feel about your Jewish fellow citizens? No one alive today can be so naive as not to know that this touches on the oldest, never-healed wound of our civilization. Nor does it suffice today to recall the penitential prayer written by Pope John XXIII shortly before his death in 1963:

> We realize that the mark of Cain stands upon our foreheads. [...] Forgive us for the curse we falsely attached to their name as Jews.

John Paul II included similar phrasings in his seven-part confession of guilt by the Catholic Church in March 2000. It should be observed here that the vast majority of Europeans today no longer participate in Christian anti-Judaism; its traces, however, can be tracked from the Gospel of John, through the later Luther, and on to some incorrigible theologians of the twentieth century. It was based on the idea, so difficult for believers to bear, that members of the people who should know better had refused their assent to the fundamental doctrine of Christianity, according to which Jesus is the Messiah. The intimate marginalization of Judaism with respect to the central tenets of both Greco-European and Latin-European religious culture predisposed it to function as a repository for ressentiment. In times of Christianity's waning, it also became a collection point attracting all kinds of xenophobia, conspiracist fantasies, hatred of the elite, accusatory passions, and competition among supposed and actual victims.

Anyone still searching for arguments to support the thesis that Europe is the continent marked by a propensity to confess its aberrance will, for the time being, find nothing better than the works of René Girard, the analyst of scapegoat mechanisms and jealousy conflicts. He is supported by the Austrian historian Friedrich Heer, who, in his magnum opus *God's First Love: Christians and Jews Over Two Thousand Years* (1967), attempted, as a kind of representative proxy, to make a general confession on behalf of one of the primary errors of Christian–European civilization. If we have refrained from placing bookmarks in the books by René Girard and Friedrich Heer, it is because we posit that, in days like these, they must remain ever open on our desks.

Lesson five
Go, and set the world aflame!
From the book of expansions

Those who apply themselves to the task of discussing Europe's long second millennium, especially the turbulent latter half that launched with Columbus's voyage, cannot avoid recourse to a word of motion without which one cannot adequately describe the way of life for those who inhabit this rugged semicontinent on the edge of Asia: "expansion." The concept kept its secrets concealed from René Descartes when he classified the world into *res cogitans* – the thinking something – and *res extensa* – the extensional something, and thereby trivialized the dimension of extension as if it were a quality of material entities or bodies in general. Goethe showed a finer sense for the unsettled potential of the category when he stated in his *Maxims and Reflections* that we humans have been constituted for "expansion" and "movement" – and, from this, he drew the corollary, almost unthinkably bold for his time, that whatever has sprung up can rise above the conditions of its origin.[1] The old man from Weimar did not rest satisfied with the higher generalities of evolutionary thinking. He was aware that wherever the will to expand determines the course of things, the variables that disrupt harmony, such as disinhibition, aggression, and acceleration, also come to the fore – for these latter, Goethe coined the prophetic neologism "velociferous," as if he were keen to name the correlation between acceleration and devilry at the earliest possible historical moment.[2] Long before Cecil Rhodes (1853–1902), the herald of British imperialism in South Africa, had devised his motto "expansion is everything," a quintessential theory of modernization could be found in characteristic Mephistophelean style in *Faust: The Second Part of the Tragedy* (1832):

> We set sail with only two ships,
> Now we are in port with twenty.
> The great things we have done
> You can see from our cargo.
> The open sea frees the spirit,
> Who knows what reflection means there!
> There, a quick grab is all it takes,
> You catch a fish, you catch a ship,
>
> [...]
>
> If you have power, you have right.
> One asks not how, but what!
> I need know nothing of seafaring:
> War, trade, and piracy
> They are the triune, inseparable.[3]

These verses, composed before 1830, make it plain that it would be a mistake to understand what later came to be known as pragmatism as if it were merely North America's late contribution to "continental" philosophy; even less does it constitute a down-to-earth antithesis to it. In Germany, primary responsibility for ideas that strive to reach the ground of facts lay with the corps of Young Hegelians, who became known for their best trick: setting fanciful metaphysical propositions on their head. For their part and in their own way, British empiricists and French positivists had long sought to demonstrate that they too did not have their heads in the clouds. As a way of speaking put by Goethe into the mouth of his enlightened devil, the turn to pragmatism emerged from Europe's aggressive self-understanding at the uttermost extent of its forays into oceanic spheres. Seafaring is recommended as the contemporary counterpart to heavenly ascension. The free spirit learns on the open seas that reflection is superfluous. Why bother with concepts when a quick grab will suffice? While thinkers of the Young Hegelian generation devoted themselves to the attempt to bring the heaven of ideas down to earth, down to the soil of the old world, where work had overtaken prayer, Goethe had already grasped that the decisive difference in the future would not bear upon any difference between heaven and earth, whether interpreted as a descent downward from above, or a transcendence upward from below. The future fate of a humanity under sail will be decided by the relationship between ports and seas. The Beyond that one must now take into account is the other shore that comes into view after crossing an ocean.

The first pragmatism, which emerged in Europe as the spirit of maritime entrepreneurship, was not naturally at home in the universities of either Old or New England – and certainly not in Heidelberg and Jena, where one might reason with sovereign permission, but only on the condition that obedience was assured. Instead, it lodged in ports where ships from transatlantic voyages came in – as one sees on the frontispiece of Bacon's *Novum Organon* (1620): there, a returning ship, laden with goods and new knowledge, heads into a harbor marked by the emblematic pillars of Hercules and the opening up of the world through Atlantic seafaring.[4] Mephistopheles gives perspicacious expression to the principle of maritime movement:

> High wisdom is crowned,
> the shore is reconciled to the sea,
> from the shore, on a swift course,
> the sea willingly takes the ships.

A philosophy that truly wanted to capture its time in thought would have had to make itself heard as a logical port authority. That its freedom-loving doctrines would not carry over into practice without an admixture of moral disinhibition can be deduced from the cynical consultant's warning:

> Why are you standing here feeling embarrassed?
> Shouldn't you be out colonizing by now?[5]

When Goethe's sober pragmatist translates the figure of the Holy Trinity into an alliance of war, trade, and piracy, he makes the realistic assumption, albeit not quite free of small-mindedness, that people of

European origin would venture out to sea only under the influence of base motives – be it lust for power and profit, be it arrogance and the urge to self-aggrandize under cover of the flag, or simply because they see no meaningful purpose for themselves on dry land, to say nothing of credible chances for happiness.[6] Anyone who wants to understand how striving for expansion took ahold of Europeans at the beginning of the modern era will not, after studying the records, be satisfied with simply endorsing the devil's own image of humanity.

In the first decades of the sixteenth century, at the commencement of what Carl Schmitt and others later called the "appropriation of the world" by constituents of the emerging European nations, there was hardly any hint of the inclination toward "expansion for expansion's sake" that Hannah Arendt claimed as the defining characteristic of imperialism – where imperialism, in a narrower sense, was understood to mean the *modus operandi* of European powers in the years between 1880 and 1914 – as exemplarily manifest in the "scramble for Africa."[7] At the beginning of the modern era, the motif of expansion in space was primarily associated with the spirit of seafaring and its as yet unforeseeable geographical implications; it expressed itself more in what Ernst Bloch once called "horizontal treasure seeking" than in the urge to build empires in distant lands – which, once it had actually begun, could rightly be said to have taken place as "a mixture of settlement and extermination."[8] The initial impulses of European extroversion were more closely bound to the sensational stirrings of exploratory curiosity and the religious libido awakened with the discovery of unbaptized peoples than to the need of Europe's rival thrones to preempt other monarchies in the opening up and seizure of the globe. Oswald Spengler's hyperbolic statements about the fatal nature of expansion cannot be applied to the early phases of what Jacob Burckhardt called the "discovery of the world and humanity." The opening of the Iberian monarchies of the sixteenth century to the lands beyond the Atlantic had nothing to do with the curse of aging advanced civilizations, according to which they were doomed to pass into a phase of empty externalization and imperial torpor. When Spengler noted

> The expansive tendency is a doom, something daemonic and immense, which grips, forces into service, and uses up the late mankind of the world-city stage [...].[9]

he was not thinking of Prince Henry the Navigator or the *Reyes Católicos* of Castile and Aragon, nor of Charles V and Philip II, whose mottos *Plus ultra* (Old French: *plus oultre*, "further still") and *Orbis non sufficit* ("the world is not enough") already attested to some of the élan of great extroversion; nor can the fact that the Philippine archipelago, named after the Spanish *infante*, was incorporated into the dominion of the Iberian crown in 1585 be explained in any way as the aging bloat of a dying civilization. Spengler's definitive idol was the gold and diamond magnate Cecil Rhodes, who died near Cape Town in 1902: in Rhodes, Spengler believed he had found the alliance of entrepreneurial ruthlessness, political megalomania, and racist self-aggrandizement that was best suited to the tasks of his time. When these qualifications were complemented by the piquant blend of messianism and cynicism that marked Rhodes' charisma, there could be no doubt about the man's suitability for the challenges of the Faustian late phase.

To tap into the older, pre-political sources of expansion, however, it is necessary to inquire into the motives of the early seafarers, without whom these momentous voyages would not have taken place. The word "motives," however, could just as well be replaced by expressions such as "delusions," "daydreams," "pious wishes," or "guiding errors." The case of Columbus is instructive in this regard: at the base of his motivation one finds an inextricable tangle of ambition and superstition; interwoven through this was an autohypnotically fixed conviction concerning the correctness of his conception of the sphericity of the Earth. Gold, the cross, and the globe formed the operative trinity of his schema of the world. The fact that this synthesis inspired successes in reality was due, on the one hand, to the fact that belief in the globe had been validated by the captain's voyages, even over-verified, in a startling way; it became the *creator spiritus* of the centuries to come; indeed this belief in the sphericity of the Earth will, for better or worse, become the demon of the third millennium – and Bruno Latour's discourse on *Gaia* will have to stand the test of whether she is indeed the goddess who alone can save us.[10] On the other hand, it was able to become influential because, even in the New World, belief in the cross proved to be a message of high translatability; one might well speak of its intercultural elasticity; finally, Columbus's triad was able to establish itself because the powerful superstition surrounding metal, advanced through the enslavement of indigenous populations, proved its suitability for promoting the import of silver and gold from "peripheral" zones into an existing monetary culture. What is characteristic of the figure of Columbus is the fact that he developed, *pro domo*, a specific mission: in his *Book of Prophecies* (1502), written three years before his death, he noted:

> What Isaiah prophesied has come to pass [...]. The Lord has made me an emissary for a new heaven and a new earth [...].[11]

Sentences like these testify to their author's proximity to the spirit of the early modern era, even though in other respects he remained a man of the Middle Ages – as, for instance, in wanting to see the treasures of the New World used for a crusade to recapture Jerusalem. In the seafarer's self-statements, a phenomenon comes to the fore that could be called "autogenous religion."[12] In the centuries to come, it proved to be a matrix capable of supporting the emergence of entrepreneurial subjectivities. Indeed, without it, it is impossible to imagine the existence of typical modern characters – captains, viceroys, wholesalers, bankers, researchers, artists, consultants – to say nothing of the princes who ruled between the sixteenth and eighteenth centuries, almost all of whom made use of autohypnosis in the key of the local political theologies. It bears remembering: their medieval predecessors had already endeavored, often with the help of high clergy, to construe their position at the top of the social pyramid as a political sacrament and to interpret its exercise as an apostolic function – occasionally even by emphasizing analogies among the Titan Atlas, Christ, and the prince, all of whom were depicted as bearers of the "weight of the world" (*onus mundi, cargo imperii*). Those possessing power, a sense of mission, and initiative in modern times often acted as priests in their own cause, writing the scripts for their own actions. Columbus made himself an apostle under sail; he believed that, in accordance with his baptismal name, he had been given the task of carrying Christ across the water once more, this time fording the Atlantic. To borrow from Jean-Paul Sartre, Columbus had "engaged" his freedom to the magnificent error of setting out for India; the seafarer himself would have had little use for the imputation that he had acted out of freedom – he saw himself as nothing more than a loyal servant of the Spanish crown and an agent of God.

One of the two key expressions that open the door to a more complex understanding of modern patterns of expansion on the oceanic front is a 1541 statement attributed to Ignatius of Loyola, founder of the Society of Jesus, the new order that had just, in 1540, gained recognition from the Holy See under Paul III: it is a command of epochal consequence which, according to Jesuit legend, was spoken before the Basque Francis Xavier (1506–1552) departed on his mission to India: "*Ite, inflammate omnia!* – Go, and set the world aflame!" Francis had been recently appointed apostolic nuncio for Asia in response to a request from the Portuguese king, John III, begging the Pope to send missionaries to India. In May 1542, Francis arrived in Goa as a passenger with the royal fleet – since 1510, Goa had been the most important Portuguese outpost on the west coast of India. There, in the course of a few years, he developed a missionary practice that was greatly successful at first glance – he is said to have baptized over 50,000 locals.[13] Doubtless, in this context, the Latin verb *inflammare* is related to, indeed virtually synonymous with, the verb *evangelizare*, which has been commonly used in the Latin European hemisphere since classical times to designate apostolic activity – based on the Greek noun εὐαγγέλιον, the meaning of which amounts to "good news."

The second key expression for illuminating the new situation is found in the term *missio*, which spontaneously entered modern national languages as a Latin loanword: English: mission, French: *mission*, Spanish: *misión*. The idea as a distillate of Jesuit conceptual work, however, entered the vocabulary of the Church and the world only around the middle of the sixteenth century; it found general acceptance so promptly and with such naturalness, it was as if it had been common since the earliest days of apostolic and church history. Its coming into usage closed – almost unnoticed – a hitherto open gap in the vocabulary of Christian cultures. In speaking of "mission," people thereafter had a term at their disposal that denoted, all at once, an action, its rationale, and its organization.

In the Ignatian imperative to undertake missionary work at the beginning of the Asian mission, the classic New Testament passage,

Matthew 28:19, was indirectly but unmistakably cited, wherein the risen Lord sends his followers to go and carry out the work of conversion, making disciples of all nations, baptizing them in the name of the Father and of the Son and of the Holy Spirit, work as urgent as it is far-reaching; the command initially bore upon a narrowly delimited horizon of time, since the return of the Lord "in his glory" (Greek: *doxa*) on the Day of Judgment upon the world was presumed to be an imminent event. Later centuries were compelled to shroud the motif of return under a veil of metaphorical meanings. For the founder of the order (1491–1556), an unprecedentedly broad horizon had opened up for him and for his contemporaries – Ignatius could not possibly believe that God would have allowed the discovery of new continents and countless foreign and unbaptized peoples if he had planned the Last Judgment for the proximate future. He condensed the dual command – to teach and to baptize – into the compact mandate *inflammate omnia*. The Latin *omnia* can stand in reasonably well for the Greek *panta ta ethne* ("all nations"), though only on the premise that there should still reverberate a synonymy of 'peoples' (Greek: *ethne*, Latin: *gentes*) and "pagans" (Greek: *eidōlatres*, Latin: *pagani*), an echo unmistakable for early Christian ears. If *inflammare* entailed not only baptizing (*baptizein*) but also teaching (or "making disciples"[14] – *matheteuein*), the updated mission statement took on a tone that was decidedly aggressive, even polemogenous – in correspondence with the state of the world after Columbus, Vasco da Gama, and Luther. Loyola's charge gave the impression that missionary work with peoples on distant continents would open up a second front in the European wars of religion. Nowhere else could such large numbers of new believers be recruited to the Catholic cause as in South America and Asia, even if they could not yet be deployed for assignments on the home front. As with the emerging states, population growth proved to be a compelling motive for the Church in the early modern period.

Almost nowhere else in spiritual literature does the coupling between the rhetoric of setting something aflame and the dynamics of missionary mobility as such come forth so vividly as in a passage printed in Vienna, 1677, from an apologia for St. Francis Xavier, composed by the German Baroque preacher Abraham a Sancta Clara (born Johann Ulrich Megerle, 1644–1709) of the Order of Discalced Augustinians: *Die heilige Hof-Art: das ist: Ein schuldige Lob-Red von dem grossen Wunderthätigen*

Indianer-Apostel Francisco Xaverio – "The Manner of the Holy Court, or, A Blameworthy Eulogy for the Great Miracle-Working Indian Apostle Francis Xavier."[15] In it, the speaker describes how the missionary in Asia rushed from one nation to another to baptize everything he saw.

> What drove him so? What drives a rocket / that flies high in the air, above its unattached pieces and its wooden [?] base? And there causes a banging and clattering sound to be heard? A fire drives it; by the fire of love, this very miracle man was driven to souls, / so that he preached everywhere, / in ships on the sea, / at pulpits in churches, / on the streets in towns [...].
>
> A true preacher should be like the brazen bull, which a tyrannical brain hatched / to be hollow inside, / so when a poor man is locked inside it / and a fire is lit under the bronze bull, / the woeful wretch cries out pitiably from the heat, / and this cry comes out of the mouth of the bull, and it seems strange, / as if this lifeless bull were crying out, but it is the voice of another. *Voce mugit alienâ*[16]: in like fashion a preacher should be so natured, / that it is not his voice that is heard, but rather the voice of the One / who came upon the apostles like tongues of fire, saying / *non enim vos estis, qui loquimini, sed Spiritus Patris vestri qui in Coelis est.*[17]

Abraham a Sancta Clara's deliberations illustrate how the expansionist activities of Jesuit missionaries were elucidated with the help of pyrotechnical analogies. To give an interpretation of then-current spiritual work, archaic-seeming mediumistic premises were brought into play. According to the concept of a personal medium, the message conveyed by speakers is ascribed not to the speakers themselves, but to a Sender who speaks *through* them. From its very inception, Christianity was transparently constituted as a system of Sender-driven communications – it explained itself, from its earliest days on, through the concept of the apostolate. From its beginning with the first twelve, it attained an enlargement in the figure of Paul, the self-appointed "thirteenth apostle," to include persons who had not known Jesus, the first of the absolute mediators, during his lifetime; from these, it branched out into chains of emissaries of the second, third, and subsequent "generations." These gradations multiplied themselves to the extent that it became clear, in the decades and then centuries after Christ's birth, that the return of the Messiah was not to be expected in the near future.

The early propagation of the Christian message was conditioned on a twofold persuasive effect: it was achieved through the synergies of mediumistic inspired speech, *alias* proclamation (*kérygma*), with the contagious effects of communitarian amicability, *alias* love (*agápe*). In recent missiological literature, such processes are described in terms of a diffusion through "capillarity"[18] – extending this image, one could say that the arterial pulsations of the preached message have passed into the capillaries of sympathy, where they maintain a self-reinforcing cycle of suggestive vitalization. What William Harvey had expounded in 1628 in his landmark treatise *De motu cordis et sanguinis*, on the circulation of the blood, was taken up tentatively in the twentieth century by religious scholars and mediologists in relation to the phenomena of a contagious self-regulating faith.

At first, the inconspicuous brilliance of the abstract general concept of *missio*[19] passes directly into the self-explanation of a mediumistic interpretation of action. Hence, the Jesuit pathos of unconditional obedience was conditioned not only by an authoritarian idiosyncrasy on the part of the order's founder or by the continuing effects of his military past; it was also based on the newly developed explication of the mediumistic schema, without which the apostolic expansion, now called missionary, would have been inconceivable under the conditions of the post-Columbian, post-Vasco da Gama, and post-Magellanic situation. One might even contend that Ignatius, in a kind of collateral campaign with early modern state formation, created a new type of sacred official who was specifically assigned to the sovereign of a church, which itself had come to resemble a party or faction: in the Jesuit agency, monastic obedience intensified into a specific obedience to the pope – sealed by the Fourth Vow – which was in turn to devolve into an unconditional obedience with respect to the superiors of the order.[20]

In the development of this system of graduated selflessnesses, the insight offered itself that a particularly high grade of interested disinterest was demanded for service on the missionary front. This was to ensure that the agents become, as it were, pure channels with a minimum of signal noise, perfectly conductive media for their message. If Kant's categorical imperative in one of its articulations essentially stated that one must never treat one's fellow human beings – or oneself – simply as a means, but must always respect them as ends in themselves,[21] this is preempted by a Jesuitical qualification: except in the case where you yourself serve as a pure means for the Pope, who in turn – *idealiter* – wields his office as a pure means for God. Through the transcendence of ends, there is a legitimation of complete self-instrumentalization, to the degree that such a thing could ever be accomplished. It forms a schema that, under atheistic premises, recurred in the early twentieth century among the professional revolutionaries influenced by Lenin. The idea of being without qualities, to which Robert Musil erected a much-admired and rarely understood monument, goes back to the sacred mediumship of post-Tridentine Christians out in the field; this, in turn, incorporated motifs from fourteenth- and fifteenth-century mysticism, according to which God can be brought to flow into an empty vessel through the complete self-emptying of the human subject. Where the utopia of a life motivated from above took shape in Europe, the "two bodies of the subject" came into play. As with the king, the inspiring element in the messenger had to be distinguished from the inspired. Apart from that, the history of modernity as a whole can be described as a progressive profanation of mediumistic qualities in their personal aspect; a later chapter would take up Pink Floyd's song "Brain Damage" (1973), with its standout line: "There's someone in my head but it's not me."[22]

The keyword "obedience" points precisely to the imperative to redefine the subjective conditions of the *vita activa* in the age of incipient globalization. Regulation became necessary when the danger of unrestrained expansionism appeared on the horizon. Hadn't the Lutheran heresy already demonstrated, with the clarity of a catastrophe, what can happen when unauthorized readings of Holy Scripture are allowed to run amok? No sooner had the new continents been discovered and the routes to them laid out than many of the actors involved were stirred by the temptation to disregard their mission with the highest mandate and instead set out for conquest and pillage on their own behalfs. Under whatever noble pretenses they might be veiled, the princes and their seafaring delegates' attempts to seize newly discovered lands were, all in all, bound to come under early suspicion of serving solely the impulses of self-interest and predatory appropriation. Only the complete ascetic self-instrumentalization of the apostolic messengers would have been able to counter such tendencies. The fact that efforts of this kind were not always in vain is indicated by the well-known *reducciones* or "reductions" established by the Jesuits in Peru, Brazil, and Paraguay from the early seventeenth century onward, which consciously withdrew from colonial exploitation; their shelter from exploitation, however, was attained at the cost of keeping the indigenous peoples in the condition of an "eternal childhood useless to the state," as Alexander von Humboldt termed it.[23] Traces of successful Jesuit discipline are still further reflected in the fact that there are over four hundred high schools named after Francis Xavier in India today; even Kim, the orphan boy from Rudyard Kipling's 1901 masterpiece, attended – plausibly, within the narrative – one such boarding school in Lucknow in what is now the state of Uttar Pradesh. The swift transition from the temptation to violence to the most villainous reality was evident in Central and South America just a few years after their "discovery": to be sure, the conquest of the continent was carried out *pro forma* in the name of august dispatchers, in this case at the behest of the Iberian kings; in practice, however, as executed by the conquistadores on the scene, it assumed the features of a disinhibited "self-attainment," far removed from any obedience – granting that the Spanish invaders may have fallen to their knees to pray for success at arms before commencing their slaughter. Already in the early days of nautical globalization, the actions of the conquistadores and the settlers on the *encomiendas*[24] manifested a tendency among Europeans on the frontier to export the worst and not the worthiest things the Old World had to offer, sometimes a bit of both, but with a preponderance of the first, in a barely extricable alliance.

The ambivalences of expansionism were noticed early on – as demonstrated in the writings of the Dominican Bartolomé de Las Casas and by his interventions in the Valladolid Debate (1550–1551) convened by Charles V, in defense of the indigenous peoples who were suffering dire exploitation by Spanish settlers.[25] His fellow Dominican, Antonio de Montesinos (1475–1540), had anticipated him: already in 1511, in a sermon in the presence of Viceroy Diego Colón, the elder son of Columbus, Montesinos had dared to reproach the Spanish settlers of Santo Domingo of standing, without exception, in a state of mortal sin because they neglected to treat the indigenous Taíno in a spirit of brotherly love instead of enslaving and exploiting them.

The full extent of the ambiguities became apparent to most Europeans only with a considerable delay, if indeed they ever reached a moment of reflection at all. As early as 1803, Alexander von Humboldt passed withering judgment on colonialism as such, rejecting the "idea of the colony" as an inherently immoral concept.[26] Little remained of former certainties about the mission, whether Christian or civilizational, when, in the age of incipient decolonization, people began to take stock of the effects of expansion.[27] The concept of mission as such has fallen into such disrepute, that, in recent times, quite a few authors dare use the m-word only behind closed doors. Others have sought refuge in the claim that the missionary orders were forerunners of "social media" in some favorable sense of the word.

For the time being, the concept of "mission" remains applicable with a more positive tenor in its secularized version: it presupposes a shift from the apostolic concept of action into a designation for any active work undertaken with any expansive motivation – regardless of whether its orientation is political, diplomatic, entrepreneurial, charitable, intelligence-related, or military; even in space travel, whether imaginary or real, it has become common practice to use the term *mission* to refer to expansive operations in space.

When, however, around the year 1800, the poet Novalis wrote: "We are on a *mission*. Our vocation is the education of the earth," his maxim struck a tone whose frequency lies above the ordinary hearing of his and our contemporaries.[28] The fact that this proposition belongs to a modern, post-apostolic regime is revealed by its geo-gnostic tone: it is no longer just the nations that need to be converted – the planet, too, requires a transformation, though it remained unclear in what direction this should take place. From today's perspective, it is evident that the planet itself should be understood as a message – and that the difference between heaven and earth has to become an internal concern for inhabitants of the Earth.

Apart from that, it should be noted that "the medium is the message,"[29] the guiding principle of contemporary communication theory coined by Canadian cultural theorist Marshall McLuhan, expresses a cryptotheological theorem. It constitutes an unnoticed secularization of the Johannine doctrine, according to which, in the Logos, in the incarnate Word of God, the messenger and the message are one.[30] McLuhan grasped the logical deficit of modernity with regard to the functioning of media in general: it had become clear to him that modern culture needed an abstract, general concept of message or mission, beyond the distinction between sacred and profane, in order to be able to come to appropriate understandings through its communicative action in the "global village." He believed he had found his key in the term *message*.[31] This constitutes an expression of the highest level of abstraction assignable to the mathematical concept of "information" (itself with a theological prehistory). With it, a level of "real abstraction" was achieved in the realm of modern (tele)communication, one equal to what was articulated in the sphere of manufacturing in the industrial system through Adam Smith and David Ricardo's concept of "labor." And, as Marx emphasized, it was only in the fully developed system of capital accumulation that this became comprehensible as value-creating "labor in general," "labor *sans phrase*";[32] likewise, McLuhan should have highlighted that it is only in modern times that one is dealing with a media-borne "message in general," a "message *sans phrase*." The discreet Catholic McLuhan (1911–1980) would certainly have been increasingly saddened to observe how the reciprocal conditioning of medium and message in the digital regime is dissolving to the extent that network providers are displaying almost boundless indifference to the content on offer. What has been called "nihilism" since the nineteenth century has been fully realized only since the medium, in this case the internet, has shed all interest in the message. Even Nietzsche would have to acknowledge that the "European nihilism" he invoked in his Lenzerheide fragment of 1887 hardly deserves its name any more, now that Silicon Valley nihilism has so far outstripped it. Dostoevsky's good old demons, who had possessed the militant anarchists, changed providers at the start of the twentieth century. Whether they still played a part in the deeds of Lenin, Dzerzhinsky, and Stalin is disputed even among cartographers of the "bloodlands" and other experts on evils realized through the state. These days, they seem to be supplementing their pensions by abetting Putin's dispirited power politics in its attempts to demoralize the West.

Among the aspects of Europe's global expansion between the voyages of Columbus and the outbreak of the First World War, the ones that are at once most awkward and least deniable for today's sense of events are the inextricable bonds between the expansive energies emanating from Europe and the conditions of strict unilateralism. Because of them, the kinetic momentum and the abundance of initiative lay solely on the European side, while their "partners" on other shores were mostly relegated to the role of retainers, indeed often slaves, or at best collaborators wielding power or tolerated local "rulers" with their subaltern helpers. Few historians of our day possess the cynical composure with which Carl Schmitt stated in his late magnum opus:

> Discoveries were made without the prior permission of the discovered. Thus, legal title to discoveries lay in a higher legitimacy. They could be made only by peoples intellectually and historically advanced enough to apprehend the discovered by superior knowledge and consciousness. [...] The intellectual advantage was entirely on the European side [...].[33]

It would therefore be wrong to say that the Aztecs and Incas could just as well have discovered and mapped Europe as the Spanish did with them and their countries. That there was an early unease concerning the asymmetry of relations is revealed not only in the fictions of missionary theology, according to which the unbaptized peoples of the New World excitedly – if unconsciously – awaited their discovery, conversion, and salvation; it is also evident in a passage, as prominent as it is symptomatic, in the Portuguese national epic *Os Lusíadas*, published in 1572, which celebrates Vasco da Gama's discovery of the sea route to India in 1497. In the fourth canto of the great poem, two figures appear in a dream to the Portuguese king Manuel the Fortunate (*Manuel o Venturoso*):[34]

> From the rivers, he seemed to see emerge
> Two ancients, bending towards him
> With slow paces like countrymen,
> And of venerable appearance;
> Water dripped from their uncombed locks
> Making their whole bodies glisten;
> Their skin was leathery and cinnamon,
> Their shaggy beards dishevelled and undone.
>
> [...]

And having the graver bearing of the two,
He spoke up to Manuel from afar:
– 'You, to whose crown and kingdom
So much of the world is reserved:
We others, also known to fame
Whose necks were never before yoked,
Counsel you now, the moment is at hand
To accept the tribute flowing from our land.
'I am the famous Ganges whose waters
Have their source in the earthly paradise;
This other is the Indus, which springs
In this mountain which you behold.
We shall cost you unremitting war,
But persevering, you will become
Peerless in victory, knowing no defeat,
Conquering as many peoples as you meet.'

The famous, sacred river said no more
And both disappeared on the instant.
Manuel awoke with the thrill of discovery
And a new direction to his thoughts. [...][35]

The dream vision of Luís de Camões (c. 1524–1580) illustrates how European expansionism sought to legitimize itself not only through the legal fiction of the right of discovery and the religious suggestion that the souls of the heathens could be saved through apostolic missions; it was also based on the geopolitical–poetical fiction according to which there was complaisance or accommodation on the part of those to be discovered, who were, as it were, eagerly awaiting their future masters. The speech of the "famous Ganges" indicated that the conquest would probably not happen without resistance, but that once this had been overcome, the Indian dominions would offer themselves to the king as great gifts (*tributos grandes*). Quite obviously, Camões's phantasm is in the service of the conquerors' perceived need to reinterpret their imperial unilateralism as a transactional event. Indeed, ambivalence with respect to the "appropriation of the world" by agents from European centers was already indicated at an early stage, in the fact that those who carried the initiative forward wanted to be perceived more as bringers of good fortune than as perpetrators of violence – even if only in the image of their own self-reflection. It was not only sailors, missionaries, traders, colonists, and viceroys who were exported, but also the fatal assumption that the previous life of these peoples had, all in all, been a brooding over hopeless fates, indeed that it could never have meant anything more than a real existing utter brokenness. The existence of the many out there under the "bondage of transience" – to quote the theologian Jürgen Moltmann[36] – deserved to come to an end, even for intrinsic reasons. Those sent by Europe should not consider themselves too good to make a necessary break in the Dasein of "barbarians."

Martial metaphors were common currency in Jesuit language games: what they wanted to accomplish among the foreigners was nothing less than a *conquista espiritual.* Hence the colonizing authorities' special interest in reports of cruel, suspicious, and shocking customs among the natives – whether ritual infanticide, widow burning, or polygamy. A special attraction came from accounts of cannibalistic practices, which were readily interpreted as evidence of a semi-animalistic *modus vivendi* among "savages," who were in desperate need of missionary work.[37] People devoted themselves to such phenomena in order to be able to congratulate themselves on their abolition. The more morally sensitive among the apologists for colonization salved their consciences with the idea that, on a deeper level – whether metaphysical, human, or civilizational – they had been *awaited.* They would have believed, far too readily, that, for the converted, the missionary was the message. Of course, they ought to have reckoned from the outset that, from the perspective of the subjugated, the bringer of oppression would remain the real message.

Lesson six
Loose-fish
Of ships, globes, and surplus sons

The deliberations in these lessons so far suggest an insight that assimilates the concerns of our time to a matter of long-standing disquiet: the task of explaining to Europeans their place in the world, caught up, as they are, in the modernization of their states and world trade – a task which, as has been seen, dates back to the dawn of Atlantic seafaring. As a man on the threshold between two eras, Ignatius of Loyola read chivalric romances in the days of his youth and made pilgrimages to Jerusalem on foot and by sea; in converting himself into the organizer of the Asian missions, he crossed the historical date line and became a man of the era known as the Modern Age. It is rightly so called because its dramatic content, the assertion of a "world view" defined by the then new medium of the "terrestrial globe," occupied the next four or five centuries. As a feat, the globe is the prelude to what is now known as the Anthropocene, a warm period in the world history of the Earth. The content of the feat is the terrestrial limit and constraint, the implicit lockdown, that follows from nautical facts. The significance of the globe is found in the completed encirclement of the Earth.

Indeed one might argue that what was crucial about the "modern era" was the way it forms the unprecedented stage in the history of post-Babylonian humanity in which "globalization" occurred in the literal sense. Leaving aside the rhetoric of economists and the grandiloquence of politicos, it represents the practical realization of the spheriform image of the Earth as a planetary singularity. It precipitates the apocalypse of the Earth – its revelation as a life-bearing celestial body. It is seldom considered that globalization, in the intensive interpretation of the word, has involved more than just the oceanization of transport and the expansion of European zones of command – more than just the advent to power of rapid news, communications, and transport systems in the twentieth century and their synchronizing effects. Its real and incalculable significance follows from the observation that European voyages across the Atlantic and Pacific ushered in an era of gathering and regathering: it brought an end to the effects of the Tower of Babel, indeed of the whole out-of-Africa period for *Homo sapiens*, by setting in motion an event that, from an anthropological point of view, can only be conceived as an "inversion of the diaspora." While members of the human species after the African exodus had earlier lived in dispersion, largely fixed in mutual ignorance and often under conditions of agricultural sedentism and pedestrian boundedness (breached now and again by short-lived equestrian nomadic raiding groups and early forms of seafaring), in the early sixteenth century a regime commenced which, like it or not – and primarily due to the geopolitical and cognitive consequences of Europe's outbound nautical reach – induced an unforeseen compulsion to return to the conscious coexistence of almost everyone with almost everyone else, across great distances, whether in active or passive mode. In place of the biblical tower there arose new sites of gathering, among which the UN building in New York, humming with multilingualism, is probably the closest to the Babylonian original.

When it comes to the moral, political, and cultural interpretation of the globalized situation, there is no consensus among interpreters – the divergence of views depends primarily on whether one is located on the active or passive side of events. There is no doubt that the world's becoming world, called *mondialisation* by the French, took place first and foremost as the process of an extension of power carried out by ships, goods, and weapons. This deepened the relationship between image and power, which dates back to magical times and was richly elaborated in the early empires.[1] We recall that, in his now classic lecture "The Age of the World Picture" from 1938, Martin Heidegger pointed out that the signature of the modern age shows itself not in that a new, so-called modern world picture has replaced an earlier, "medieval" one; rather, with the modern age as such, the "age of the world picture" had dawned. The decisive "event" is revealed in the circumstance that, thereafter, the world could be comprehensively captured in visual representations and thus delivered over to the grasp of technopolitical powers; in this process, science is progressively transformed into the handmaiden of technology, while technology becomes wholly the organ of a sovereign will emanating from Europe, which proclaims ever more loudly "I can" and "I will be able to." There remains something dubious in the fact that Heidegger omitted to speak expressly about the effective media of this new setting-into-images of the world – he mentions not a single word about the new terrestrial globes emerging around 1500 that helped Europeans come to an understanding of their situation as a whole;[2] he also does not mention double hemisphere projections, world maps which project the domed globe onto two flat halves to bring the verso of the sphere into visibility at the same time; he ignores the sea charts long cloaked in secrecy, the continuously updated atlases, the ship's logs initially kept like state secrets, and countless other media for extending the reach of power through the informed eye. These ranged from the emblem books that exploded into popularity with the age of print, challenging the monopoly of meaning held by writing, to descriptive geometry, from which calculus, the mother tongue of mathematical modernity, developed in the seventeenth century. After Copernicus came to prominence with his heliocentric model around 1543, the impulse for nautical circumnavigation of the Earth, which had been active since Columbus and da Gama, provided the best possible geographical foundation – even as one may also question whether the event often called the "Copernican revolution" ever really took place. The main fact of the new situation was not that the Earth revolves around the Sun. This remained a doctrine that defied appearances, of interest only to theory-driven, ivory-tower zealots. What defined the epoch was the circumstance that, in the form of ships and with the help of ships, there was an encircling of the Earth by European money, goods, and people.

Through the entire episode, there ran a streak of tragic irony that was discernible beyond just the marriage of the message of salvation and the colonial crimes associated with the early Spanish expansions, among others. Their true fatality, for better or for worse, seemingly arrived at by chance and yet irreversible, lay in the fact that with each ship that reached India after rounding the Cape of Good Hope or, after crossing the Atlantic, anchored in Central America, and later also in North and South America, a set of geographical truths was exported, concerning the spherical form of the Earth and the distribution of land and water masses. Even if the missionaries had not preached Christianity, but had set sail with syncretic offerings of Greek, Roman, and Gallic myth, the mere fact of their appearance on the shores of other continents implied the certification of a "worldview" that *eo ipso* ceased to be merely an image, merely a phantasm, merely a grasp at the void. When one of the five ships from Magellan's expedition, which had set sail for the South Atlantic in 1519, returned to the port of Sanlúcar de Barrameda near Seville in 1522 after a three-year circumnavigation, it supplied striking evidence for the regnant fact of the centuries ahead. The ships that had set sail – in accordance with Charles V's motto, *plus ultra!* – rediscovered their own starting point as the *non plus ultra* in practice. The proscription against navigating beyond the "Pillars of Hercules" was replaced by the newly discovered impossibility of setting out from one's starting point and traveling an absolute distance greater than half the circumference of the Earth. After the maritime circumnavigation of the planet, the counterintuitive notion of the spheriformity of the Earth, formerly a logical audacity, lost its status as a mere hypothesis and attained the rank of an unshakeable foundation – even if supporters of continental conservatism would regard it with mistrust and reluctance, right up to the present day. The ensuing half-millennium thus saw the division of Europe into people who accorded with the opening up of their countries by way of the oceans and people who wanted to maintain their immemorial orientation toward the axioms of territoriality – a schism that still claims a certain topicality in our own day as the opposition between European Atlanticism and Russian territorialism. When Nietzsche's Zarathustra one day implored his friends to "remain true to the Earth," he had long since envisioned a picture of the Earth and the world that encompassed a totality of seas and landmasses, and so the sum total of terrestrial immanence. For this reason, for him, the Columbus of the boundary-dissolved condition of the world as viewed by the religions of the hereafter, like the emphasis on the antitheses of land and sea promoted by authors like Carl Schmitt and his western and eastern epigones, could lead only to outraged provincialisms.

But this was plain: from the sixteenth century onward, it was impossible to be a missionary without proclaiming, alongside the Christian message, the truth about the shape of the Earth, the planetary fact, even if only indirectly. At first, it was concealed in the almost miraculous fact of their own presence among distant strangers. It was not entirely without reason that in some places the white men who arrived on ships were taken for gods – of whom their own priests had sometimes dreamed. Where they were not taken for gods, they were in some places treated as foes who, due to local tradition – later interpreted as acts of "resistance" – were devoured and incorporated in cannibalistic feasts[3]; in Japan, there soon awakened a sense of anti-missionary parody as, for example, when the ruling warlord Toyotomi Hideyoshi (1537–1598) crucified seventeen Japanese converts together with nine missionaries – six Franciscans and three Jesuits – near Nagasaki in February 1597.[4]

If writing itself is the message, then the ship crossing the ocean must likewise be grasped as a message in its own right. It conveyed the diktat that the addressees must acquiesce both to the premises of seafaring on global waters and to their consequences. It is not only the cloaked, the concealed, the subterranean that is discovered – first and foremost, it is the overt and obvious that is discovered: that for those who know how to get there, every point on the earth lies on the surface. The medium of the ship – as a floating sack for bringing home acquired goods[5] – embodied the message, essential for traders and pirates, that no object of exchange, no spoils, could be taken farther than an antipodal "position" on the circumnavigated earth. In his 1651 novel *El Criticón*, the Spanish Jesuit Baltasar Gracián coined the most lucid metaphor for a ship that sets sail to open up new worlds: "the portable Europe."[6]

In fact, the new medium of the terrestrial globe – its prototype being the "Erdapfel," the globe produced by Martin Behaim between 1490 and 1492 and now on display at the Germanisches Nationalmuseum in Nuremberg[7] – brought with it a boost to the correspondence theory of truth: a sentence or an image that depicts a situation or an object no worse than a globe depicts the planet Terra may be deemed, if not absolutely true, then at least "true enough." On the other hand, Goethe's crypto-Platonic motto, "One sees only what one knows," was ironically anticipated by the maxim of explorers, colonial masters, and pirates, according to which one truly owned, on land as at sea, only what one had stolen with one's own hands or with those of one's minions.

From the outset, the praxis of the conquistadores tended to place itself under the indulgent heavens of halfway subtle fictions of legitimacy and a salved conscience. Among them, more or less sophistical concepts such as the doctrine of discovery, the rule of finders, and prize law ranked at the forefront, followed by postulates based on natural law such as right of visit, right of settlement, commercial law, and communications law – figures and fictions lauded even by such studious readers of seafaring literature as Immanuel Kant.[8] The American novelist Herman Melville is to be credited for deriving, only semi-satirically, all these mellifluous fabrications from deep-sea fishing, and whaling in particular. There, the distinction between "fast fish" and "loose fish" is said to have been a law both longstanding and ironclad. During a quiet moment at sea, the narrator of *Moby-Dick* relates that, in the eyes of seamen, "fast-fish" rightfully belong to those who are the first to "fasten" upon them (by way of harpoon lines), whereas "loose-fish" are considered fair game for any hunter on the seas who first can seize them. Melville added that this distinction was likewise followed in the hunt for new lands.

> What was America in 1492 but a Loose-Fish, in which Columbus struck the Spanish standard by way of waifing it for his royal master and mistress? What was Poland to the czar? What Greece to the Turk? What India to England? What at last will Mexico be to the United States? All Loose-Fish.
>
> What are the Rights of Man and the Liberties of the World but Loose-Fish? [...] What is the great globe itself but a Loose-Fish?[9]

Melville's allusion to the raising of the Spanish standard on the soil of the New World invokes a gesture of ritual appropriation, which was used to camouflage crude appropriations as legitimate acts under international law. The Portuguese expansions made extensive use of the ceremonial raising of *padrões* – stone stelae crowned with a cross, taller than human height, which were brought along on board the expeditionary ships. To this day, the hollow and fatal gesture of appropriating unclaimed property has remained virulent in the repertoire of political symbolism; an instance of this fact was on display in 2007 with the planting of a

Russian flag in the sea near the North Pole at a depth of 4,000 meters – it served to mark Russia's claims to the supposedly rich deposits of oil and natural gas there. Be that as it may, the legal implications of this flagging are unlikely to extend any further than the symbolic raising of a Chinese flag on the moon, which since 2020 has been keeping company with the long-disintegrated US flags left behind in six earlier landings (from Apollo 11 in 1969 to Apollo 17 in 1972) – unless Russia's committed geologists succeed in proving that its continental shelf, which would be recognizable as national territory, extends so far into the Arctic Ocean.

Anyone wishing to discuss the spirit of expansion in due detail would have no choice but to spend days and nights beyond count in archives piled high with documents relating to the two most powerful post-Catholic, essentially modern imperialisms – the Napoleonic French and the Victorian British, both long primed through earlier nautical–mercantile–military incursions by their country into distant zones. In these paper underworlds, there is a wealth of evidence to be found in support of the thesis that the "civilizing mission," whether Anglophone or Francophone, had overtaken the Christian-articulated Iberian–Roman efforts *circa missiones* from the early nineteenth century onward. This propelled a momentous shift in the rationales deployed in support of colonial discriminations: if, from the early sixteenth century onward, arguments had been based almost exclusively on the difference between Christians and pagans, and soon thereafter between the civilized and the savage (the barbarian, later the "primitive"), the nineteenth century came to establish a discourse of culturally mature adults and culturally immature children – with the implication that the colonizers wanted to see themselves more as educators than as oppressors. Indeed, if a certain degree of oppression were called for, it would be only to the extent that the pupils' recalcitrance or unruliness seemed to necessitate a firm hand from the teacher. Here, there came into play a difference that implied more than just a nuance: the necessity of educational constraint was given little thought in Europe until the age of progressive pedagogy around 1900, notwithstanding Rousseauism and the Romantic idealization of the child, but in the home country it affected only minors among children, whereas it was applied to entire populations among foreign peoples; of these, Rudyard Kipling, not in his best moment, could still claim without embarrassment that one could find equivocal traits in them – "half devil and half child."[10] It is entirely understandable that later decolonial struggles were often also staged as demands issued in the name of political maturity. Lodging complaints on the grounds of adulthood did produce, here and there, crude emulations of colonial masters by their former subjects. In his drama *The Tragedy of King Christophe* (premiering at the Salzburg Festival in 1964), the Franco-Caribbean poet Aimé Césaire showed the psycho-cultural depths that must be penetrated for effective liberation from invasively implanted models from times of foreign rule. The play presents the former slave Henri Christophe (1767–1820) as he declared himself King of Haiti and then reigned as a cruel despot in the north of the country. Ingrained gestures of colonial pedagogy persisted during the last third of the twentieth century in systems of "development aid," which can hardly be interpreted as anything other than a scholarship system for the politically and economically immature. This implies the insight that thinking in terms of development remains incompatible with thinking in terms of equality – a circumstance which, if it can be grasped at all without cynicism or fatalism, becomes tractable only through the art and the craft of transition – which is to say: through diplomacy.

To be noted *en passant*: the democratic pedagogy of our time, aiming to cultivate fitness for the "realities ahead," has for some time exhibited traits of a hasty and ill-considered internal colonialism by teaching those alive today to adapt to the semi-anonymous dominion of tomorrow's evolutionarily unpredictable, near-term predictable technical structures.[11]

But even those political and educational systems of the sixteenth to nineteenth centuries that were directed in upon European nations themselves were based on programs of national homogenization that originated in the capitals; this was especially true of those designed to enforce the axioms of the Counter-Reformation – whether the "enculturation" of the southern German states through the Jesuits' post-Reformation *missio in Germaniam* or the subjugation of France under the state-Catholic regime at Versailles and the Île-de-France. Alongside extensive compulsory schooling, the most effective means in the long term proved to be the deployment of a gendarmerie to even small towns and villages, especially in districts where, well into the nineteenth century, brigandry continued to flout the rule of law; this formed a strain of "counterculture" that has remained influential to the present day, notably in Italy. In order to grasp the intra-European effects of colonialism, one should never forget that the officials of the short-lived Napoleonic Empire looked down on the local elites of Tuscany and Spain with much the same disdain that the British Sahibs in India felt when they looked down upon the natives there, and as the Spanish and Portuguese governors felt when they looked down upon the Indios. As a rule, Europeans of today are people who – conceiving of themselves as citizens of their nation states – one would presume to be definitively reconciled to the effects of internal colonization.[12] The new populist movements expose this assumption as premature: quite a few European citizens feel themselves to have been colonized by their countries' elites; increasingly, they are behaving as restively as residents of a periphery. In wealthy countries in particular, a divergence is opening up between metropolitan and rural areas – something hardly expected, politologically. There, it is often only a short step from *Landlust* to *Landfrust*, from "yearning for country life" to "frustration with country life." From this perspective, it is not really surprising that, in France and the United Kingdom, there have recently come to prominence spheres of social unrest that feel themselves to be colonies of the capitals and pawns of their elite. What is called populism today often means nothing more than the dream of the provinces to teach the metropolis a lesson it will not soon forget.

Even the shortest excerpt from the European Book of Expansions cannot do without inserting a bookmark in the chapter entitled Cecil Rhodes. The legendary son of a British clergyman, born in 1853 in the county of Hertfordshire on the northern outskirts of London, sickly from a young age and physically delicate throughout life (he suffered his first mild heart attack at the age of 19), a man who had written seven wills before he died at the age of 49, he was among the most self-aggrandizing and self-expanding figures of his century – indeed, the exemplary figure of the imperial age then reaching its zenith. His character was entirely to the taste of his fellow neurotic interpreter Oswald Spengler – which is also why he deserves a mention here, beyond applause and the toppling of monuments. From the phenomenon of Cecil Rhodes, more clearly than with any other figure of his era, one might illustrate the tendencies of a post-Christian, yet pretentious and ever more missionary expansionism of European (or more narrowly, British-imperial) stamp. His profile gains little in definition as the unlikely rise of a fragile youth who, as an eighteen-year-old, began with cotton plantations in the British Colony of Natal to gain a foothold in a distant outpost of the Empire, but soon thereafter sought his fortune in diamond and gold mining, until, after a series of clever moves and lucrative alliances, he reached the top of global monopolies in the gold and diamond industries in his thirties and forties. If there is still reason to remember the man who was also Prime Minister of the Cape Colony from 1890 to 1896,[13] it is because he is a key figure for understanding the secular metastasis of missionary thinking. Rhodes was one of the entrepreneurial princes of the late nineteenth century, for whom economic enrichment was merely a prelude to greater power – it is needless here to mention current names, from both sides of the Atlantic, on the Olympus of philanthropy. During the years of his prime ministership, intellectual fancies of global reach began to take shape in his mind. The dominant theme concerned the synthesis of a linguistic motif with what he considered to be the racial–political imperative of his era. Just as Rhodes had no doubt that the white race was at the top of the anthropological pyramid, it was likewise evident to him that only through anglophonicity could the world as a whole be brought together into a meaningful unity. There is an important distinction mediologists will make between anglophony and anglography, but Rhodes himself gave little thought to this or to the fact that empires had long been ruled more by post, hence by long-distance writing, rather than by telephone, or long-distance speaking.[14] The basic geopolitical outline for a project of this scope was provided, as if spontaneously, by the expansion of the British Empire. At the emotional heart of Rhodes' deliberations, one finds a counterfactual reverie of piquant presumption and world-historical aspiration. Its crucial point lay in his refusal to accept as irrevocable the United States's secession from the British Crown on July 4, 1776. In his fancy, the English-speaking "race," regrettably dispersed across a multitude of nations, continued to represent a virtual union – one whose restoration might be advanced through suitable policies, even if under American leadership. In this, Rhodes, as a vicar's son and an early convert to the Darwin-influenced belief that God was with white excellence, was aided by thinking in grand analogies. He saw the fracturing of Christianity through the Reformation in the sixteenth century as a disaster that had proven irreversible, notwithstanding the Jesuit counteroffensive. In his eyes, the American secession was a comparable misfortune – but one that he thought was not yet settled as irreversible. To restore the shattered anglophone catholicity, a comprehensive initiative was called for: a kind of improved Jesuitism, a male society on the model of a monastic order to be created through an effort of the British élite – an organon aiming at the restoration of world unity. This synthesis could be executed only through the synthesis of whiteness, anglophonicity, and technical civilization; as a paradigm of the latter, Rhodes envisioned the extension of the telegraph line from Cape Town to Cairo, one of his favorite projects – with the classic imperial implication that effective expansion in space requires and results in the overcoming of distances, whereas a distance yet unconquered represents an opportunity for resistance with respect to imperatives issued from the center. In the first instance and in most cases, imperialism and telecommunications wage the same battle.

In his seventh and final will, the imperialist with grandiose dreams stipulated that the bulk of his fortune should go to endow a foundation committed to such objectives. This foundation, which ostensibly took the form of a secret society, or better still, a round table of homophile string-pullers, is still surrounded by suggestive rumors, whether they refer to the Round Table movement or Bilderberg meetings, as if these were nothing more than the visible surfaces of conspiracies committed to invisibility. Indeed, the Rhodes Scholarships, awarded since 1903 – in the shadow of the Nobel Prizes – continue to this day; their statutes make no mention of occult cultural–political projects. Their most famous recipient was the future 42nd President of the United States, Bill Clinton.

Let us note that, even a hundred years after Rhodes' death, the Rhodes type continues to demonstrate his irrefutable topicality: his psychodynamic–oligarchic drive system has been successfully transposed into the twenty-first century – the Rhodes of our own day, more anglophone than ever, crowd the pages of business newspapers. At no point has the secularized concept of mission lost its appeal; as a way of thinking in terms of action groups that transmit influence emanating outward from a center, it is as relevant today as it was in the days of Loyola and the Moravian mission. As regards the schema of "autogenous religion," which arose in the Renaissance to help entrepreneurial life arrange for a transcendence paid for from its own pocket – after the Columbian model – it has come through the journey of the past five centuries largely intact. It is what lies beyond the bank account that burnishes the brilliance of a billionaire. Where the sect was, the foundation shall come to be. It is said of Rhodes that, from his early years, he always carried upon his person a crumpled pocket edition of Marcus Aurelius's *Meditations*. His wills, though they contain no confessions, testify to his need to transcend the possession of monetary power and high office. His words on his deathbed, "So much to do, so little done,"[15] can be taken as an ambivalent entry in the European Book of Confessions. To get an idea of the impression Rhodes made on intelligent contemporaries, it is worth quoting from a chapter appended to Rhodes' *Last Will and Testament* by his editor, William T. Stead (1849–1912), one of the most important British journalists of the time:

> He does not emerge an immaculate saint, carved in the whitest of Parian marble. He is revealed not as an archangel of radiant stainless purity, but neither was he a cloven-footed devil. Judging him by his stature in influence, in authority and in driving force, he belonged to the order of archangels; but he was a grey archangel, with a crippled wing, which caused him to pursue a somewhat devious course in the midst of the storm-winds of race-passion and political intrigue. A grey archangel crossed with a Jesuit, who was so devoted to his ends that almost all means were to him indifferent [...].[16]

It should be apparent that this characterization says at least as much about its author as it does about the person portrayed. Rhodes had initially appointed William T. Stead as one of the executors of his will, but he ultimately withdrew his trust because the former confidant had ventured too far into the waters of spiritualism for his taste – Rhodes found no pleasure fishing in the great beyond; his megalomania remained pragmatically grounded and his flights of fancy required no uplift from otherworldly powers. Stead lost his life on April 15, 1912, in the sinking of the Titanic.

The deliberations undertaken on European activities of expansion have thus far, with intentional one-sidedness, restricted themselves to the aspect of motivation or intellectual purpose. They deviate from the conventions of "materialist historiography" in that, in Aristotelian terms, they grant precedence to final causes (*causae finales*) over material and efficient causes (*causae materiales, causae efficientes*) – not only at the level of representation, but in the matter itself. This one-sided emphasis on "mental" motives should ultimately be compensated for through some indication of an aspect of efficient-cause expansion motivity.

To explain, in terms of social causes, Europe's tempestuous expansion – in the first instance, the sudden rush to the ships in the late fifteenth century – one is obliged to consider the impetus, the energy, flowing into events due to a precipitous change in demographic conditions. Indeed, the transition to an efficient-causal consideration of longer-term processes can be illuminated most plausibly by way of the term "populationism" – an expression that circulated from the eighteenth century onward, though in substance it was related to the nascent interest taken much earlier by princes in promoting expansionist population policies. It characterizes a tendency of early modern "biopolitics," expressed through rulers' wish for the greatest possible expansion of their population. Its origins lay in the long-term consequences of pandemic bubonic plague, known as the "Black Death" (*mors atra*) from 1346 to 1353 – which, according to historians' estimates, claimed the lives of at least one-third of Europe's population. The total population is said to have fallen from 78 million to 45 million within these years. The centuries that followed – right up to 1900 – can be summarily interpreted as an era of demographic "reforestation." This was disrupted by frequent recrudescence of the plague – as well as by the devastations of the Thirty Years' War – but not decisively held back. Europe's population is said to have sunk to its lowest point in the dire plague year of 1400, when, again in the wake of several epidemics, it fell even lower than the level seen in 1353.

It was not until the last third of the fifteenth century that efforts to repopulate the country by promoting births bore real fruit. From the 1970s onwards, the economist and cultural historian Gunnar Heinsohn (1943–2023) argued that the eradication of wise women – midwives – which began in the fifteenth century under the pretext of witch-hunting, was primarily to be understood through an acute "biopolitical" interest in "repopulation."[17] Many of the seemingly irrational traits of the "witch craze" that raged through Europe during the Renaissance lose their irrationality when they are interpreted as instruments in a campaign to increase the state's reserves of "human capital" – granting that this cynical expression was a later coinage.[18] Their ideological orientation is documented in texts such as Pope Innocent VIII's *Summis desiderantes affectibus* of 1484, and even more so in the ominous *Malleus Maleficarum* (*Hammer of Witches*) by the Dominican inquisitor Heinrich Kramer from 1487, as well as in the *Constitutio Criminalis Bambergensis* from 1507. Writings of this tendency attest to the fascination of clerics with the idea that the devil is particularly interested in the improper use of the sexual organs. Who, if not the devil, would take pleasure in sabotaging creation by preventing births?

From the 1480s onward, Europe suddenly found itself once again with, as Heinsohn dryly puts it, "hordes of sexually frustrated non-inheriting sons"[19] – a circumstance that was particularly applicable to Extremadura, Spain's desperate west; this arid region provided an unexampled array of extroverted, violent men, including figures such as the Pizarro brothers, Cortés, de Soto, Valdivia, and Balboa. For the flood of young men who, because they were second-born (Spanish: *secundones*), could not find positions in their own country to match their ambition, the window of migration to the New World opened just as the tide was rising.

The fact that Europe, during its most virulent centuries, possessed a near monopoly on human export was manifested in the demographically explicable asymmetry between what was later called "the other cape" (or "the other heading") and "the rest of the world." A glance at statistics suffices to solve the puzzle in terms of quantity. Europe's population increased tenfold between 1400 and 1900: even despite the severe decline in the early and mid-seventeenth century, it grew from 45 million to 450 million over that period – and this, as noted, was by no means a foregone conclusion, but instead primarily the result of a coherently pursued policy of promoting childbirth, on which thrones and altars agreed, notwithstanding their very different rationales. With respect to the fine-tuning of the repopulation "project," populationist practices – the actual 'biopolitics' about which Foucault, the founder of the "discourse," says strangely little – contributed to a malfunction with chronic consequences: for the nascent states, the desired superfluity of births became – by 1550 at the latest – more of a burden than a political resource. All too many people had "taken the trouble to be born" – to echo the formulation that Beaumarchais' Figaro aimed at the arrogance and presumption of a noble lineage.[20] Due to this fatal excess, the crime of being poor assumed epidemic proportions in the leading nations of the modern era – the establishment of early hospital systems and municipal poor relief constituted the first responses of local authorities and states to growing population pressures in the early modern era. In his 1526 treatise *De subventione pauperum*, dedicated to the magistrate of Bruges, the Spanish–Flemish humanist Luis Vives (1493–1540) laid the foundations for what later times would call "social policy."

Even the vast human wastage of the Napoleonic Wars – said to be four to five million victims between 1795 and 1815 – was only a trivial check on the surge in population growth. The diminishing of demographic surpluses and the easing of growth did not occur until the late nineteenth century, when the reinvention of contraception suddenly reduced the pressure.[21] Even the emigration of fifty million people by the end of the nineteenth century did not alter the basic fact that European nations were producing more or less steadily mounting surpluses in offspring not entitled to an inheritance, to say nothing of the swelling of the poverty zone, far removed from the world of work, at the broad lower margin of early modern societies;[22] among the superfluous ones, the deep reserves of second and third sons, like the bastards of the nobility and clergy,[23] formed an energetic, ambitious, and virulent group – unless they became soldiers destined for wastage, they were recruited in numbers beyond all reckoning as clergymen, missionaries, scholars, writers, artists, and seditious settlers of "counter-societies" of the mind, ranging from the miracle courts and garrets of the big city, to suburban dive bars, to the universities. When such groups saw reasons to rebel against "established conditions," it was not against a system that exploited their skills, but against conditions in which they were simply superfluous. The tens of thousands of application letters stored in the archives of the Jesuit Order in Rome show just how attractive a career in missionary service was to superfluous young men in Catholic regions during the seventeenth and eighteenth centuries.[24] From a distance, they must have resembled the tortuous personal statements or letters of motivation that foreign students today submit with their applications for a place at an elite university in the USA.

Anyone who, guided by cues such as these, continues to leaf through the Book of European Expansion, will notice that the past five centuries in this part of the world have set in motion more than just an unfinished experiment in the progressive dissolution of hierarchies of social origin – more than just a tendency to erase the distinction, so decisive for earlier orders of genealogical relations, between legitimate children and the offspring of the wrong bed, between noble and bourgeois births, and between traditional marriages and same-sex cohabitations, which are now taken on equal terms with marriages. During the same long period, there was also an experiment in the rigorous suppression of previously well-known forms of birth control; the result was that, for centuries, the ecosystem of culture as a whole was thrown out of balance by rampant reproduction.

In short: it is hardly possible to meaningfully use the word "expansion" in its material aspect unless it is made clear that it was not solely religious and missionary motives that determined its development; nor was it just the inflated and clerically fueled monarchical ambitions that rose to prominence in light of reports from the new worlds – whereby, especially in Spain, the idea of alleviating the "permanent state of emergency"[25] in the royal treasury through the influx of mintable metals from distant colonies carried considerable weight. The proceedings as a whole exhibited traits of a half-blind overflow more than they suggested a well-defined project. When the New World came into the sights of Europeans hungry for action, it was not only as a projection screen for dreams of happiness indulged by captains, royal advisors, lenders, shipowners, and treasure seekers; primarily, and above all, it served as an overflow basin for European surpluses of people, frustration, and vague energies in search of worthwhile and rewarding tasks – energies that one day, on the east coast of the American side of the Atlantic, were cloaked in constitutional guarantees under the slogan of "the pursuit of happiness."

If one contemplates the metaphor of the "overflow basin" more closely, it straightaway becomes discernible that the overflow of European power would have been unthinkable without the return flow of profits from foreign trade. It is a widespread misconception in post-colonial studies to take the bulk of transatlantic spoils, as well as the profits from voyages to India, simply as depredations – as naked "extractions," to borrow from current terminology. From a European perspective, they early on possessed the character of a return on investment, and thus had a monetary and credit-driven nature. To understand this, it is important to take account of the fact that transoceanic ships, the high-tech constructs of their time – galleons, carracks, caravels – were generally already cruising the seas as floating loans. Their voyages were driven by the need to generate sufficient profit so that, after repayment of loans and interest, there would remain a surplus to make the whole effort worthwhile. Thus, from the outset, the European Book of Expansion was linked to the Book of Invention[26] – not least in relation to shipbuilding, sailing technology, naval artillery, and navigational instruments.

Fortunately, it is not the case that its entire scope falls under the category of the "universal history of infamy." From this history, Jorge Luis Borges offered several stories in the style of dark *baroccismo* in his 1935 collection of the same name. They confirmed Franz Kafka's aphorism that when one has once accepted and absorbed evil, it no longer demands to be believed – for there isn't any more evil than there is. Because it is there in its terrible near-ubiquity, yet embodies no principle, there is nothing to counter attempts to diminish it. As a whole, the Book of Expansions is included in the still unedited Book of Ambiguities, which was made accessible to the broad public of the twentieth century under the heading of "globalization" – a word that, as has been shown, says at once too much and too little.

Lesson seven
Get a-way, you old peoples![1]
From the book of dissenting voices: Europe in the accusative

"If Europe were a book": over the course of the deliberations here, extensive use has been made of the book metaphor – and made along paths already well established by traditional European symbolism;[2] this has supported the suggestion not only that the complex known as "Europe" is legible like a book, but that it could be arranged into chapters, or assembled into separately readable books that might together form a super-book – a document naturally incomplete. "Bookmarks" were placed at points that should be revisited by those interested in understanding the broader context. We benefited, moreover, from an element of excess or extravagance in the analogy when we pretended that a geographically rugged region of the world, a promontory of Asia wrongly called a continent, could be a self-writing book – a book whose readers are its inhabitants and whose editing is undertaken now and again by generals, captains, and crowned and uncrowned megalomaniacs of both sexes.

And yet, it was not merely a baroque suggestion when it was claimed that for half a millennium, in this part of the world that invented "the world," ever new inducements had been found, and at regular intervals, to inform the set of people increasingly referred to as "Europeans" about the state of their internal and external affairs. In fact, when Europeans were not daunted by fear of the winds of change and caught up in their own prejudice and defiance of the new, the unproven, and the freshly arrived from overseas, they allowed themselves to be taught, step-by-step, by the script they themselves had written about where they stood with themselves and their role within the whole – a whole whose main mass one has demurred, for some time now, to call "the rest of the world."

Talk of a self-authoring book is less hybrid than it might appear at first glance. Before the mid-nineteenth century, when the inhabitants of Europe learned through new sciences such as political economy and sociology that they lived in "societies" – up to that point, this term had been used to refer to militant communities such as the Jesuit order, then to chartered companies and shareholders of listed companies, designated S.A. or *sociétés anonymes* – most of them would probably have been willing to allow that, although they had been commonly referred to as "peoples" up to that point, they formed something like commodious discussion groups. The dead and the unborn took part too, if discussions can be understood to mean more than just the irrecoverable words shared between passers-by, salon visitors, and subscribers to flat-rate telecom plans. Inhabitants of Europe in earlier times allowed themselves to be guided in their themes: princes, priests, merchants, poets, researchers, and rumor-mongers prescribed the topics that constituted them as real speaking communities; through their speaking existence, these societies became, each in their own sphere, fields of shared concern, shared curiosity, shared indignation – and, in rarer cases, such as enthronements, princely weddings, and peace settlements, also reverberators of shared jubilation. The line from Friedrich Hölderlin's hymn "Celebration of Peace," written around 1802 – "Since we have been a discourse and have heard from one another" – definitively conceptualized the state of affairs as it presented itself before the suffocating talk of "society" began its triumphal march.

What has been labeled "society" since the nineteenth century embodies, from the perspective of recent media theories, something like a structured heap of sand. Due to market effects and – to borrow a critical-religious term coined by Régis Debray – due to mental "communion"[3] (instituted through school systems and culminating in party conventions or state celebrations), societies accomplish the feat of turning countless grains into something that resembles an animated whole; or, to borrow once more from Debray's almost too elegant turns of phrase, they succeed more or less well in temporarily transitioning *du tas au tout*, from the heap to the whole.[4]

In this final section of our project, we would like to remain, as much as possible, faithful to the metaphor of the Book of Europe. Because, as announced in the title of this lesson, its authorship is now being handed over to non-Europeans, this can only happen at the cost of divesting our book of its privilege of being drafted entirely on its own terms. In short, we would like to address the fact that Europe has long been in the process of losing, to portraitists from elsewhere, its quasi-monopoly on configuring its own image.

At least since the American Declaration of Independence in 1776, Europe, already by then called the Old World, knew itself to be exposed to a multiplicity of retrospective, reciprocal, and foreign gazes. These eroded its certitude that it might effectively counter any possible outside view with a robust self-presentation. From the early sixteenth century on, Europeans in the field, notably Dominican missionaries such as Antonio de Montesinos and Bartolomé de Las Casas, wrote alarming reports of the New World colonists' behavior and relayed them to their superiors back in their homelands. In addition, the voyages of the "Pilgrim Fathers" and other emigrants provided evidence that there were mounting reasons to take leave of the Old World and to do so without plans for return.

No one would claim that the ability to see oneself from the outside and bow one's head was among Europe's innate virtues. Still, it should be noted that gestures from the examination of conscience and confession, which continue to this day – and from which "critique" later emerged – were imprinted since the early thirteenth century upon the mental grammar of the then still almost all-encompassing Catholic sphere.[5] But even when Thomas Aquinas (1225–1274) wrote his *Summa contra Gentiles* around 1260, directed "against the pagans,"[6] and even when there could be no doubt about the Church's magisterial monopoly, Aquinas too expressed the Church's acquired and continuing consternation with respect to metaphysical second opinions. They were embodied in the existence of Jews and Muslims, who presented the Christian community with stubborn evidence that there was a dissident Outside – with the one as unsettling as the other. Because of their monotheistic orientation, both alternative faiths presented Christian-trained theologians with a scandalously close Other. And yet tensions between the discourses on Yahweh, the Trinitarian God, and Allah were about more than just the narcissism of small differences. Each of these theologies conceived a different schema of human Dasein in relation to God – and thus a different way of being in the world and a different way of having to come to terms with finitude, as is the lot of mortal beings. The establishment of the Inquisition toward the end of the twelfth century also clarified the extent to which the still undivided Church believed, like a fortress under siege, that it had to arm itself not only against external enemies who spread lies about the Most High, but also, even more torturously, against manifestations of internal deviation, which from the very beginning formed a heretical shadow world.

All in all, one had to wait until the early eighteenth century to be able to claim that the age of two-way traffic, two-way communication, that is to say, two-way observation and two-way assessment, even a two-way mission, had truly begun for Europe and Europeans – and this after centuries of enjoying a one-way privilege of expansion, observation, and assessment. We will not tarry long here with the inherently fascinating and multifaceted phenomenon that one could describe as Europe's "oriental mirror stage."[7] It was heralded – after precursors dating back to the fairy-tale dreams of the Middle Ages – by the appearance of a sophisticated polyphonic epistolary novel in French, published anonymously in Amsterdam in 1721 under the title *Persian Letters*. In it, the author allowed himself the serious lark of documenting the correspondence of two visiting noblemen from Persia as they comment on the oddities they observe in local conditions in Europe, particularly in France. This light, early work by Montesquieu (1689–1755) became immensely popular and promptly fell victim to censorship – though this was possibly due more to its eroticism than to its politics and morality; it also, unmistakably, documents an expanded European soliloquy. The incipient Enlightenment devoted itself here to an attempt to elevate the culture of differences of opinion – which had flourished in ritualized disputes in the milieu of universities since the High Middle Ages – to the level of a cheerful public conversation between people with differing views. When the author related the disparity of views to the disparity of climates and the "cultures" that arose from them, this provided an early ecological rationale for the demand for tolerance.

What began as a light exercise in comparative studies broadened in the years after Montesquieu into an enlightened critique of civilization – with a focus on distilling a general normative theory of human coexistence within regulated social associations: while local cultures as a whole, as agglomerations of dogmas, customs, and mores, could be assigned to the sphere of "prejudices in the body" – where elements relate in ways partly incompatible, partly complementary, and partly ironized – over the course of time, through ongoing accumulation and comparison, a mountainous mass of civilizational principles emerged that could no longer be interpreted merely as local legacies of the past, as heirlooms of former conditions of the world, or as scripts for success from bygone ways of life. It was only after Montesquieu and the writings of the first explorers and early alumni of the *giro del mondo*[8] that the question could arise of whether there might be – beyond the locally ingrained prejudices that constitute the world – an all-encompassing horizon within which the scattered local motifs of the art of existence could be sorted and assembled as contributions to a system of higher order.

If such a horizon could be established, it would be a construct to which, as yet, no more apt expression could be applied than the archi-European term "civilization" – a word circulating since the eighteenth century. Its connotations echo both the Roman name for city dwellers (*civis*) and the postulation of a certain process of "formation," indicating the attainment of interactivity in a polyphonic and polymorphic world, something corresponding to the Latin words *educatio*, a "leading out of a primitive state," and *eruditio*, a "bringing out of the rough," an "expansion of knowledge" – and both united in the Ciceronian concept of *cultura animi*, literally: an "ordering and cultivation of the soul," from which everything is derived that is understood to this day under the key words of "culture" and "humanity."

What has been known since the eighteenth century in Europe as "the Enlightenment" was in essence nothing more than a program to clarify the meaning of the concept of *civilization*. Its explosiveness would become apparent only in the course of the nineteenth and twentieth centuries – and fully taking center stage in the twenty-first in what the late Nietzsche would have called "great politics." Its protagonists bear the names of history-making nations, named after the more recent centers of imperial power: the British Empire, the French Nation, the German Reich, the Russian Empire, the United States of America, followed by a group of second-tier contenders for power. Their clashes were called world wars. World wars can also be procedures for determining the meaning of the term "civilization." Victors would have to demonstrate not only that they had superior military resources at their disposal, they would also have to be able to show that, from a civilizational perspective, they deserved to be the more successful. They show this by submitting their *modus vivendi* for voluntary imitation.[9]

In 1871, a book was published in St. Petersburg, that had been written between 1865 and 1867 by the Russian naturalist Nikolay Yakovlevich Danilevsky: *Russia and Europe: A Look at the Cultural and Political Relations of the Slavic World to the Romano-German World.* It was one of the first radically Euro-critical programmatic writings and, by no mere coincidence, it addressed head-on the problem of "civilization" – a problem which, by the way, cannot be said to have been since resolved in any generally satisfactory manner. It is characteristic of Danilevsky's argument that he did not hesitate to label the concept of "civilization" as a product of the European sphere: without any substantial objections, he identified it initially as lying within the ambit of Romano-German cultures. Even so, he was unwilling to concede that Romano-Germanic definitions of "civilization" fully encompassed the potential scope of the term. Au contraire: for Danilevsky, the radiant appeal of the Western model had already exhausted itself, even as, in the Russian East of Europe, the seed of a completely self-willed, counter-Western civilization was waiting to germinate. Danilevsky argued that it was the mission of the Slavic peoples, and the Russians first and foremost, to counter the supposedly exhausted and discredited Western complex with an Eastern alternative. He circulated two pieces of good news at once: first, that another world was possible, and second, that it was already developing in the form of the Slavic world. It needed only to shape itself at last into a self-sufficient, well-rounded universe by shaking off its Western influences like a temptation overcome. Grounded in early Christian orthodoxy, the civilization that was emerging – east of Europe, yet anything but merely eastern Europe – would be free from the power-craving constructs of Roman Catholicism; it would eschew the egomaniacal anarchy that had broken out with the triumph of Protestantism in Northern Europe and North America. Russia had indeed never been a European colony, but it had been all too submissive with respect to Western influence. To realize its destiny, Russia would have to free itself from its tendency to self-colonize under German, French, and British models, and it would have to reflect upon its true "essence," its fundamentally unique human qualities, which at the same time had remained close to the truest and earliest Christianity.

In the twentieth century, the fate of Pan-Slavic ideas became intertwined with that of the socialist Soviet Union between 1922 and 1991, albeit in a paradoxically twisted way. Although the Union of Soviet Socialist Republics brought virtually all Slavic peoples step-by-step under its control – albeit through military coercion, not voluntary annexation – its leaders were unwilling to champion Danilevsky's semi-biological concepts of civilization. Quite a few Bolsheviks were oriented within internationalist ideas and they discarded Danilevsky's theories as relics of a racialist, nationality-based mode of thought derived from romantic notions of the people.

What gives Danilevsky's external view of the European civilizational complex its edge is the author's determination to attribute to the Slavic world in its entirety a wealth of virtues that, in his eyes, the West lacked – above all, forbearance, cooperativeness, piety, a neighborly disposition, and an absence of belligerence; while the negative counterparts to these – intolerance, unilateralism, heresy, egoism, and a contentious demeanor – were located on the Germanic-Roman side. Thus, through Danilevsky's opposition between "Russia" and "Europe," a third "near Other" emerged over and against the European and North American realms, one that was clearly distinct from the distant Otherness of Asia. His plea sought to revoke any forced convergence with the civilizational norms of the Romano-Germanic sphere, which had been on the Russian political agenda since Peter the Great (1672–1725). Not quite unexpectedly, but with eruptive vehemence, Danilevsky's intervention formulated nothing less than a claim for a compelling antithesis to Europe – a peculiar "civilization" in its own right, which, in order to come into its own, must renounce the corruptive influence of the West. Indeed, its turn from Europe was necessary in order for it to fulfill its mission in world affairs: to preserve the Orthodox heritage that had been transferred – free from Roman falsifications – via Byzantium and Kyiv to Moscow.

Danilevsky's book, sometimes celebrated as the "Bible of Pan-Slavism," excited a great sensation in Russia, not least because the country, humiliated by its defeat in the Crimean War (1853–1856) against the politically and culturally suspect European–Ottoman alliance, had become more receptive to ideological compensations with a Europhobic slant. It was read favorably by the intellectuals known as *Narodniks*, who, from the 1870s onward, had devoted themselves to the dream of a direct transition from peasant society to socialism – bypassing the "developmental stage" of industrial, egoistic, capitalist ways of life that dominated the West. Similarly inclined, and at about the same time, Fyodor Dostoevsky gave literary expression to his own bitter hatred for everything Western.[10] The fact that the March 1881 assassins of the reformist Tsar Alexander II emerged from a radical faction that had split from the Narodniks and called themselves *Narodnaya Volya* (the "People's Will"), had far-reaching consequences for the later history of Russia: the young Lenin turned away from the anarchist assassination–politics line and instead devoted himself to a strategy of conquering the state apparatus. When the new line entered openly onto the stage in the autumn of 1917, it sought from the outset to reinforce the conspiracy newly in power with state-terrorist protection – at that time under the name of Cheka – a choice that lives on insofar as the dominance of Russia's Federal Security Service persists into the twenty-first century.

In European literature of the late nineteenth century, voices expressing Russian antipathy for the West did not go unnoticed. It was the young British writer Rudyard Kipling, born in 1865 near Mumbai,[11] and having spent his youth in India, who more than any other developed an early sensitivity for the vicissitudes of the Great Game between Russia and England on the South Asian "chessboard." In his 1891 story "The Man Who Was,"[12] he captured the stormy mood in European–Russian relations. It manifested itself in a memorable way at a British cantonment in the then Indian-administered garrison town of Peshawar, the headquarters of Her Majesty's White Hussars, near what would later become the Pakistani frontier with Afghanistan.

At a festive evening hosted by British officers to celebrate a winning polo match, a Russian guest, a Cossack officer named Dirkovitch, is present. It is said that he serves under various names as a correspondent for Russian newspapers. How he arrived in India from the north, by which pass, no one knows. Credentials from high officials commend him as a welcome guest. Whether drunk or sober, he rhapsodizes about an Anglo-Russian alliance that would one day jointly undertake the task of civilizing Asia – though he knew as well as anyone else that these were mere empty words. He proves himself to be a man with a boundless tolerance for alcohol – a trait that qualifies him for a role in the intelligence service, since even under the influence of alcohol, he could not be induced to betray state secrets. Over the course of the British officers' celebration, Dirkovitch gives evidence of this capacity for drink by emptying countless glasses of brandy – indeed in such quantities that he sinks under the table for a time, seemingly stupefied.

The evening cheer is disrupted by the appearance of a wretched figure, who is suspected to have been out to steal a carbine – a common offense in British garrisons, since the natives liked to settle their disputes with modern Western weapons. After a little while, it transpires that the weeping heap of rags is in fact a white man – indeed, it is discovered that he is a former member of this regiment: after the battles for Sevastopol, he had been passed over in a prisoner exchange due to dishonorable conduct and abandoned to the Russian enemy. Somehow, this almost dehumanized individual must have managed to escape from the Siberian camps and, after decades, as if effaced, find his way back to his garrison. In fact, lists dating to the time of the Crimean War are discovered in the Peshawar troop registry, in which the man's name is found: "Lieutenant Austin Limmason. Missing."

At this moment, however, amid the general confusion, the Russian awakens from his stupor and launches into an unexpected speech: in the Tsar, he no longer believes in the slightest, any more than he believes in Napoleon, who was but an episode. The Slavic peoples, however – they were the ones he wanted to believe in! The Slavs had perhaps not yet accomplished anything in the world worth mentioning – but, listen carefully! There were seventy million of them and more! Their work would soon be done! Look at this heap of rags! As with him, this "man who was," this former and now effaced personage, so it would happen to all of them, but they, they would never come back, not here and not home to England – but there: he points to a coffin shadowed on the ceiling of the hall. "Seventy millions – get a-way, you old peoples!"[13]

Kipling's artful narrative saves the revelation of Dirkovitch's sentiments for the end of the story. While the Russian agent would have been capable of keeping political secrets even in the most intoxicated state, alcohol proved suitably conducive for surfacing ideological avowals. The unexpected punchline is set up at the start of the story through an ambiguous sentence in an ethnological tone:

> Let it be clearly understood that the Russian is a delightful person till he tucks in his shirt. As an Oriental he is charming. It is only when he insists upon being treated as the most easterly of western peoples instead of the most westerly of easterns that he becomes a racial anomaly extremely difficult to handle. The host never knows which side of his nature is going to turn up next.[14]

The figure of the Russian officer can best be grasped as a Danilevskian who has strayed onto British territory. In Kipling's story, it fell to him to drop his mask in a moment of disinhibition: the East, wallowing in its grievances, wished death upon the British and upon peoples of their sort. Transformed into a drunken oracle, he unveiled the anti-Western civilizational rancor of the Slavophile movement, not without admitting that it was at bottom just the *ressentiment* of an ensemble of inert peoples against the active hegemons – a vindictiveness that would soon rise to global significance. The figure "seventy millions," mentioned so emphatically, carried weight from the fact that Great Britain, far and away the leading power among the "old peoples," at that time boasted, in demographic terms, less than half the Russian masses.

Recollection of Kipling's story "The Man Who Was" is apt to evoke a historical moment in which Europe, now more often referred to as "the West," was targeted – or pilloried – as a "continent" caught between two demands. From the outside, the cry "Away with you!" became so clearly audible that it gradually penetrated general consciousness as a programmatic expression of decolonization, even in parts of the world where the idea of the sovereign state, imported from Europe, is stubbornly interpreted as a pretext for coups d'état, military putsches, and dictatorial regimes.[15] From the other side, which unsurprisingly formed mainly from elements within the withdrawing colonial powers, came the opposing cry: "Continue to accept your task in the world out there, even if they spit in your face!" What has been called "imperialism" in the jargon of historians, political scientists, and sociologists since 1900 – an expression whose inflationary usage distorted its meaning early on – was initially and in substance the space of conflict between these demands. Whereas the name Europe formerly appeared primarily in the nominative case – "Europe knows …," "Europe wants …," "Europe has decided …" – in recent times one finds it especially in the object position of a sentence or as the addressee of an accusation, an insult, or at best a vocative sigh, as Hans Magnus Enzensberger articulated it in his now classic book *Ach Europa!*[16] The first call – which combines accusation with undisguised rudeness – conveyed the demand that Europe and its delegates, whether colonists, missionaries, or ultimately tourists, should clear out from all places where they had no business being, except for half-baked educational dreams and one-sided economic interests; the second call insisted that the West should continue to fulfill its obligations in all those places where, through its appearances, its interferences, and its ill-kept promises, it had brought upon itself a world of "thankless tasks."

Rudyard Kipling's 1899 appeal to the "Western powers," "Take up the White Man's burden,"[17] which was mostly understood in terms of crude power politics, has been transformed, within a century, into a routine of assigning the problems of the non-Western world, solvable or not, to the debit column of the Leukosphere, i.e., the Euro-American sphere of influence. Construed realistically, this would be coterminous with what used to be described as the Western-dominated "world order," in the years following the collapse of the 69-year-old conspiracy system known as the Soviet Union – which temporarily succeeded in mystifying itself as the "Second World," even the wellspring of a "world revolution" – and before the rise of China and the "global South" set new standards. The current situation is marked above all by the fact that conspiratorial agencies acting as state powers in the post-Soviet era – China foremost, but attended by its Russian vassal (still under the guidance of its security services), and with the acclamation of not a few postcolonial police states and dictatorships – are together devoting themselves to more or less synchronized efforts to adjust the primacy of the West in their own favor.

Anyone looking back from the dawn of the twenty-first century to the second half of the twentieth will notice a major trend that, in political science terminology, is denoted with the term "decolonization." In substance, it amounts to an inflation of complaints with respect to political and cultural sovereignty by formerly dependent political entities. While the League of Nations, founded in 1920 and dissolved in 1946, originally comprised 29 victorious states of the Treaty of Versailles plus thirteen neutral members, the list of member states of the United Nations in 2024 includes no fewer than 193 names – more than quadrupling the pool of states within little more than a century. In effect, the existence of the United Nations can be grasped as an operationalization of what Rudyard Kipling meant by "the white man's burden." It constitutes the historical culmination of a fundamentally thankless task – summed up in the formula: where there was a colony, there shall be an independent state. It shares its awkward situation with other European exports like science, technology, and industry. Their critical feature becomes apparent once they fall into the hands of non-European users: they cannot be recalled. First and foremost, alongside the concept of the state, taken up by a number of entities incapable of actually forming one, is the idea of the university – something founded in the medieval institution of the *universitas studiorum* (where *universitas* initially meant something like "meeting place") and undergoing a momentous supplementation by the academies that flourished in the West from the fifteenth century on. Just as the modern state represents a genuinely European product of political engineering, which between the fifteenth and nineteenth centuries produced an array of more or less easily replicable models, the university or school of higher learning, as an entity of pedagogical and cognitive invention and inventiveness, represents a widely and willingly deployed instrument that brings about the direct or indirect Europeanization of its users. Quite consistently, it is deployed as a means of self-empowerment – as if it were in place to implant the equation of knowledge and power established in seventeenth-century Europe in as many non-European agencies as possible.

Where newer agencies organized themselves in the form of states – and furnished with the privilege of catching up with modernization – they also appeared on the scene as buyers of Western weapon systems – an eventuality to which the sovereignty fictions of international law would seem to entitle them. For their part, Western arms manufacturers – stimulated by the desire for statehood in the former peripheries – often displayed remarkable recklessness when it came to weighing economic interests against peace policy goals. One might almost think that impartiality is less a philosophical virtue than an arms dealer's.

Anyone who undertakes to add a few bookmarks to works from the Europe-critical or the forthrightly anti-European library should take some account of the fact that the modern universe of books and, by extension, the ideas published in the press would be inconceivable without the media and technologies exported around the world by Europeans. McLuhan's famous principle that the medium is the message implies that the message can be returned to the sender with the help of the medium. Phenomena such as "world literature" – to recall Goethe's coinage – and "world politics" or "great politics" in Nietzsche's sense, can be grasped, from a civilizational perspective, only as effects of *export inversion*, and sometimes also as *mission inversion*.

What Europe is facing today from the chorus of dissenting voices is mostly responses to the incoherence of its messages: it had purported to disseminate the loftiest thing it had to share – the Christian injunction to dissolve the boundaries of love and its translation into the enlightened inclusion of everyone within an empire of reciprocal human recognition and just exchange; yet it often exported the most villainous aspects of its culture to its contemporaries near and far: the violent subjugation of others under a regime of exporters. Amid the anti-Western sentiments that one hears articulated from all points of the compass these days, albeit with the delay typical of reactive acts, an ensemble of initiatives is forming that cannot be denied their element of truth. If the term "resistance" has attained such high prestige in the political vocabulary of the twentieth and twenty-first centuries, this is because it designates a productive figure in the arena of reality-creating forces; this holds true especially in contexts where it can be interpreted not merely as a reactionary reflex, but as a spontaneous impulse to counterattack and a refusal to submit, as in France, where – against the backdrop of the myth of the *Résistance* – terms such as *insoumission* and *contre-attaque* – noncompliance and counterattack – are experiencing a remarkable resurgence. If the medium is the message and the message is conveyed by force, then the impulse to respond with counterforce has a plausible inducement, even a legitimate right, to choose a medium that will in turn become the better message.

Naturally, this can also be sustained, accompanied, and clarified by force or violence.

To examine these deliberations on the concept of resistance, we place our penultimate bookmark in a document that can now be named as a classic of anti-Europeanism. Inevitably, the discussion here turns to Frantz Fanon's polemic *The Wretched of the Earth*, originally published in Paris in 1961 by Maspero.[18] The treatise by this author, born in Martinique in 1925, has since become a *vademecum*, a handbook, for peripheral uprisings; from the outset, he wanted it to be read as an anti-colonial manifesto. And, in fact, though slightly delayed, it appeared in a good season: a year before its publication, eighteen African states declared their independence from the European colonial powers – foremost among them, fourteen new political entities that dissociated themselves from France. Decades had to pass before the view of the conflict had become sufficiently clear as to bring to light a crucial cultural–theoretical insight concerning Fanon's theses: that they could be properly appreciated only as products of a mental counterexport, indeed of a massive countermission. Fanonian dogmas are distinguished by a lucidity that can only be achieved by thinking an axiom through to its conclusion.

> decolonization is always a violent event.
>
> […]
>
> Its definition can […] be summed up in the well-known words: "The last shall be first."
>
> […] For the last can be the first only after a murderous and decisive confrontation between the two protagonists [the colonizer and the colonized].
>
> […]
>
> As soon as they are born it is obvious to them that their cramped world, riddled with taboos, can only be challenged by out and out violence.
>
> […]

> In the period of decolonization the colonized masses thumb their noses at these very [white] values, shower them with insults and vomit them up.
>
> [...]
>
> [During the period of decolonization] the colonist never ceases to be the enemy, the antagonist, in plain words public enemy number 1.[19]

Jean-Paul Sartre's preface to Fanon's book betrayed, even in the moment of its appearance, just how readily the advocates for European self-critique would preempt even the most radical figures of the anti-colonial countermission.[20] If one accepts Sartre's 1961 political feuilleton at face value, one notes a sharp nuance. The French philosopher suggested an analogy between the African revolt against the colonizers and the abolition of the nobility in the French Revolution – the one apparently as legitimate as the other in his view. The irregular assassination of French colonial administrators, whether in French West Africa or elsewhere in the world, would, therefore, from the perspective of revolutionary theory, be *mutatis mutandis* equivalent to the execution of Louis XVI, which was discussed, decided upon, and carried out in January 1793 in the course of the Jacobin intensification. Whether with or without a trial, the act of violence demanded from the colonized would be tantamount to a necessary murder – indeed a holy murder. Two reciprocal liberations would follow from it: from one side, a collective could take shape, composed of subjects who leave their oppression behind as they become conscious of their equality and sovereignty through the bloody violence they inflict upon their foreign masters; from the other side, citizens of the former colonial power can breathe again because they finally grasp that they need no longer subjugate others for their own existence and state of being.

An objection to the Fanonian program of armed revolt and its exaltation in Sartre's dialectical fantasies suggests itself all the same. For those on the side of the new "nations" to be liberated – and for the author, the term "nation" is bound together with a wealth of revolutionary hopes – if they had concerned themselves with the history of the French Revolution in detail and without being led astray by its violence-prone communist vulgate, they would have been forced to draw somewhat different lessons from its history than the usual ones. The lesson of the French people for their political contemporaries and for posterity – for those willing to learn it – would reveal something vexing about the course of revolutions of this type. The radical upheaval conceived by the Jacobins remained not only incomplete in practice, it was inherently and intrinsically impossible to complete. Four relapses into monarchy in the nineteenth century (Napoleon I, the Bourbon Restoration, the bourgeois monarchy of Louis-Philippe I, Napoleon III) and two semi-monarchical relapses in the twentieth century (de Gaulle, Mitterrand) should have shown that it was not unreasonable to express doubts about the world-historical exemplarity of the Great Days of 1789 to 1794 in world history.[21]

The essential lesson to be learned concerned the deployment of lethal force, which radical circles so readily believed would be the midwife of progress and the wetnurse of liberation. Revolutionary terror, whose salubriousness and necessity the Jacobin activists did not doubt – some considered themselves Martyrs of the Good who took upon themselves the use of evil means – was evidently discharged only in small part against members of the nobility, whose complicity in traditional abuses – along with the glamorously absurd theater of Versailles – could not justly be waved away. The main thrust of the terror, it turns out, was directed against rivals for supremacy in the struggle to overcome the existing order and establish the order to come – as well as against a myriad of marginal figures who aroused suspicion through their lack of enthusiasm. Even during the dress rehearsal for political modernity, it was comparatively rare to find killing in the service of a better future visited upon the defenders of the old order. It was mainly the moderates and the less eccentric who fell by the wayside amid the intensifying revolutionary urgency. Nine-tenths of the victims of the Terror were not staunch royalists or incorrigible apologists for outmoded conditions; they fell victim to the frictions that are inevitably generated with the acceleration of revolutionary conduct. The difference in political tempos became apparent only in the course of the race. Thus was revealed the paradox of prevailing in contests of this kind: those who rushed most resolutely ahead were sooner or later exposed as having gone too far. Wild, unruly group dynamics – together with hypnoidal groupthink – formed the typical traits of the turbulence that conferred upon the great upheavals of modern times their tendency to overheat.[22]

What had been apparent in the "mother revolution" in France pertained all the more intensely for the "daughter revolution" in Russia.[23] If we survey the tableau of violence-suffused events from a greater height – from a sphere befitting the owl of Minerva – a noteworthy fact pattern becomes evident: the greater part of the revolutionary effacements during the Great Days of the French nation were clearly attributable to rivalries between political sects and denunciations from obscure sources – as if it had to be proven that in times of high ideological excitement, yesterday's good neighbors and even comrades-in-arms could no longer be relied upon. In states where Jacobin ideologies were in power, denunciation remained an everyday reality, even after the peak of excitement had abated, as evidenced by conditions in the Soviet Union, East Germany, and other regimes where those in power succeeded in taking their populations hostage and training them to become informers. The historical analogy is a consequence of the nature of the matter, insofar as the Russian Revolution was conceived as an adventure mimetically oriented toward the French model: far and away the largest part of the terror, as logically justified by Lenin in September 1918,[24] as implemented by Trotsky in the war against the White Army from 1918 to 1922, and as taken to extremes by Stalin from 1936 onward, was also attributable to divisions among supporters of the cataclysmal movements on Russian soil – expressing, in this respect, its affinity with the course of events in France after 1789.

This makes it all the more surprising that Fanon, analyst of the complex psychodynamic relationships between white masters and black inferiors, managed to take such scant notice of the foreseeable complications of the unleashed violence for which he supplied the slogans. Shouldn't he, of all people, have known that there is no moment more dangerous than when the wretched of this earth awaken? Wouldn't they, too, be much more likely to abuse and maltreat each other than to turn on their colonial masters? Or, to shift to the level of general revolutionary theory: wouldn't they, too, give the lie to Marx's suggestion that in the "final fray" there would only be a single sharply drawn front line: that between capital and the proletariat? Would they not bring before the eyes of the world just how deadly and delusional it is to claim that, even at the end of the colonial drama, there would still be only the one clear front – one where the colonizers and the colonized face off against each other?[25] On this point, statistics are clearer than political theory: in the course of the intra-African conflicts that followed the withdrawal of the colonial powers after 1960, almost twice as many people perished as were deported to the Americas through the slave trade between 1519 and 1867 – according to more recent, more precise estimates, this figure is believed to be eleven million.

In this chapter devoted to dissenting voices, the last bookmark we place in the Book of Europe will, as announced, be placed in a document of lesser celebrity in our corner of the world – a short text, barely twelve pages in its original form, but consequential for political thought in South America; through its idiosyncratic logic, it escapes the familiar and frustrating dialectic of colonizing violence and revolutionary counter-violence. Hence, the discussion at last turns to the "Cannibalist Manifesto," published in São Paulo in 1928, by Oswald de Andrade (1890–1954),[26] a poet and essayist who remains one of the most noted voices of "peripheral surrealism," indeed of "peripheral literature" in general. In choosing the form of a manifesto, the author seized upon a procedure practiced by European avant-garde artists of the pre-First-World War era, which consisted of transferring the genre of the pamphlet or programmatic text from the sphere of partisan politics to the arena of art and cultural politics – as exemplified in the "Manifesto of Futurism" by Filippo Tommaso Marinetti, which appeared in the Paris daily morning newspaper *Le Figaro* on February 20, 1909. With the turn to anthropophagy, the Euro-critical impulse forsook the terrain typical for conflict literature, which tends to concern itself throughout with violence and counter-violence, strike and counterstrike, states of subjugation and rebellious strivings for sovereignty.

Oswald de Andrade's manifesto announces straightaway that it wants nothing to do with conventional figures of a "clash" – whether of classes, parties, or civilizations. Hence, its first sentence reads: "Cannibalism alone unites us."[27] This opening proposition is amplified in the proposition that follows:

> The world's single law. Disguised expression of all individualism, of all collectivisms. Of all religions. Of all peace treaties.[28]

How precisely Andrade had apprehended the rules of the modernist genre was apparent from the start with his use of stylistic tropes characteristic of the manifesto: exaggeration, abbreviation, sentence interruption, undetermined meaning.[29] His insight into the art of writing manifestos went beyond the use of formal devices, in that he adhered to the unspoken rule according to which a manifesto is good only insofar as it manages to surpass previous manifestos.

This claim announces itself in the third proposition of the "Cannibalist Manifesto":

> Tupi or not tupi, that is the question.[30]

What sounds at first like a mediocre play on words or a punning citation from Hamlet's monologue reveals itself, in lingering longer on the objectionable passage, to be an unexpected application of the anthropophagic scheme. To understand this, one must know that "Tupi" is the abbreviated name of a historical group of indigenous Brazilian peoples living on the Atlantic coast, the Tupinambá, whose mythos included its "cannibalistic" customs.[31] Their descendants were more or less lost from view in the centuries following the arrival of the Portuguese, even as vestiges of the Tupi language remained active. Andrade availed himself of the Shakespearean parody to signal that, for him and his people, it was not about the difference between being and non-being, i.e., between life in this world and life in a "hereafter." The choice was between belonging to the world of the Brazilian indigenous peoples or to the sphere of the Luso-European colonizers. In advocating for the indigenous, anthropophagic side, the author made it clear that, in his view, contemporary Brazilian culture could thrive only if it understood how to assert its archaic gestures against the overpowering influence of imported modernity. Even citing a classic Western text can turn out to be an anthropophagic act. Concomitantly, Andrade was aware at all times of how his own impulses were conditioned by imports. He intuited, however, that Brazil's self-affirmation no longer needed to take the form of symmetrical revolt, counterexports, or counterstrikes. As soon as opposition to the superior power of the Western colonizers takes place in "Tupi mode" – as cannibalizing the foreign master – the contest between that which is one's own and that which is foreign shifts to a literally internal level. For the anthropophagist, the scene of the struggle lies in the bowels. The fourth proposition makes this quite clear:

> I am only concerned with what is not mine. Law of Man. Law of the cannibal.[32]

Incorporation supersedes confrontation – where once there was polemic, there devourment shall come to be.

The fact that the incorporative contest with the external master does not remain without a claim to have surpassed the devoured other, at least not in the sphere of rhetorical gestures, becomes apparent in the eleventh proposition from Andrade's writing:

> We want the Carib Revolution. Greater than the French Revolution. The unification of all productive revolts for the progress of humanity. Without us, Europe wouldn't even have its meager declaration of the rights of man.
>
> The Golden Age heralded by America. The Golden Age. And all the *girls*.[33]

The word "America" here refers to the continent that today includes itself with the "Global South." At the same time, the anthropophagic act loses its barbaric quality in Andrade's exposition; in the Manifesto, it is exalted as an almost sacred act through which resistance transforms into appropriation:

> Absorption of the sacred enemy. To transform him into a totem. The human adventure. The earthly goal.[34]

Even so: only "the pure elites" would be capable of realizing the kind of anthropophagy "which carries within itself the highest meaning of life." Such lines hint at an anthropophagic utopia: only through the total devourment of humans by humans can the hyper-totem "humanity" emerge. Where genuine elites of devourment are at work, that all-around appropriative libido can be realized, expressing itself in a broad and high "thermometrical scale"; it can become friendship, love, science. What must be avoided are the baser excesses of the gluttonous drive: envy, usury, calumny, murder – in other words, all the sins that had spread worldwide as the "plague of a supposedly cultured [*cultos*] and Christianized peoples."[35] With a contemptuous gesture, their inventory is left to Dr. Freud in faraway Vienna. In any case, nothing good could be expected from the Portuguese conquistadores as Europeans.

> But those who came here weren't crusaders. They were fugitives from a civilization we are eating, because we are strong and vindictive like the Jabuti [a kind of tortoise admired by the indigenous peoples].[36]

Andrade does not cease in his effort to surpass the European revolutions – the French Revolution foremost among them – with the Carib Revolution[37]; he asserts a claim, through his doctrine of universal anthropophagy, to surpass the European traditions of eating God, as these were represented in the Christian Eucharist.[38] The clash of cultures shifts to a field that serves as the playground for a contest of incorporations. Andrade was convinced that the Tupis, whether real or imaginary, had no need for either colonization or missionary work:

> We already had Communism. We already had Surrealist language. The Golden Age. [...] Before the Portuguese discovered Brazil, Brazil had discovered happiness.[39]

The anthropophagic act can be understood only as an amalgam of Eucharist and revolt. By consummating a synthesis of incorporation and effacement, lucid cannibals prepare a grave in their own bowels for the foreign, the imported, the imposed formality, and the articles of the catechism – naturally with the prospect of later excretion. Where this were to happen, it would amount to a successful immunization against the unacceptable. The process, taken as a whole, prompts the notion that the innards of the cannibal may be conceived as a waste treatment system in which the bad and unwelcome is excreted, while the good and useful is incorporated into what is one's own. This is precisely what is indicated in the proposition "Absorption of the sacred enemy. To transform him into a totem."

Beyond all doubt, Brazilian anthropophagy parodies Christian theophagy, whose meaning lay in the symbolic incorporation of the spiritual body of Christ. It should lead to the coalescence of the communicant with the received Eucharist and to the subtle indwelling of the ingested God in the receiving vessel; in this case, however, excretion could never be a factor. Christians, as discreet theophagists, may indeed become unfaithful to their totem, the crucified and risen God; they may deny his teachings or turn to other idols – but on no account would the question of what becomes of their incorporated God after passing through them ever arise for them; they are content with the notion that the host will transform those who receive it into the likeness of Christ. After the anthropophagous act, however, the question imposes itself as to what will become of what has been devoured. One eats the other at one's own risk – and with a price imposed by a digestive system that does not know how to dissolve without leaving behind some trace.

Unless some detail has escaped all notice, Oswald de Andrade remained delinquent in resolving inquiries about the fate of those devoured and located still in the cannibalistic interior. What's more, he had to remain delinquent in this respect because further execution of his great project would have led to inevitably paradoxical consequences. As soon as one tries to think through the anthropophagic event, a cascade of bizarre and obscene images will emerge: critical surrealism merges into intestinal cabaret, while Caribbean resistance transforms into an absurd theater of digestion. And one must be prepared for the fact that not every devourment accomplishes a complete metamorphosis of the devoured in the rebellious bowels of an indigenous people.

Andrade's bold designs open upon something that can hardly be called anything other than the rediscovery of indigestibility. From there they come to a renewed distinction between body and spirit, whereby the spirits of the devoured awaken to a bizarre afterlife in the bodies of the anthropophagists. The indigestible elements of the consumed colonial agents, the elements that cannot be broken down by indigenous intestinal processes, remain alive and ghostly in their new vessels, as it were; they begin to speak from the mouths of those participating in the cannibalistic communions. This may explain the frequently observed effect that, across all regions that have expelled their exploitative old masters, the same voices seem to continue to speak, albeit now from indigenous sources that speak on their own behalfs. The doctrines of Western universalism prove to be non-biodegradable figures, like swallowed diamonds.

They could indeed be recontextualized ideologically and politically, but they retain their truth value and their assertive energy even when, in a hostile incorporation, they are inserted into the self-statements of speakers antagonistic to Europe and North America.

A coherent unfolding of hints and signals from the "Cannibalist Manifesto" gives rise to observations of some irony. The post-colonial strategy of cheeky incorporation (diametrically opposed to the neurosis, described by Fanon, of the slave identifying with the master) was practiced on a broad front, whether consciously taken up or else internalized through emulation. It led to the emergence of a ventriloquistic ecumenism. Countless voices speaking out against the West, and more recently against the Global North, echo the ineliminable Western doctrines held by Europeans. They, for their part, are compelled to admit the recognizable features of reason in the other's plea.[40]

A good part of what has been circulating recently at Western universities and progressive cultural institutions all around the world under the heading of "postcolonial studies" is discourse with a ventriloquistic quality. It constitutes the latest metastasis of the spirit of European self-critique, preformed by the culture of religious confession, but now transformed into external self-critique in a ventriloquistic mode.[41] No doubt it will take a while before those concerned perceive that what they consider postcolonial thinking still represents an indirect European soliloquy – only projected outward through anthropophagic alienation, reintroduced as an external voice, and made to serve the desire for moral self-critique. The *Persian Letters* have been replaced by Indonesian, South African, and Caribbean dispatches, mostly written in English, French, or Spanish. The era of counterexport has likewise begun at the level of philosophical discourse – sometimes it barely bothers to conceal its parodic punchline. A *Critique of Black Reason* is now available to take the place of the *Critique of Practical Reason*.[42]

As his publication nears its centennial, what Oswald de Andrade's foray reveals is an elevation of the principle of incorporation to a feature of universal parody. Under his banner, a phony world war unfolds before our eyes. It remains to be seen how the Old World will assert itself in this struggle. Most Europeans are like the Phaiakians of the planet, still indulging in their post-historical predilections; it is uncertain whether they will find solace in the insight that one cannot fight Europe without citing it, and can hardly cite it without stumbling into the broad field of parody. A hundred years ago, a *bon mot* circulated in Italy: "Times are tough, but they are modern." Another word might be characteristic of the times to come: the world will be full of parodies, or it will not be.

Acknowledgments

The pieces published here largely correspond to the German-language drafts of lectures that I had the honor and pleasure of giving in French, between April 4 and June 17, 2024, at the Collège de France in Paris, where I held the Annual Chair of L'Invention de l'Europe par les langues et les cultures. My special thanks go to Olivier Mannoni, who once again brilliantly rendered my work in French – this time, moreover, under the pressure of a tight schedule. Special thanks go to the faculty of the Collège de France, in particular its administrator Thomas Römer, as well as William Marx and Philippe Descola, who gave the newcomer a friendly welcome on the occasion of his inaugural speech in April. I would also like to express heartfelt thanks to my colleagues who participated as respondents in colloquia that followed the lectures: Karlheinz Stierle (Professor Emeritus at the University of Konstanz), Johann Chapoutot (Sorbonne University), Rémi Brague (Professor Emeritus at the Paris 1 Panthéon-Sorbonne University), Gilles Kepel (Sciences Po) and Robert P. Harrison (Stanford University). I would also like to thank the project manager at the Collège de France, Mme Marina de Castro Cartier, who managed the administrative aspects of the annual chair with a steady hand, as well as the audio-visual staff, who, with unfailing friendliness, ensured the technical success of the lectures, seminars, and recordings. Finally, a grateful greeting goes out to the always ample audiences gathered at the Salle Marguérite de Navarre, who, Monday after Monday, enlivened the enterprise with their alert presence and stimulating attention.

Readers of the pieces here should be aware that they are dealing throughout with revised extended versions of original German texts. In their actual presentations in French, the individual papers were shortened, in consideration of the time requirement of 55 minutes for a *lectio magistralis*, though audiences were alerted to the availability of complete versions on the Collège de France website.

Notes

Epigraph

1 Johann Wolfgang von Goethe, *Faust, Part II*, Act 3 [8971–3].

First inaugural address

1 Homer, *The Odyssey*, trans. Richmond Lattimore. New York: Harper Perennial, 2007, p. 146 [IX.366–367].

2 With the case of Odysseus in mind, one might just as well depict the history of thought among the Greeks as making a transition from *metis* (or *mechané*) to *logos*, as from fairy tale (*mythos*) to rational argument. *Polytropos, polymetis, polymechanos* (the one who has seen it all, the one who is full of tricks, the man of many ideas) – these are some common epithets for the ancient hero. Cf. Harro von Senger, *The Book of Stratagems: Tactics for Triumph and Survival*, ed. and trans. Myron B. Gubitz. New York: Viking, 1991.

3 "Beyond Human Rights," in Giorgio Agamben, *Means without End: Notes on Politics*, trans. Vincenzo Binetti and Cesare Casarino. Minneapolis: University of Minnesota Press, 2000, pp. 15–28.

4 His reflections are based on Hannah Arendt's remarks on the Jewish question, in which Arendt treated the Jews as paradigmatic strangers in the midst of European societies.

5 Susan Sontag, "What's Happening in America," *Essays of the 1960s & 70s*, ed. David Rieff. New York: Library of America, 2013, pp. 452–461.

6 Michel Winock, *Décadence: Fin de siècle*. Paris: Gallimard, 2017. See also Mario Praz, *The Romantic Agony*, trans. Angus Davidson. London: Oxford University Press, 1978.

7 "La France se meurt. Jeune homme, ne troublez pas son agonie!"

8 Douglas Murray's book on the subject begins: "Europe is committing suicide …" Douglas Murray, *The Strange Death of Europe: Immigration, Identity, Islam*. London: Bloomsbury, 2017.

9 Edmund Burke, *Reflections on the Revolution in France*. Buffalo, NY: Prometheus Books, 1987, p. 80.

10 Friedrich Nietzsche, *The Gay Science*, trans. Josefine Nauckhoff. Cambridge: Cambridge University Press, 2001, p. 205 [§347].
11 *Twilight of the Idols or, How One Philosophizes with a Hammer*, in Friedrich Nietzsche, *The Portable Nietzsche*, ed. and trans. Walter Kaufmann. New York: Penguin Books, 1982, p. 468 [Maxims and Arrows §12].
12 *Beyond Good and Evil: Prelude to a Philosophy of the Future*, in Friedrich Nietzsche, *Basic Writings of Nietzsche*, trans. and ed. Walter Kaufmann. New York: The Modern Library, 1968, pp. 301–302 [§200]. [See also: "the hybrid European" p. 340 §223.]
13 In his autobiographical work *Ecce Homo* from 1888, Nietzsche portrayed himself as a decadent, the migraine sufferer, who nevertheless did not want to lose his taste for war and attack.
14 Friedrich Nietzsche, *Daybreak: Thoughts on the Prejudices of Morality*, ed. Maudemarie Clark and Brian Leiter, trans. R.J. Hollingdale. Cambridge: Cambridge University Press, 1997, p. 179 [§176].
15 Jacques Derrida, *The Other Heading: Reflections on Today's Europe*, trans. Pascale-Anne Brault and Michael B. Naas. Bloomington: Indiana University Press, 1992.
16 In 1960, eighteen former colonies became politically independent, including fourteen former French colonies, two British colonies, one Belgian, and one Italian colony.
17 Francis Fukuyama, *The End of History and the Last Man*. New York: Free Press, 2006.
18 With the Treaty of Madrid in 1750, some areas where there had been Indian resettlements (*reducciones de indios*) by Spanish missionaries came under Portuguese rule – with the result that Brazilian gold prospectors and slave hunters (*bandeirantes*) expanded their zones of activity into previously protected areas.
19 Tzvetan Todorov, *The New World Disorder: Reflections of a European*, trans. Andrew Brown. Cambridge: Polity, 2005.
20 Jacques Derrida, *The Other Heading: Reflections on Today's Europe*, pp. 7–8.
21 Fyodor Dostoyevsky, *Notes from Underground*, trans. Richard Pevear and Larissa Volokhonsky. New York: Vintage Books, 1994, p. 29.
22 James Joyce, *Ulysses*, The Corrected Text, ed. Hans Walter Gabler. New York: Vintage Books, 1986, p. 28.

Second inaugural address

1 "The Book of Sand," in Jorge Luis Borges, *The Book of Sand*, trans. Norman Thomas Di Giovanni. New York: E. P. Dutton, 1977, p. 119.
2 *The Birth of Tragedy* in Friedrich Nietzsche, *Basic Writings of Nietzsche*, p. 98 [§15]. On the tremendous struggle of the gods in Greek theater: "Alas, it is the magic of these struggles that those who behold them must also take part and fight."
3 Virgil, *The Aeneid*, trans. Robert Fitzgerald. New York: Vintage Books, 1985, p. 190 [VI.1151–1154]. *Tu regere imperio populos, Romane, memento / haec tibi sunt artes, pacique imponere morem, parcere subiectis et debellare superbos.* "Roman, remember, by your strength to rule Earth's peoples – for your arts are to be these: To pacify, to impose the rule of law, To spare the conquered, battle down the proud." In a classic "prophecy after the event," Aeneas is addressed in advance as a Roman, though the founding of the city is then still in the distant future. After landing on Italian soil, Aeneas takes control of the city of Lavinium; his son Ascanius founds the city of Alba Longa (on Lake Albano) around 1152 BCE. Rome itself dates its founding to 753 BCE.
4 *The City of God*, by Augustine of Hippo, was completed in 426 CE.

5 Howard W. French, *Born in Blackness: Africa, Africans, and the Making of the Modern World, 1471 to the Second World War*. New York: Liveright Publishing, 2021.
6 The work of British historian Robert Bartlett illustrates the violence that marked the development of the early kingships on European soil, from which the later nation states emerged. See: Robert Bartlett, *The Making of Europe: Conquest, Colonization and Cultural Change, 950–1350*. Princeton, NJ: Princeton University Press, 1993.
7 Ernst Robert Curtius, *European Literature and the Latin Middle Ages*, trans. Willard R. Trask. Princeton: Princeton University Press, 2013. For commentary critical of the concept of the "Middle Ages," see: Bernhard Jussen, *Das Geschenk des Orest: Eine Geschichte des nachrömischen Europa, 526–1535*. Munich: C.H. Beck, 2023.
8 Franz Overbeck, *Werke und Nachlaß, Band 6.1: Kirchenlexicon: Materialien: "Christentum und Kultur,"* ed. Barbara von Reibnitz. Stuttgart: J.B. Metzler, 1996, p. 246.
9 The way in which the papacy itself attained revolutionary intensity from the eleventh century onwards will become clear when, in the next chapter, we bookmark the long sequence of "European revolutions," after the suggestion of Eugen Rosenstock-Huessy.
10 Two generations after the Battle of Lechfeld, Hungary gained its first Christian king in Stephen I of Hungary (1000–1038), who was canonized in 1083.
11 Otto II ascended the throne in 973 and died in Rome in 983 at the age of 28.
12 Eugen Rosenstock-Huessy, *Out of Revolution: Autobiography of Western Man*. Eugene: Wipf and Stock, 2013, p. 504.
13 Ibid., p. 548.
14 Ernst H. Kantorowicz, *The King's Two Bodies: A Study in Medieval Political Theology*. Princeton: Princeton University Press, 2016, p. 204.
15 Claudio Magris, *Danube: A Sentimental Journey from the Source to the Black Sea*, trans. Patrick Creagh. New York: Farrar, Straus and Giroux, 2008.
16 Fernand Braudel, *The Mediterranean and the Mediterranean World in the Age of Philip II, Volumes I & II*, trans. Siân Reynolds. Berkeley: University of California Press, 1995.
17 Alexander Randa, *Das Weltreich: Wagnis und Auftrag Europas im 16 und 17 Jahrhundert*. Freiburg: Walter Verlag, 1962.
18 The first national language grammar in Europe was the result of Spanish language policy: Antonio de Nebrija's *Grammar of the Castilian Language* was published in 1492. Europe owes the phenomenon of national bankruptcy to Spanish fiscal and monetary policy; it was declared three times in the sixteenth century alone: in 1557, 1575, and 1596.
19 The idea of the Fifth Empire renders superfluous the figure of the *katechon* – the "restrainer of the End" – that fiction from the fund of historical theology that Carl Schmitt abused for his improvised over-interpretation of the "Third Reich."
20 George L. Mosse, *The Nationalization of the Masses: Political Symbolism and Mass Movements in Germany from the Napoleonic Wars through the Third Reich*. Madison: University of Wisconsin Press, 2023.
21 The new Balkan states and those of the North were exceptions, insofar as their nationalisms remained predominantly self-centered and without major empire-building ambitions – provided one leaves aside pan-Serbian impulses as a curiosity of political pathology in the Balkans (as condensed, for example, in Serbian neuroses with regard to the Kosovo Plain).
22 "Yet Mussolini is a Roman emperor in every respect except the name." Eugen Rosenstock-Huessy, *Out of Revolution: Autobiography of Western Man*, p. 623.
23 Johann Chapoutot, *Greeks, Romans, Germans: How the Nazis Usurped Europe's Classical*

Past, trans. Richard R. Nybakken. Berkeley: University of California Press, 2016. The case of Carl Schmitt demonstrates that racial ideology was not the only means for a falsification of antiquity: for Schmitt, Rome meant exclusively the Caesarean Empire – as if there had never been a republican Rome to inspire the French Revolution; even, as the seat of the Pope, Rome was only congenial to the apologists of dictatorship insofar as they conceived of the Pope as the actual Caesar – in this sense, Schmitt was akin to the Catholicizing atheist Charles Maurras. See also: Richard Faber, *Lateinischer Faschismus: Über Carl Schmitt, den Römer und Katholiken*. Hamburg 2021 [2001]. Apart from that, it might be observed that ideologists of the Soviet system too were no strangers to racist speculation; under Stalin's auspices, quite a few academics strove to prove that Slavs and Russians had played a role in all of humanity's pioneering achievements.

24 It should not be forgotten that Mehmed II, the Conqueror (1432–1481), having conquered Constantinople in May 1453, claimed the title of *kayser-i Rûm*, Caesar of Rome, as if the Sultan were asserting his own claim to succeed the Caesars.

25 For an explanation of the concept of decorum as well as the neuro-rhetorical principles of high style, see Heiner Mühlmann, *The Nature of Cultures: A Blueprint for a Theory of Culture Genetics*, trans. Robert Payne. Vienna/New York: Springer, 1996.

26 For the best exposition of the Western aspect, see Luuk van Middelaar, *The Passage to Europe: How a Continent Became a Union*, trans. Liz Waters. New Haven: Yale University Press, 2016; for the eastern aspect, see Martin Schulze Wessel, *Der Fluch des Imperiums: Die Ukraine, Polen und der Irrweg in der russischen Geschichte*. Munich: C. H. Beck, 2023. Jean-François Colosimo's study places Putin's actions within a broader horizon of neo-imperial movements, see Jean-François Colosimo, *Occident, ennemi mondial n°1*. Paris: Albin Michel, 2024; such movements are observable not only in Russia but also in China, Turkey, Iran, and India; in each case, an essential role is played by the instrumentalization of religion or nationalism as a means for mobilizing political power.

Lesson one

1 Harri Meier, *Die Entstehung der romanischen Sprachen und Nationen*. Frankfurt am Main: Vittorio Klostermann, 1941.

2 See chapter 2, "Die Akademie: Ein Geschenk Griechenlands an das künftige Europa," in Karlheinz Stierle, *Das lebendige Wort: Begegnungen mit der Antike*. Baden-Baden: Rombach Wissenschaft, 2020, pp. 35–48.

3 Ernst Robert Curtius, *European Literature and the Latin Middle Ages*, trans. Willard R. Trask. Princeton: Princeton University Press, 2013, pp. 36–61.

4 John Amos Comenius, *The Way of Light*, trans. E.T. Campagnac. Liverpool: Liverpool University Press, 1938 [the rarity of Campagnac's Comenius translation has necessitated a new translation of this passage from Sloterdijk's German – trans.] See also Peter Sloterdijk, *You Must Change Your Life: On Anthropotechnics*, trans. Wieland Hoban. Cambridge: Polity, 2013, pp. 350–357.

5 William Shakespeare, *As You Like It*, Act II, scene 7.

6 Jacob Burckhardt, *The Culture of the Renaissance in Italy*, trans. S.G.C. Middlemore. Harmondsworth: Penguin Books, 1990, pp. 104–110.

7 Karlheinz Stierle, *Francesco Petrarca: Ein Intellektueller im Europa des 14. Jahrhunderts*. München: Hanser, 2003.

8 Robert K. Merton, "The Matthew Effect in Science: The Reward and Communication

Systems of Science are Considered, *Science*, 159/3810 (January 5, 1968): 56–63. DOI: 10.1126/science.159.3810.56.

9 Gospel of Matthew 25:29–30 (NRSVUE). The "wicked and lazy slave" is the one who took the wealth entrusted to him and hid it in the ground instead of increasing it "with interest." Moreover, it should be clear that the parable of the talents is not about monetary value, but rather about shares in the kingdom of God, which increase through the intensity of faith. In the psychoeconomics of old Europe, "faith" emerges as a paradigm of activities oriented toward self-enhancement.

10 John Amos Comenius, *The Way of Light*, trans. E.T. Campagnac. Liverpool: Liverpool University Press, 1938 [as before, the passage is newly translated here from Sloterdijk's German].

11 Barbara W. Tuchman, *A Distant Mirror: The Calamitous 14th Century*. New York: Random House, 1978.

12 Tidiane N'Diaye, *Le Génocide voile: Enquête historique*. Paris: Gallimard, 2008. Manfred Pittioni (ed.), *Die Muslimische Sklaverei: Das "vergessene" Verbrechen*. Berlin: Lit Verlag, 2019.

13 Jürgen Beetz, *Feedback: Wie Rückkopplung unser Leben bestimmt und Natur, Technik, Gesellschaft und Wirtschaft beherrscht*. Berlin: Springer Spektrum, 2021.

14 Werner Stegmaier, *Orientierung im Nihilismus – Luhmann meets Nietzsche*. Berlin/Boston: De Gruyter, 2016.

15 Karl Marx, *Capital: A Critique of Political Economy*, ed. Frederick Engels, trans. Samuel Moore and Edward Aveling. New York: The Modern Library, 1906, p. 172: "Value, therefore, being the active factor [...], requires some independent form [...] And this form it possesses only in the shape of money." See also Falk Wagner, *Geld oder Gott: Zur Geldbestimmtheit der kulturellen und religiösen Lebenswelt*. Göttingen: Vandenhoeck & Ruprecht, 2019 [1984], a theological critique of monetary pantheism that raises the question of the "real" subject to a higher level.

16 Cf. "Everything that would exist in stasis and everything of the order of social standing evaporates." [For the original context and the classic, nineteenth-century rendering of the line as "All that is solid melts into air [...]," see Karl Marx and Friedrich Engels, *The Communist Manifesto*, trans. Samuel Moore. London: Penguin Books, 2002, p. 223.]

17 Peter Burke, *A Social History of Knowledge, Volume II: From the Encyclopédie to Wikipedia*. Cambridge: Polity, 2012.

18 Since the days of Peter the Great, timber exports had been one of the main sources of revenue for the Russian state; a large part of the British shipbuilding industry in the eighteenth century was dependent on timber imports from Russia.

19 Pierre Charbonnier, *Affluence and Freedom: An Environmental History of Political Ideas*, trans. Andrew Brown. Cambridge: Polity, 2021, pp. 80–85. Dread-filled visions of the end of coal are present even in Max Weber's work, as when, in the final section of his treatise on Protestantism, he prophesies that individuals will remain confined to the iron cage of the modern economic order "until the last ton of fossilized coal is burnt." See Max Weber, *The Protestant Ethic and the Spirit of Capitalism*, trans. Talcott Parsons. New York: Charles Scribner's Sons, 1950, p. 181.

20 See also "A Conquest by Method," in Paul Valéry, *History and Politics*, trans. Denise Folliot and Jackson Mathews. New York: Bollingen Foundation, 1962, pp. 46–66.

21 The ships of the White Star Line, which owned the Titanic (sunk in 1912) and its sister ship the Olympic (in service until its scrapping in 1935), had engines with an output of over 51,000 HP and burned up to 640 tons of coal per day.

22 Rolf Peter Sieferle, *The Subterranean Forest: Energy Systems and the Industrial Revolution*, trans. Michael Osmann. Cambridge: The White Horse Press, 2001. Sieferle's observation that fossil energy reserves originated from dead forests should be supplemented with the further note that a good part also originated from marine organisms – and algae in particular.
23 And a second time, thanks to the production of charcoal.
24 Immanuel Kant, *Anthropology from a Pragmatic Point of View*, trans. and ed. Robert Louden. Cambridge: Cambridge University Press, 2006, p. 194 n15. See also pp. 142–143 (§71).
25 Cicero, *On the Orator: Books 1–2*, trans., E.W. Sutton and H. Rackham. Cambridge: Harvard University Press, 1948, pp. 224–225 [Book II, IX.36].
26 See "Historia Magistra Vitae: The Dissolution of the Topos into the Perspective of a Modernized Historical Process," in Reinhart Koselleck, *Futures Past: On the Semantics of Historical Time*, trans. Keith Tribe. New York: Columbia University Press, 2004, pp. 26–42.
27 Manfred Riedel, *Nietzsches Lenzerheide-Fragment über den europäischen Nihilismus: Entstehungsgeschichte und Wirkung*. Zollikon/Zürich: Kranich Verlag, 2000.
28 For an expanded concept of religious freedom, see Peter Sloterdijk, *Making the Heavens Speak: Religion as Poetry*, trans. Robert Hughes. Cambridge: Polity, 2023, pp. 225–234.
29 Christoph Möllers, *Freiheitsgrade: Elemente einer liberalen politischen Mechanik*. Berlin: Suhrkamp Verlag, 2020, p. 17.

Lesson two

1 Eugen Rosenstock-Huessy, *Out of Revolution: Autobiography of Western Man*.
2 See the Author's Preface to the First Edition in Karl Marx, *Capital: A Critique of Political Economy*, ed. Frederick Engels, trans. Samuel Moore and Edward Aveling. New York: The Modern Library, 1906, p. 13.
3 Cf. Giovanni Boccaccio, *Famous Women*, ed. and trans. Virginia Brown. Cambridge: Harvard University Press, 2001.
4 Karl A.E. Enenkel, *Die Erfindung des Menschen: Die Autobiographik des frühneuzeitlichen Humanismus von Petrarca bis Lipsius*. Berlin/New York: De Gruyter, 2008.
5 Wilhelm Dilthey, *Gesammelte Schriften, Band VII: Der Aufbau der geschichtlichen Welt in den Geisteswissenschaften*, ed. Bernhard Groethuysen. Göttingen: Vandenhoeck & Ruprecht, 1992. See also: Wilhelm Dilthey, *Texte zur Kritik der historischen Vernunft*, ed. Hans-Ulrich Lessing. Göttingen: Vandenhoeck & Ruprecht, 1983.
6 Hans-Georg Gadamer, *Truth and Method*, 2nd, revd. edn., trans. Joel Weinsheimer and Donald G. Marshall. London: Continuum, 2004, p. 217.
7 Aurelius Augustinus, *Confessions II*, trans. William Watts. Cambridge: Harvard University Press, 1988, pp. 46–53 [Book IX, chapter 10].
8 Karl Barth, *The Epistle to the Romans: Sixth Edition*, trans. Edwyn C. Hoskyns. Oxford: Oxford University Press, 1968.
9 Hugo Ball, *Byzantinisches Christentum: Drei Heiligenleben*. Munich: Duncker & Humblot, 1923; Hugo Ball, *Flight Out of Time: A Dada Diary*, ed. John Elderfield, trans. Ann Raimes. Berkeley: University of California Press, 1974.
10 Ernst Bloch, *The Spirit of Utopia*, trans. Anthony A. Nassar. Stanford: Stanford University Press, 2000.
11 "The Crisis of the Mind" in Paul Valéry, *An Anthology*, ed. James R. Lawler. Princeton: Princeton University Press, 1977, p. 94.

12 Adolf Hitler, *Mein Kampf*, trans. Ralph Manheim. Boston: Houghton Mifflin Company, 1999, p. 206.
13 Hermann Broch, *The Sleepwalkers*, trans. Willa and Edwin Muir. San Francisco: North Point Press, 1985, p. 545.
14 See "'The New Thinking': A Few Supplementary Remarks to *The Star* [*of Redemption*]" in Franz Rosenzweig, *The New Thinking*, ed. and trans. Alan Udoff and Barbara E. Galli. Syracuse University Press, 1999, pp. 67–102.
15 In Antonio Scurati's *M: Son of the Century*, the novelist shows how greatly Mussolini's founding of the Fasci movement benefited from the frustrations of war veterans who, although formally among the victors, felt that the terms of the Treaty of Versailles cheated them of the reward they were due for the sacrifices they'd made. See: Antonio Scurati, *M: Son of the Century*, trans. Anne Milano Appel. New York: Harper, 2022.
16 Eugen Rosenstock-Huessy, *Die europäischen Revolutionen: Volkscharaktere und Staatenbildung*. Jena: Diederichs Verlag, 1931.
17 Eugen Rosenstock-Huessy, *Out of Revolution: Autobiography of Western Man*, p. 10.
18 Under the influence of Rosenstock-Huessy, Harold J. Berman wrote his classic work *Law and Revolution: The Formation of the Western Legal Tradition*. Cambridge: Harvard University Press, 1983. See in particular: "Part 1: The Papal Revolution and the Canon Law," pp. 47–270.
19 Michael Walzer, *The Revolution of the Saints: A Study in the Origins of Radical Politics*. Cambridge: Harvard University Press, 1982.
20 With the partial exception of France, which had been laicized since 1905 but was still traditionally Catholic.
21 Eugen Rosenstock-Huessy, *Out of Revolution: Autobiography of Western Man*, p. 709.
22 In 1920, he published a work entitled *Die Hochzeit des Krieges und der Revolution* [The Marriage of War and Revolution] with Patmos Verlag, a publishing house he co-founded.
23 Max Weber, *From Max Weber: Essays in Sociology*, ed. and trans. H.H. Gerth and C. Wright Mills. New York: Oxford University Press, 1946, p. 357.
24 Such regulations, which seem to have originated in the Auvergne region in the tenth century, have entered the history books under the term *Treuga Dei* ("Truce of God").
25 On this point, Rosenstock-Huessy shares a prejudice common to Europe's intelligentsia before 1917, tending to see Russia as the matrix of a quasi-archaic faith in search of possibilities for modernization. For more on this, see "Russia in Europe" in Friedrich Heer, *Europe: Mother of Revolutions*, trans. Charles Kessler and Jennetta Adcock. New York: Praeger Publishers, 1972, pp. 312–356. Heer sums up his thoughts on nineteenth-century Russian spirituality in the phrase: "The road to Pravda." Closely aligned here with Rosenstock-Huessy, he remains committed to a radically spiritual overinterpretation of events in Russia and China even in the early 1960s: he calls Trotsky "the Red Origen" (355) and, elsewhere, Mao a "Chinese Moses" (205). Heer also quotes the young Bakunin, who wrote to a Polish friend in 1848: "[...] now I seek God in the revolution" (345).
26 Rosenstock-Huessy was hardly the only one who subscribed to the doctrine of the productive anonymization or pseudonymization of Christian messages; so too did his friend Franz Rosenzweig (1886–1929), who wrote to Hans Ehrenberg (1883–1958) on April 19, 1927: "Just as social democracy, even when atheistic, is more important for the realization of the Kingdom of God through the Church than anything ecclesiastical, so is Zionism for the synagogue." See: Franz Rosenzweig, *Franz Rosenzweig, Briefe*, eds. Ernst Simon and Edith Rosenzweig. Berlin: Schocken, 1935, p. 580.

27 Described in Acts 2:4–13, with an emphasis on xenoglossic communion.
28 In *Meaning in History* (1949), Karl Löwith revealed the theological sources behind the Marxist historical philosophy inspired by Hegel – an unwelcome enlightenment in the view of the left-wing intelligentsia of those years, since it was perceived as an exposure of the unrecognized metaphysical premises of "progressive" practice. Rosenstock-Huessy, by contrast, had already laid his historical–theological cards on the table already in his writings of 1931 and 1938. See Karl Löwith, *Meaning in History*. Chicago: University of Chicago Press, 1949. Around 1940, midway between Rosenstock-Huessy and Löwith, Walter Benjamin attempted to endow the already derailed Russian Revolution with a hint of messianic legitimacy encrypted in his historiographical theses.
29 See Eugen Rosenstock-Huessy, *Planetary Service: A Way into the Third Millennium*. Jericho, VT: Argo Books, 2001.
30 Eugen Rosenstock-Huessy, *Out of Revolution: Autobiography of Western Man*, p. 524.
31 As the so-called Hossbach Memorandum attests, Hitler had outlined his war aims and attack plans already as early as November 5, 1937, when he did so for his military commanders and Foreign Minister von Neurath.
32 Eugen Rosenstock-Huessy, *Out of Revolution: Autobiography of Western Man*, p. 628.
33 Ibid., pp. 442–443.
34 He shares this problem with, among others, the French mediologist Régis Debray, who, in seeking to explain social synthesis through media and "communion," never manages to clarify how to distinguish between good and bad forms of mass enthusiasm. See Régis Debray, *Les Communions Humaines: Pour en finir avec la "religion."* Paris: Fayard, 2018.
35 Eugen Rosenstock-Huessy, *Out of Revolution: Autobiography of Western Man*, p. 708.
36 Eugen Rosenstock-Huessy, *Die europäischen Revolutionen: Volkscharaktere und Staatenbildung*, p. 75.
37 Eugen Rosenstock-Huessy, *Out of Revolution: Autobiography of Western Man*, p. 60.
38 Ibid., p. 50.
39 Hans Küng, *Christianity: The Religious Situation of Our Time*. London: SCM Press, 1995.
40 Friedrich Heer, *Europe: Mother of Revolutions*, trans. Charles Kessler and Jennetta Adcock. New York: Praeger Publishers, 1972, p. 726.
41 Joseph de Maistre, *The Pope; Considered in his Relations with the Church, Temporal Sovereignties, Separated Churches, and The Cause of Civilization*, trans. Aeneas M. Dawson. London: C. Dolman, 1850.
42 If this expression sounds less outlandish today than in the time of its first usage, this is primarily because Harold J. Berman popularized it – referring explicitly to Rosenstock-Huessy's pathbreaking interpretation of the papacy. See Harold J. Berman, *Law and Revolution: The Formation of the Western Legal Tradition*. Cambridge: Harvard University Press, 1983.
43 The term was coined in the 1750s by the Marquis Vincent de Gournay (1712–1759), who was under the influence of British ideas, notably those of David Hume and Josiah Tucker, and who served as an intendant of commerce for France from 1751 to 1758.
44 Eugen Rosenstock-Huessy, *Out of Revolution: Autobiography of Western Man*, p. 543.
45 With his deliberations on revolutionary theory, Rosenstock-Huessy anticipated the theses of the philosopher Bruno Karsenti on the role of pivotal classes (*les classes-pivot*) in progressive turns. See: Bruno Karsenti, *Nous autres Européens: Dialogue philosophique avec Bruno Latour*. Paris: Presses Universitaires de France, 2024, p. 97–110.

46 Among others: Pierre de Gaulle, the general's grandson, and Emmanuel Todd, the sociologist who, on account of his Germano- and Americanophobia, tends to make gloomy predictions about "the West" and to praise Putin's rational path toward "authoritarian democracy."

47 Eugen Rosenstock-Huessy, *Out of Revolution: Autobiography of Western Man*, p. 217.

48 Ibid., p. 449.

49 Rosenstock-Huessy remains to be discovered as a philosopher of language. His magnum opus is entitled *Die Sprache des Menschengeschlechts: Eine leibhaftige Grammatik in vier Teilen*, vols. 1 & 2. Heidelberg: Lambert Schneider, 1964. [Excerpted in Eugen Rosenstock-Huessy, *The Origin of Speech*. Norwich: Argo Books, 1981. – trans.]

Lesson three

1 Stefan Zweig, *The World of Yesterday: Memoirs of a European*, trans. Anthea Bell. London: Pushkin Press, 2024.

2 All quotations from Martin Heidegger, "What is Metaphysics?" trans. David Farrell Krell, in *Pathmarks*, ed. William McNeill. Cambridge: Cambridge University Press, 1998, pp. 82–96. [trans. modified.]

3 One might say that the whole of Europe was in night-flight mode in those years. "What use to turn his eyes toward the east, home of the sun? Between them lay a gulf of night so deep that he could never clamber up again." Antoine de Saint-Exupéry, *Night Flight*, trans. Stuart Gilbert. New York: Harcourt Brace Jovanovich, 1932, p. 57.

4 Anton Mirko Koktanek, *Oswald Spengler: Leben und Werk*. Beltheim-Schnellbach: Lindenbaum Verlag, 2020, p. 217.

5 As Walther Rathenau put it in his *Was wird werden?* Berlin: Fischer Verlag, 1920.

6 Theodor Lessing, *Geschichte als Sinngebung des Sinnlosen*. Munich: C.H. Beck, 1921.

7 [When the two volumes of the work are published separately, as with the English translation, the respective subtitles are *Vol. 1: Form and Actuality* and *Vol. 2: Perspectives of World-History*. – trans.]

8 Eugen Rosenstock-Huessy, *Out of Revolution: Autobiography of Western Man*. Eugene: Wipf & Stock, 1969, p. 698.

9 Martin Heidegger, *The Fundamental Concepts of Metaphysics: World, Finitude, Solitude*, trans. William McNeill and Nicholas Walker. Bloomington: Indiana University Press, 1995, pp. 11–105 [§§ 4–23].

10 Oswald Spengler, *The Decline of the West: Volume One: Form and Actuality*, trans. Charles Francis Atkinson. New York: Alfred A. Knopf, 1927, p. 3.

11 The second version of Ernst Bloch's *Spirit of Utopia*, which was later declared authoritative, appeared in Berlin in 1923.

12 Oswald Spengler, *The Decline of the West: Volume One: Form and Actuality*, pp. 420–421.

13 Immanuel Kant, *The Conflict of the Faculties; Der Streit der Fakultäten*, trans. Mary J. Gregor. Lincoln: University of Nebraska Press, 1992, pp. 141–143.

14 Ulrich Raulff and Peter Sloterdijk, "Schicksalfragen: Ein Roman vom Denken: Ulrich Raulff im Gespräch mit Peter Sloterdijk," *Marbacher Magazin: Schicksal: Sieben mal sieben unhintergehbare Dinge*, no. 135 (2011): 15–72.

15 Ulrich Sonnemann, *Negative Anthropologie: Vorstudien zur Sabotage des Schicksals*. Reinbek bei Hamburg: Rowohlt Verlag, 1969.

16 Dirk Jörke, *Die Größe der Demokratie: Über die räumliche Dimension von Herrschaft und Partizipation*. Berlin: Suhrkamp Verlag, 2019.

17 Oswald Spengler, *The Hour of Decision, Part One: Germany and World-Historical Evolution*, trans. Charles Francis Atkinson. London: George Allen and Unwin, 1934, p. 228.
18 Ibid., p. 230.
19 Oswald Spengler, *The Decline of the West: Volume One: Form and Actuality*, p. xiii.
20 Anton Mirko Koktanek, *Oswald Spengler: Leben und Werk*, pp. 141–142.
21 Ibid., p. 142.
22 "Spengler after the Decline," in Theodor W. Adorno, *Prisms*, trans. Samuel and Sherry Weber. Cambridge: The MIT Press, 1983, p. 54.
23 On feedback, see the discussion above in Lesson One, as well as Jürgen Beetz, *Feedback: Wie Rückkopplung unser Leben bestimmt und Natur, Technik, Gesellschaft und Wirtschaft beherrscht.* Berlin: Springer Spektrum, 2021.
24 Élie Halévy, *The Era of Tyrannies: Essays on Socialism and War*, trans. R.K. Webb. Garden City: Anchor Books, 1965, p. 279.
25 Franz Borkenau, *The Totalitarian Enemy*. London: Faber & Faber, 1940; Hannah Arendt, *The Origins of Totalitarianism: Expanded Edition*, eds. Jerome Kohn and Thomas Wild. New York: Library of America, 2025; Stéphane Courtois, *Lénine: L'Inventeur du totalitarisme.* Paris: Perrin, 2017.
26 Pierre-André Taguieff, *Les Théories du complot.* Paris: Que sais-je? 2021. The irony of "conspiracy theories" is that those who devise them claim that the machinations of secret actors are at work behind the "façade" of political reality; at the same time, they are regularly unable to perceive manifest power-wielding conspiracy systems – such as that of the Communist Party in the Soviet Union and its filiation in the Putinist-oligarchic-security-services complex.
27 Even at the beginning of the third millennium, sixty percent of Egypt's population of over 110 million is said to consist of *fellahin*, while in large cities, such as Cairo, a suburban fellah population with no ties to agriculture is growing and proving receptive to neo-Muslim agitation. See *Aufstieg und Fall der ägyptischen Muslimbruderschaft 2011–2013*, ed. Wolfram Reiss. Baden-Baden: Tectum Verlag, 2016.
28 Jacob Burckhardt, *Reflections on History*, trans. M.D.H. London: George Allen & Unwin Ltd, 1943, p. 215.
29 Linus Hauser, *Kritik der neomythischen Vernunft, Vol. 1: Menschen als Götter der Erde: 1800–1945*. Paderborn: Schöningh, 2005; *Vol. 2: Neomythen der beruhigten Endlichkeit: Die Zeit ab 1945*. Paderborn: Schöningh, 2009.

Lesson four

1 This is the title of a series of lectures given by Michel Foucault at the University of Toronto in June 1982 as part of his studies on subjectivity and truth. [See: Michel Foucault, *Speaking the Truth About Oneself*, ed. Henri-Paul Fruchaud, Daniele Lorenzini, and Daniel Louis Wyche. Chicago: University of Chicago Press, 2021. – trans.]
2 Oswald Spengler, *Ich beneide jeden, der lebt: Die Aufzeichnungen »Eis heauton« aus dem Nachlaß*. Düsseldorf: Lilienfeld Verlag, 2007, pp. 43; 46–48.
3 Oswald Spengler, *The Decline of the West: Volume Two: Perspectives of World-History*, trans. Charles Francis Atkinson. New York: Alfred A. Knopf, 1927, p. 292.
4 See the chapter "The Second Penance" in the late work by Michel Foucault, *Confessions of the Flesh: The History of Sexuality: Volume 4*, trans. Robert Hurley. New York: Vintage Books, 2022, pp. 58–78.

5 Oswald Spengler, *The Decline of the West: Volume Two: Perspectives of World-History*, p. 294.
6 Ibid., p. 295.
7 Jean Delumeau, *L'Aveu et le pardon: Les Difficultés de la confession, XIII–XVIII siècle*. Paris: Fayard, 1990, p. 7.
8 An example from the transition period from a reading community to an anthropologically interested public is to be found in the memoirs of the court chaplain Adam Bernd, *Eigene Lebens-Beschreibung*. Leipzig: Johann Samuel Heinsius, 1738 [reprint: Berlin: Hofenberg, 2013]. This testimony has entered the annals of psychopathography due to its explicit descriptions of compulsive ideas and nervous crises.
9 Charles Baudelaire, *Late Fragments: Flares, My Heart Laid Bare, Prose Poems, Belgium Disrobed*, trans. and ed. Richard Sieburth. New Haven: Yale University Press, 2022, p. 116 (§12).
10 Ibid., p. 111 (§3).
11 Ibid., pp. 124–125 (§33; §30).
12 Pablo Neruda, *Memoirs*, trans. Hardie St. Martin. Harmondsworth: Penguin, 1978, p. 100.
13 In 2016, a Chilean feminist posted a picture of Neruda accompanied by the caption: "I confess, I have raped" [a play on the Spanish (and German) title of Neruda's *Memoirs*: "I confess, I have lived" – trans.] Obviously, this was not done for the sole purpose of destroying the image of the national poet and replacing it with a female icon of Chilean literature. Beyond that, it was about overriding the purgative function of confession, through the mercilessness of the accusation, which, as is common in total moralism, turns into an execution.
14 Rainer Maria Rilke, *Werke Band 2: Gedichte und Übertragungen*. Frankfurt am Main: Insel Verlag, 2003, p. 92.
15 Heraclitus. Fragment B45, from John Burnet, *Early Greek Philosophy*. London: Adam & Charles Black, 1920, p. 138.
16 Pierre Bourdieu, "The Biographical Illusion," in *Identity: A Reader*, ed. Paul du Gay, Jessica Evans, and Peter Redman. London: Sage Publications, 2000, pp. 297–303.
17 Augustine, *Confessions I*, trans. William Watts. Cambridge: Harvard University Press, 1912, pp. 10–11 [Book I, chapter 5].
18 G.W.F. Hegel, *Lectures on the History of Philosophy, Vol. I*, trans. E.S. Haldane. London: Kegan Paul, Trench, Trübner & Co., 1892, pp. 149–150.
19 Aurelius Augustinus, *De vera religione; Über die wahre Religion*, ed. Wilhelm Thimme, Stuttgart: Reclam, 1983, pp. 39, 72.
20 From Psalm 69:2 (Psalm 68 in Greek numbering).
21 Augustine, *Confessions I*, pp. 164–165 [Book IV, chapter 6].
22 Ibid., pp. 38–41 [Book I, chapter 13].
23 Ibid., pp. 118–121 [Book III, chapter 6].
24 Jean-Marie Vaysse, *L'Inconscient des Modernes: Essai sur l'origine métaphysique de la psychanalyse*. Paris: Gallimard, 1999.
25 Paraphrase after J.G. Fichte's sonnet: "What gave my eye this power."
26 For an examination of the shift in the image of the eye of God, from the theological to the legal sphere, see Michael Stolleis, *The Eye of the Law: Two Essays on Legal History*. New York: Birkbeck Law Press, 2009.
27 Written sometime in the ten years preceding 1353.

28 Francesco Petrarch, *Petrarch's Secret, or, The Soul's Conflict with Passion: Three Dialogues Between Himself and S. Augustine*, trans. William H. Draper. London: Chatto & Windus, 1911, pp. 7–15.
29 Martin Heidegger, *Being and Time*, trans. Joan Stambaugh. Albany: State University of New York Press, 2010, pp. 221–255 [§§ 45–53].
30 Johann Wolfgang von Goethe, *Faust, Part II*, Act 5 [11581–4].
31 Nicolas Rétif de la Bretonne, *Monsieur Nicolas or, The Human Heart Laid Bare*, trans. Robert Baldick. New York: Clarkson N. Potter, 1967.
32 1811–1814 in Tübingen.
33 Polybius of Megalopolis (c. 200–118 BCE) described a cycle of constitutions that begins with monarchy and decomposes into tyranny; against this, aristocracy comes to power and then degenerates into oligarchy; to resist this, democracy arises, the degenerate form of which is mob rule (ochlocracy or mobocracy). This in turn is overcome by a new monarchy, whereupon a new cycle is set in motion.
34 This is the key statement from the conversation between Martin Heidegger, Rudolf Augstein, and Georg Wolff held in Freiburg on September 23, 1966, which was published a week after the philosopher's death on May 31, 1976, in an edition of *Der Spiegel* (23/1976) that was released early due to Pentecost.
35 The therapeutic effect of Husserl's recollection of the lifeworld promptly manifested itself in Maurice Merleau-Ponty's magnum opus: *Phenomenology of Perception*, 1945; it was comprehensively elaborated in the oeuvre of the founder of New Phenomenology, Hermann Schmitz (1928–2021), who deals very powerfully with corporeality, feelings, atmospheres, and "embedding situations."
36 *Thus Spoke Zarathustra: A Book for All and None: First Part*: On the Gift-Giving Virtue, §2, in Friedrich Nietzsche, *The Portable Nietzsche*, ed. and trans. Walter Kaufmann. Harmondsworth: Penguin Books, 1982, p. 189.

Lesson five

1 Hermann Schmitz, *Goethes Altersdenken im problemgeschichtlichen Zusammenhang*. Bonn: H. Bouvier, 1959.
2 "I must hold it for the greatest calamity of our time, which lets nothing come to maturity, that one moment is consumed by the next [...]. [...] and so it goes on from house to house, from city to city, from kingdom to kingdom, and at last from one hemisphere to the other, all velociferously." Johann Wolfgang von Goethe, *The Maxims and Reflections*, 2nd edn., trans. Thomas Bailey Saunders. London: MacMillan and Co., 1908, pp. 64–65 (§23). [trans. modified.]
3 Johann Wolfgang von Goethe, *Faust, Part II*, Act 5 [11173–11180, 11184–8].
4 On the transition of modern thought into categories of risk, see Peter Sloterdijk, *In the World Interior of Capital: Towards a Philosophical Theory of Globalization*, trans. Wieland Hoban. Cambridge: Polity, 2013, pp. 86–93.
5 Johann Wolfgang von Goethe, *Faust, Part II*, Act 5 [11273–4].
6 In much the same mood, Ishmael, narrator of Herman Melville's whaling novel *Moby-Dick*, confesses that he takes to the ship whenever he finds himself out of sorts with life on land.
7 Hannah Arendt, *The Origins of Totalitarianism: Expanded Edition*, eds. Jerome Kohn and Thomas Wild. New York: Library of America, 2025, pp. 281f.
8 Gunnar Heinsohn, *Söhne und Weltmacht: Terror im Aufstieg und Fall der Nationen*. Zürich: Piper, 2003, p. 26.

9 Oswald Spengler, *The Decline of the West: Volume One: Form and Actuality*, p. 37.
10 Bruno Latour, *Facing Gaia: Eight Lectures on the New Climatic Regime*, trans. Catherine Porter. Cambridge: Polity, 2017.
11 Christopher Columbus, *Book of Prophecies*, trans. Kay Brigham. Barcelona: Editorial Clie, 1991.
12 Not to be confounded with the "second religiousness" that, in Spengler's construction, occurs in the late stages of cultures that have exhausted themselves. Oswald Spengler, *The Decline of the West: Volume Two: Perspectives of World-History*, pp. 310–314.
13 His corpse, venerated as a relic, has been lying in the Basilica of Bom Jesus in Old Goa since 1554; his right arm, "weary from the baptizing of tens of thousands," was transferred in 1615 to the mother church of the Society of Jesus in Rome.
14 As rendered ("Zu-Jüngern-Machen") in later editions of the Luther Bible [in English: the NRSVUE translation given above.]
15 The title "The Manner of the Holy Court" is explained by the circumstance that the speaker had been appointed imperial court preacher by Leopold I in April 1677; the sermon is presumed to have been delivered at court before it appeared in print. It is reprinted in the volume: P. Abraham a St. Clara, *Geistlicher Kramer-Laden voller Apostolischer Waaren und Wahrheiten*. Lindau: Verlag Johann Thomas Stettner, 1867, pp. 261–287.
16 "He bellows with a strange voice."
17 Gospel of Matthew 10:20: "for it is not you who speak, but the Spirit of your Father speaking through you."
18 Michael Sievernich, *Die christliche Mission: Geschichte und Gegenwart*. Darmstadt: WBG, 2009.
19 At first, the term appeared mostly in the plural: *missiones*. Its locus classicus is found in the Fourth Vow of the Jesuits, following the solemn profession of the three traditional vows of poverty, chastity, and obedience: "... I further promise a special obedience to the sovereign pontiff in regard to the missions (*circa missiones*)."
20 Johannes Günter Gerhartz, "*Insuper promitto ...*": *Die feierlichen Sondergelübde katholischer Orden*. Rome: Verlagsbuchhandlung der Päpstlichen Universität Gregoriana, 1966.
21 Literally: "Act in such a way that you always treat humanity, whether in your own person or in the person of any other, never simply as a means, but always at the same time as an end." Immanuel Kant, *Groundwork of the Metaphysic of Morals*, trans. H.J. Paton. New York: Harper & Row, 1964, p. 96.
22 Lyric by Roger Waters.
23 Alexander von Humboldt, *Über die Freiheit des Menschen: Auf der Suche nach Wahrheit*, ed. Manfred Osten. Frankfurt am Main/Leipzig: Insel Verlag, 2017, p. 132. From pp. 151f., the author develops a comprehensive critique of the "arbitrary rule of monks," which primarily directed itself at conditions in Venezuela, but also touched upon the mission villages of Colombia and Peru.
24 The term (from Spanish *encomendar*, "to entrust") could be rendered by formulations such as "serfdom-based enterprises" and "commanderies."
25 Bartolomé de las Casas, *In Defense of the Indians*, trans. Stafford Poole. DeKalb: Northern Illinois University Press, 1974.
26 Alexander von Humboldt, *Über die Freiheit des Menschen: Auf der Suche nach Wahrheit*, ed. Manfred Osten. Frankfurt am Main/Leipzig: Insel Verlag, 2017, p. 121.

27 Boris Barth, Jürgen Osterhammel (eds.), *Zivilisierungsmissionen: Imperiale Weltverbesserung seit dem 18. Jahrhundert*. Konstanz: Universitätsverlag Konstanz, 2005.

28 Miscellaneous Observations §32, in Novalis, *Philosophical Writings*, ed. and trans. Margaret Mahony Stoljar. Albany: State University of New York Press, 1997, p. 28.

29 Marshall McLuhan, *Understanding Media: The Extensions of Man*. Cambridge: The MIT Press, 1994, pp. 7–21.

30 The unity of message and messenger is reflected in John in several parables with a participatory tendency; cf. John 15:5: "I am the vine; you are the branches. Those who abide in me and I in them bear much fruit, because apart from me you can do nothing." The branches are "one" with the vine in a mode of organic belonging.

31 An apt choice of term from an etymological perspective too: the Old French word "message" goes back to the Vulgar Latin *messaticum* (derived as a past participle from the classical verb *mittere*), which could equally mean "message" or "mission" as well as "envoy" or "messenger."

32 See the General Introduction (§3 The Method of Political Economy) to the *Grundrisse* in Karl Marx, *Selected Writings*, ed. David McLellan. Oxford: Oxford University Press, 1977, p. 355.

33 Carl Schmitt, *The* Nomos *of the Earth: in the International Law of the* Jus Publicum Europaeum, trans. G.L. Ulmen. New York: Telos Press Publishing, 2006, p. 132.

34 Manuel I of Portugal reigned from 1495 to 1521.

35 Luís Vaz de Camões, *The Lusíads*, trans. Landeg White. Oxford: Oxford University Press, 1997, pp 91–92 [Canto IV.71–75].

36 Cited from: Carl Amery, *Das Ende der Vorsehung: Die gnadenlosen Folgen des Christentums*. Reinbek: Rowohlt, 1974, p. 217.

37 It was only with the 1928 publication of the "Cannibalist Manifesto" by the Brazilian surrealist Oswald de Andrade that a reinterpretation of cannibalism began: it was no longer to be regarded as a manifestation of inhuman barbarism, but rather as a primal form of resistance against Eurocentrism and colonialism. See below, Lesson Seven: Get a-way, you old peoples: From the book of dissenting voices: Europe in the accusative.

Lesson six

1 Paul Zanker, *The Power of Images in the Age of Augustus*, trans. Alan Shapiro. Ann Arbor: University of Michigan Press, 1990.

2 It should be noted that until the start of the nineteenth century, globographic art mostly produced terrestrial globes and celestial globes side by side. Globographic modernity began in the first half of the nineteenth century with the abandonment of the heavens and their representation.

3 Oswald de Andrade made reference to a cannibalistic meal when he signed off his *Cannibalist Manifesto* of 1928 with the valedictory formula "In Piratininga, in the 374th Year of the Swallowing of Bishop Sardinha."

4 The "26 Martyrs of Japan" were beatified at the beginning of the seventeenth century; they were canonized much later, in 1862, by Pius IX, the pope of aggressive anti-modernism.

5 "Éloge du sac et de la corde," in François Dagognet, *Médium: Transmettre pour innover*, 2/2005, pp. 33f.

6 Baltasar Gracián, *The Critick*, trans. Paul Rycaut. London: T.N., 1681, p. 2 [Rycaut's translation is "the grand *Cargason* of Europe"; *cargason* is a now obsolete noun for a load of cargo to be carried elsewhere]. The phrase *la portátil Europa* refers initially to the South

Atlantic island of Saint Helena, the "pearl of the sea, or emerald of the earth" (1), where the novel's hero begins his adventure; it takes on its full meaning as a metaphor for the nautical expansion emanating from Europe.

7 Several times during the Nuremberg rallies after 1933, Adolf Hitler is said to have had the Behaim globe brought to his room at the Hotel Deutscher Hof. A large globe was also set up in Hitler's study in the New Reich Chancellery in Berlin, which opened in 1939.

8 Immanuel Kant, "Toward Perpetual Peace: A Philosophical Project," *Practical Philosophy*, trans. Mary J. Gregor. Cambridge: Cambridge University Press, 1999, pp. 317–351.

9 Herman Melville, *Redburn: His First Voyage; White Jacket or The World in a Man-of-War; Moby-Dick or, The Whale*. New York: Library of America, 1983, p. 1219.

10 Rudyard Kipling, "The White Man's Burden." The Kipling Society, https://www.kiplingsociety.co.uk/poem/poems_burden.htm.

11 Johann Chapoutot, *Free to Obey: How the Nazis Invented Modern Management*, trans. Steven Rendall. New York: Europa Editions, 2023.

12 This finding has a delicate linguistic-political aspect. When the progressive Abbé Henri Grégoire (1750–1831) called, in his address to the National Convention in June 1794, for the eradication of the dialects (*patois*) and the promotion of French as spoken in Île-de-France as the national norm – which he argued was the "idiom of freedom," though it was then spoken by barely a fifth of the political population – he inaugurated linguistic Jacobinism, which became a reality only through the cultural policy of the Third Republic after 1875. See Jürgen Trabant, *Der Gallische Herkules: Über Sprache und Politik in Frankreich und Deutschland*. Tübingen/Basel: A. Francke Verlag, 2002.

13 A position from which he had to resign in December 1895 because of his backing for the Jameson Raid, a failed rebellion, against the government of the South African Republic led by Paul Kruger.

14 Harold A. Innis, *Empire and Communications*. Toronto: Dundurn Press, 2007.

15 Cecil Rhodes, *The Last Will and Testament of Cecil John Rhodes*, ed. William T. Stead. London: Review of Reviews Office, 1902, p. 184.

16 Ibid., p. 139.

17 Gunnar Heinsohn, Rolf Knieper, and Otto Steiger, *Menschenproduktion: Allgemeine Bevölkerungslehre der Neuzeit*. Frankfurt am Main: Suhrkamp Verlag, 1979.

18 The German term, *Menschenmaterial*, first appeared several times in Karl Marx, *Capital, Volume I* (1867), and was later frequently used by the German General Staff over the course of the First World War.

19 Gunnar Heinsohn, *Söhne und Weltmacht: Terror im Aufstieg und Fall der Nationen*. Zürich: Piper, 2003, p. 88.

20 Beaumarchais, *The Marriage of Figaro*: "Nobility, affluence, rank and position, that's something to be proud of. What have you done to deserve all these advantages? You've taken the trouble to be born and nothing more" (V.3).

21 In the First World War, combatants were still drawn overwhelmingly from generations with surpluses of systemically "expendable" sons, on the scale of about nine million casualties on the front lines. Six million civilians lost their lives without the overall population balance crashing. By the beginning of the Second World War, however, France had been bled out to the point of being unfit for military service, while Hitler already had to pad out his troops with reproductive substance, and, by the end, child soldiers.

22 The derogatory term "Lumpenproletariat" coined by Marx and Engels implies the

authors' involuntary confession that the visible poverty of the lower classes can be explained only by the exploitation, through low wages, of the industrial part of the proletariat. A vastly greater share of the impoverished in modern Europe, however, were produced through misguided monarchical and clerical policies of overpopulation. The failure of Marxist approaches to explain modern conditions was already in place at the level of terminology: if *proles* means offspring, then "proletariat," properly understood, would refer to that part of the population whose interests would be better served by setting aside sexuality as a means of production and foregoing offspring who were predestined for poverty.

23 Peter Sloterdijk, *The Terrible Children of Modernity: An Antigenealogical Experiment*, trans. Oliver Berghof. New York: Columbia University Press, 2025.

24 *Sendung – Eroberung – Begegnung: Franz Xaver, die Gesellschaft Jesu und die katholische Weltkirche im Zeitalter des Barock*, ed. Johannes Meier. Wiesbaden: Harrassowitz Verlag, 2005, pp. 67–96.

25 On this parodically tinged expression (alluding to Trotsky's idea of "permanent revolution"), see Ernst H. Kantorowicz, *The Two Bodies of the King: A Study in Medieval Political Theology*. Princeton: Princeton University Press, 2016, pp. 284–289.

26 See the discussion above, on European invention and inventiveness, in "Lesson one: The grande école of the world."

Lesson seven

1 Rudyard Kipling, "The Man Who Was." The Kipling Society, https://www.kiplingsociety.co.uk/tale/the-man-who-was.htm.

2 Ernst Robert Curtius, *European Literature and the Latin Middle Ages*, trans. Willard R. Trask. Princeton: Princeton University Press, 2013, pp. 302–347.

3 Régis Debray, *Les Communions Humaines: Pour en finir avec "la religion."* Paris: Fayard, 2005.

4 "From the heap to the whole." It remains to be considered that the grain in the heap, whether conceived as an atom or as an individual, only becomes a theme, physically and sociologically, in later abstractions.

5 See above, Lesson Four: *Dire vrai sur soi-même* – Speaking the truth about oneself: The European Book of Confessions.

6 *Summa contra Gentiles* is also known as *Liber de veritate catholicae fidei contra errores infidelium* – "book on the truth of the Catholic faith against the errors of the unbelievers."

7 In his book *Orientalism* (New York: Vintage Books, 1979), the Foucault-inspired, Palestinian-born, American cultural-studies scholar, Edward Said (1935–2003) claimed that this had always been a fantasy of Western actors who tailored their Eastern "Other" to their own – i.e. Eurocentric-imperial – predilections, without ever touching the "real Orient." This view did not remain unchallenged by academic Near Eastern studies. It was not merely that Said's theses could be convicted of tendentious distortion of the documents under discussion; they could be reproached – and with good reason – with violating the ethos of the humanities. By breaking out of the sphere of *pax academica*, they distorted the sphere of the university into a battlefield of warring ideological discourses. Said denounced the founding of Israel, created as a refuge for the persecuted Jews of Europe, as a Western colonization project in line with imperialism. Since October 7, 2023 and the Hamas attack on Israeli communities on the edge of the Gaza Strip, it has been plainly evident that Saidism, from the indirect path of academic "postcolonial

discourses," admits terrorism as a legitimate act of "resistance." As an antidote to distorted presentations of European yearnings for the East, see: Mathias Énard, *Compass*, trans. Charlotte Mandell. New York: New Directions, 2018.

8 The first report of a "journey around the world" comes from the Calabrian jurist Giovanni Francesco Gemelli Careri (1651–1725), whose *Giro del Mondo* appeared in six volumes between 1699 and 1700 – it is considered a founding document of modern "tourism."

9 Such proposals were occasionally offered by the Soviet Union in the post-Stalin era and were adopted here and there in Central America and Africa; for several decades, they also emanated from Maoist China. See Julia Lovell, *Maoism: A Global History*. New York: Vintage Books, 2019. It was, however, neither the Soviet nor the Chinese ways of life that exerted an attraction; such alliances were about cooperation, i.e., strategic military aid, development aid, and political maneuvering as a bloc. The masses of the world still do not dream of living like the Russians or the Chinese.

10 Fyodor Dostoyevsky's 1862 travelogue "Winter Notes on Summer Impressions" conveys some idea of the author's aversion to conditions in France and Britain.

11 A settlement founded by Portuguese sailors in the sixteenth century under the name "beautiful bay" (*bôa bahia*), ceded to the British Crown in the seventeenth century as Bombay, and renamed or restored as "Mumbai" in 1995 under the influence of Marathi nationalist arguments.

12 Rudyard Kipling, "The Man Who Was." The Kipling Society, https://www.kiplingsociety.co.uk/tale/the-man-who-was.htm.

13 Ibid.

14 Ibid.

15 In May 2024, demonstrators in Niamey, the capital of the Sahel state of Niger, carried placards addressed to American security assistance forces with the slogan: *You leave, you move, you vanish*; at the same time, the Alliance of Sahel States welcomed a new power, Russia, to assist in its defense needs.

16 Hans Magnus Enzensberger, *Europe, Europe: Forays into a Continent*, trans. Martin Chalmers. New York: Pantheon Books, 1989.

17 Formulated in view of the Philippine crisis, during which US intervention was under debate. Rudyard Kipling, "The White Man's Burden." The Kipling Society, https://www.kiplingsociety.co.uk/poem/poems_burden.htm.

18 Frantz Fanon, *The Wretched of the Earth*, trans. Richard Philcox. New York: Grove Press, 2004.

19 Ibid., pp. 1–14.

20 Thirty years after Sartre's intervention in support of Fanon's polemic, the peace researcher Johan Galtung, in his lecture "Europe 1492–1992–2492: Brain or Disease of the World Society?," launched a sweeping attack that shows how easily the European culture of confession transitions into a riot of self-accusation. The occasion for the speech was the 500th anniversary in 1992 of Columbus's voyage, as it was commemorated at the ÖSFK (the Austrian Study Centre for Peace and Conflict Solution) in Stadtschlaining, Burgenland. Galtung contented himself with two essentialist statements in his characterization of Europe: its primary psychological and moral quality consists in the synthesis of megalomania and paranoia; its essential activity between 1492 and 1992 was genocide. See Johan Galtung, *Eurotopia: Die Zukunft eines Kontinents*, trans. Horst Friessner. Wien: Promedia, 1993.

21 See François Furet, *The Passing of an Illusion: The Idea of Communism in the Twentieth Century*, trans. Deborah Furet. Chicago: University of Chicago Press, 1999. In this incisive work, Furet demonstrates the affinities between the Jacobin intensification of the French Revolution and the terror-based Soviet system.

22 See Ivan Nagel, "Der Intellektuelle als Lump und Märtyrer," *Gedankengänge als Lebenslauf: Versuche über das 18. Jahrhundert*. Munich: C. Hanser, 1987, pp. 77–106. See also Arno J. Mayer, *The Furies: Violence and Terror in the French and Russian Revolutions*. Princeton: Princeton University Press, 2002.

23 From Rosenstock-Huessy's perspective (see Lesson Two above), what both have in common is that they discounted their derivation from the three earlier European revolutions: the Papal Revolution in Italy, Luther's "German Revolution," and the Glorious Revolution of the British; in consequence of this, they suffered a fatal contraction in their perspective vis-à-vis the history of freedom, a contraction that manifested itself in France as dogmatic laicism and in the Soviet Union as state atheism. As regards the Chinese revolution, which began as an Asian clone of the Leninist model, its progress can be best understood as a resumption of Stalinism, with the further resolve that there should never be phenomena such as *glasnost* (openness) and *perestroika* (restructuring). Xi Jinping's paramount concern can be articulated in the axiom that an effective de-Maoization must be prevented at all costs, lest China suffer a fate similar to the one that de-Stalinization brought upon the Soviet Union.

24 The first camp of the Gulag system was established during Lenin's lifetime – in 1923.

25 Fanon had detected a certain propensity for violence among the colonized on a pre-political level: "one of the ways the colonized subject releases his muscular tension is through the very real collective self-destruction of these internecine feuds." Frantz Fanon, *The Wretched of the Earth*, trans. Richard Philcox. New York: Grove Press, 2004, pp. 17–18.

26 "Manifesto antropófago," first published in the *Revista de Antropofagia*, co-founded by de Andrade, of which there appeared only the 1928 and 1929 volumes (called *dentiçõe* – rows of teeth, dentition). For the English translation, see: Oswald de Andrade, "Cannibalist Manifesto," trans. Leslie Bary, *Latin American Literary Review*, vol. 19/38 (1991), pp. 38–47.

27 Ibid., p. 38.

28 Ibid.

29 In technical terms: hyperbole, ellipsis, anacoluthon, irony.

30 Oswald de Andrade, "Cannibalist Manifesto." [In English in Andrade's original as in Sloterdijk's citation of it. – trans.]

31 Karl-Heinz Kohl, *Neun Stämme: Das Erbe der Indigenen und die Wurzeln der Moderne*. Munich: C.H. Beck, 2024, pp. 15–34.

32 Oswald de Andrade, "Cannibalist Manifesto."

33 Ibid., p. 39.

34 Ibid., p. 43.

35 Ibid.

36 Ibid., p. 41.

37 The author writes *revolução Caríba* with a capital C, as if the postulate were an event that had already entered into history.

38 For their placement within a broader anthropological context, see Jan Kott, "The Eating of the Gods, or *The Bacchae*," *The Eating of the Gods: An Interpretation of Greek Tragedy*,

trans. Boleslaw Taborski and Edward J. Czerwinski. Evanston: Northwestern University Press, 1987, pp. 186–230.

39 Oswald de Andrade, "Cannibalist Manifesto," pp. 40, 42.

40 One exception: the sermons of jihadists, who invoke Koranic motifs in their "war against the West" to legitimize the killing of infidels (*kuffār*); cf. Gilles Kepel, *Holocaustes: Israël, Gaza et la guerre contre l'occident*. Paris: Plon, 2024. Another exception: the doctrines of Chinese party ideologues, who frontally reject the heart of "Occidentalism," the doctrine of universal human rights, as if it were a regional ideology; on the other hand, they have no qualms about the mass-scale implantation of universalist conceptions found in European science and European technology. This suggests that China is on the way to succumbing to the West's own demonic possession of times past: incorporating into its arsenal everything that promises to expand its power, while defaming principles – such as human rights – that limit that power.

41 Postcolonial discourse proceeds from the doctrine propagated by twentieth-century Western Marxism on the necessary class betrayal by the bourgeois intelligentsia in favor of the "proletariat": it leads to the thesis that, at this point – in view of the advanced destructive tendencies of modernity – Western intellectuals, not exclusively, but primarily Western intellectuals, are now due for nothing less than a betrayal of civilization, a defection to the camp of the Global South, which for a while now has made no secret of its leukophobic, Europhobic, and Occidentophobic tendencies. For a radical left that wants to save its soul, the transition from class betrayal to civilizational betrayal is the dictate of the moment. In doing so, however, they get into the difficulty that the "global South" is a phantom, and that defecting to its camp makes no sense: there is no one there who would welcome you as a comrade in arms; nor is there any obvious common cause to which local preferences could be subordinated.

42 *Critique de la raison nègre*: a book written in French by Cameroonian intellectual Achille Mbembe (b. 1957), who now teaches in South Africa, published in German in 2014 under the somewhat despondent title *Kritik der schwarzen Vernunft*.